FRANÇOIS DE CALLIÈRES: A POLITICAL LIFE

HISTORY OF INTERNATIONAL RELATIONS, DIPLOMACY AND INTELLIGENCE

Series Editor

Katherine A.S. Sibley

St. Joseph's University

VOLUME 15

THIS BOOK IS ALSO PART OF THE

ADST-DACOR

DIPLOMATS AND DIPLOMACY SERIES

SERIES EDITOR:

MARGERY BOICHEL THOMPSON

FRANÇOIS DE CALLIÈRES

A POLITICAL LIFE

Laurence Pope

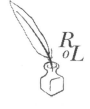 

DORDRECHT • ARLINGTON
2010

Cover illustration / Design:
Callieres's sketch of the site where Jan Sobieski was elected King of Poland in 1674, from his report to the Duke of Savoy. Letters refer to the text, and identify the positions of the principal dignitaries. Warsaw Castle is visible in the background. (Courtesy of the Polish Library of Paris.)

This book is printed on acid-free paper.

Library of Congress Cataloging-in-Publication Data

ISSN	1874-0294	
hardbound	ISBN	978-90-8979-039-2
paperback	ISBN	978-90-8979-040-8

To the memory of my father, Everett Pope,
whose edition of *On Negotiating with Sovereigns* is on my desk,
and who wanted to be a diplomat before he saw too much of war.

CONTENTS

PREFACE

François de Callières (1645-1717) is remembered today as the author of a celebrated diplomatic treatise with a cumbersome title. *On Negotiating with Sovereigns: Of the Utility of Negotiations, on the Choice of Ambassadors and Envoys, and on the Qualities Necessary for Success in Those Employments*[1] was published almost immediately after the death of Louis XIV; Callières had been the Sun King's private secretary. His earlier books had often been bestsellers by the standards of the time, but despite a respectful notice in the *Journal des Savants,* this one sank virtually without a trace. Five hundred fliers were posted in Paris, but of a thousand copies forty-nine were sold between March 3 and September 26 of 1716. On his death the remainders were turned over to the apothecary's shop at the Hôtel-Dieu, then as now the hospital for the poor of Paris, where the paper was used to wrap medicinal powders.[2] The author of a treatise with a similar title published in 1738 suggested that the book might have done better if its style had been less dense, as "even the best precepts succeed with difficulty when the means of presenting them is disagreeable."[3]

Callières spoke no English. He wrote to his friend Cardinal Gualtieri that the English were "unpredictable and bizarre by nature"—and so there is some irony in the fact that it was the English translation, which appeared almost immediately in London, that saved *On Negotiating with Sovereigns* from oblivion. This translation, by an anonymous Grub Steet hack, is used in the contemporary editions of the book, and it continues to this day to be a celebrated text among Anglo-Saxons, to use the quaint French terminology for English speakers. Lord Chesterfield commended *On Negotiating with Sovereigns* to his son in one of his sententious letters of advice.[4] Harold Nicolson, a British diplomat and author better known today as the husband of Virginia Woolf's lover Vita Sackville-West, suggested in a 1953 lecture that *On Negotiating with Sovereigns* was the best book on diplomatic method ever written.[5] Management experts have

---

[1] *De la manière de négocier avec les souverains, de l'utilité des négociations, du choix des ambassadeurs et des envoyéz, et des qualitez nécessaires pour réussir dans ces employs.*
[2] Waquet, *François de Callières,* 13, 70.
[3] Pecquet, *De l'art de négocier,* 41.
[4] Chesterfield, *Letters,* 215.
[5] Nicolson, *The Evolution of Diplomatic Method,* 62.

even seen in Callières a precursor to be emulated by modern business executives.[6]

It would be hard to think of another book published in France three centuries ago that is available today to be downloaded in English to an electronic book reader, and in recent years, thanks in large part to this admiring attention in the English-speaking world, the book has been rediscovered in France too. In the introduction to an admiring 2002 French edition, the first since 1750, a political scientist with a foot on both sides of the Atlantic argued somewhat implausibly that Callières prefigured the emerging school of what is known as 'peace politics.'[7] A more critical study of the book in historical context by Jean-Claude Waquet appeared in 2005, with a meticulously researched biographical chapter correcting previous accounts of Callières's life.[8]

Callières left a considerable paper trail in various archives. His political activities are documented in the *correspondance politique*, the records of French diplomacy formerly preserved at the Quai d'Orsay. Decoded letters in the library at Chantilly outside Paris tell the story of his first undercover mission to Poland in 1670. The Polish Library in Paris has his long eyewitness account of the election of Jan Sobieski in 1674, illustrated by his drawing of the election ground outside Warsaw with the city's skyline in the background,[9] used here for the first time. Letters from a gossipy cleric in Rome document his activities as one of a close-knit group of intellectuals and courtiers in the orbit of the Colberts. The papers of Colonel Nathaniel Hooke, a Jacobite in French service, and the memoirs of a Scot who called himself Lord Lovat, testify to the central role of the 'Marquis de Callières' in various Jacobite intrigues. Some of the letters he wrote from 1704 until 1715 to Cardinal Gualtieri were sold to the British Museum by the Cardinal's descendants and are now in the manuscript collection of the British Library. The court diarist of Louis XIV, the Marquis de Dangeau, mentions him from time to time, though the two men detested each other. His seventy-five letters to the Marquise d'Huxelles give some sense of the private man, with traces of the court he paid to a well-born lady who married another.[10]

---

[6] The edition of *On Negotiating with Sovereigns* (New York, 2000) introduced by Charles Handy is subtitled *From Sovereigns to CEOs, Classic Principles of Diplomacy and the Art of Negotiation*. The publisher's blurb suggests that "In today's business world, those same princely principles can make or break corporations and launch careers."

[7] Lempereur, *De la manière de négocier avec les souverains, édition critique.*

[8] Waquet, *François de Callières.*

[9] See the cover illustration.

[10] *Letters.*

Finally, many of his state papers, *mémoires* to the King, are preserved in the *Fonds Renaudot* of the Bibliothèque nationale de France, well over one hundred pages in his hand. Uncatalogued as such, they have not previously been known to exist.[11] These materials make it possible for the first time to piece together a reasonably comprehensive account of a long and active life in politics, and the narrative that follows adheres closely to these archival sources. Its intention is to allow Callières to speak for himself as much as possible, on the old-fashioned premise that when their context is understood, primary documents can be a window into the foreign country that is the past.

This is a biography, not a work of diplomatic history. Callières's career spanned over forty years of involvement in the great issues of his time, from Poland in 1670 to Scotland in 1715. Of necessity, the historical context is sketched in broad strokes. Specialists will find things to quarrel with perhaps, but even they may find something new here. Nor is this an academic work of postmodern theory. Its unfashionable assumption is that these were once real negotiations, conducted by real people for high stakes, and that the life of a man who was involved in the great affairs of his time has an intrinsic interest.

While Callières would be forgotten today if it were not for *On Negotiating with Sovereigns,* to see him through the lens of what a later age would call "diplomacy," that powerful modern trope, is anachronistic and distorting. This account of his political career is an attempt to place him in his own time. The light it sheds on the contrast between the career of the man and the high-minded precepts of his famous book may be uncomfortable for his uncritical modern admirers, but it would not have surprised anyone at Versailles in 1700.

My own interest in Callières dates to the beginning of this millennium, which also saw the end of my diplomatic career. I had been the American Ambassador to Chad, and after a few years as the political advisor to the General in charge of the U.S. Central Command, I was nominated by President Clinton to be Ambassador to Kuwait. But the U.S. Senate was controlled by a Republican majority, and rightly suspecting that I harbored doubts about the wisdom of an invasion of Iraq, the chairman of the Senate Foreign Relations Committee declined to schedule a confirmation hearing. As a relief from Arabic verbs, I had been reading *On Negotiating with Sovereigns,* and when I decided to resign from the

---

[11] English versions of several of these state papers are included in the appendix. (All translations are the author's unless otherwise indicated.) Omont's inventory of the *Fonds Renaudot* does not indentify their author, Omont, *Inventaire sommaire.*

American Foreign Service to protest these proceedings, I had the leisure to gratify my curiosity about the historical Callières. This book is the result, almost a decade later.

Laurence Pope
Portland, Maine

ACKNOWLEDGEMENTS

Without great libraries a book of this kind would not be possible. The staff of the *salle de manuscripts occidentaux* at the Bibliothèque nationale de France was unfailingly kind to a researcher who was often incapable of distinguishing between *nouvelles acquisitions françaises* and *manuscrits français*, or even of remembering that you turn in your orange badge first and only then get a green one – unless it is the other way around. Mme Valentine Weiss kindly emailed the catalogue of the Fonds Renaudot, and the BnF made available the microfilm of *nouvelles acquisitions françaises* 7487. It contains three of the four *mémoires* included in the annex, facilitating the work of transcription and translation. The BnF's invitation to a colloquium on Coronelli's globes in January of 2007 helped finance a research trip to Paris.

At the Polish Library on the Quai d'Orléans in Paris, the gracious Mme Eva Rutkowska was bemused by the reaction of an American researcher to the discovery of Callières's report to the Duke of Savoy, and she was kind enough to make available Callières's drawing of the election ground outside Warsaw in 1684 for the cover of this book. My grateful thanks to her. Professor Stefania Ochmnann-Staniszewska of the University of Wroclaw sent a copy of her edition of the letters of Jan Andrasz Morsztyn, and explained the mysteries of the Polish electorate in 1674. Dr. Ben Trotter alerted me to the existence of the Vauban connection, and Mme Michèle Virol told me where to find Vauban's papers, which were made available for consultation with the permission of Vauban's descendant, the Marquis de Rosanbo.

I'm grateful to the British Library for making available the letters of Callières to Cardinal Gualtieri. Closer to home, the library at Bowdoin College contains the majestic nineteenth century edition of Saint-Simon by André Boislisle, all forty-four volumes. I owe particular thanks to the Rylands Library in Manchester, U.K., and the *Bibliothèque municipale* of Avignon, where Huxelles's letters are preserved. By chance both libraries were closed for repairs during the only window I had for a visit. At Avignon, Mme Émilienne Molina, the conservator, brought the volumes to her own office and vacated it for a visiting researcher, and the same thing happened at Rylands. At the French national archives, when the materials I wanted to consult having to do with the *Collège d'Harcourt* happened to be in transition, M. Philippe Béchu, conservator, made his own office available and tracked them down. If there is a pattern here it is one of unfailing kindness.

I am a newcomer in a field in which others have worked a lifetime. The late Roger Duchêne, whose biography of Mme de Sévigné is unmatched in its acuity, was encouraging to a newcomer who asked about Mme d'Huxelles and her letters to La Garde. Professor Jean-Claude Waquet whose book on Callières I have admired and used extensively, has been extremely helpful, without a trace of proprietary feeling. I'm grateful as well to Professor Lucien Bély of the Sorbonne for his advice and counsel to someone without the slightest academic standing. I wonder if the leading experts in the field in the U.S would welcome a visiting French researcher with as much generosity. The Irish scholar Thomas Byrne whose PhD thesis on Nathaniel Hooke is a model of the genre, was particularly helpful, and I thank him for sharing it with me. Germaine Warkentin of the University of Toronto set me straight on the Canadian explorers Radisson and Groseillers.

Finally, without the help of two distinguished British scholars from very different disciplines this book would never have seen the light of day. Professor William S. Brooks of the University of Bath edited the manuscript with painstaking attention to detail, and I have continued to lean on his moral support and infinite capacity for taking pains. Professor Geoff Berridge, the pre-eminent scholar of diplomatic practice pruned and reshaped a narrative that had wandered too far into unproductive byways, and he edited the final version with a firm hand. My grateful thanks to them both. They embody the finest tradition of the Republic of Letters. Margery Thompson of the ADST was a valued source of advice and encouragement. My friend Amy MacDonald took time from her own writing and lecturing to copyedit the manuscript with patience and consummate skill. Even she could not eliminate all its mistakes and infelicities. To Elizabeth Pope, my sometime research assistant who now knows far more than she ever wanted to about François de Callières, thanks are inadequate. She knows what I owe her.

LIST OF ABBREVIATIONS

AAE	*Archives des Affaires Etrangères*
AN	*Centre historique des Archives nationales, Paris.*
BAC	*Bibliothèque et Archives du Canada*
BnF	*Bibliothèque nationale de France, Paris*
BL	*British Library, London*
CP	*Archives des affaires étrangères, Correspondance politique*, formerly at the Quai d'Orsay in Paris, now at La Courneuve outside Paris.
Bernou	*Nouvelles acquisitions françaises 7487, Bibliothèque nationale de France, Paris.*
Chantilly	*Bibliothèque et archives du Château de Chantilly, papiers de Condé, Serie R, Tome XIV.*
Hooke	'Correspondence of Nathaniel Hooke, Agent for the Court of France to the Scottish Jacobites,' Roxburghe Club, ed. William D. Macray, I, 1870-1871.
Listy	*Stefania Ochmann-Staniszewska, 'Listy Jana Andrzeja Morstina' Wroclaw, 2002.*
Mémoires	*Collection des mémoires relatifs à l'histoire de France,* Petitot, Monmerqué, etc Paris, 1823
Rylands	The John Rylands Library, Deansgate, University of Manchester, UK.
S/S	*Saint-Simon, Louis Rouvroy, duc de, Mémoires* ed. Yves Coirault, Gallimard, 1983, 8v.
Sévigné	*Lettres de Madame de Sévigné*, various editions, cited by date.
TNA	The National Archives [British]

LIST OF ILLUSTRATIONS

1. Images from the *Le Monde illustré*, 1890, Montréal, of the parents of François de Callières. The originals, miniatures once in the Museum at Cherbourg, are lost. We have included them here, in spite of their quality, since they are the only pictures of Callières' parents. (Bibliothèque et Archives Nationales, Québec.)

2. Jan Andrasz Morsztyn, Grand Treasurer of the Polish Republic, and his wife Lady Mary Catherine Gordon of Huntley, Callières's patrons and friends from their first meeting in Poland in 1670 to the end of their lives in France. (Czartoryski Museum, Krakow.)

3. Detail from "Crossing of the Rhine," Adam Frans van der Meulen. The Duke de Longueville is prancing on a charger before the King. (Réunion des Musées Nationaux/Art Resource, NY.)

4. Jan Sobieski as Grand Marshal of the Crown.

5. Toussaint de Forbin-Janson, Bishop of Marseille, later Cardinal de Janson, who recommended against employing Callières as the French Resident in Poland.

6. Marie Jeanne Baptiste de Savoie-Nemours, Madame Royale.

7. Eusèbe Renaudot, at the time of his election with Callières to the Académie Française. (Musée des Chateaux de Versailles et de Trianon, Versailles.)

8. "Arrival of the Ambassadors at Rywsick," showing the arrival of the French delegation. (Museum Rijswijk.)

9. Jean-Baptiste Colbert, Marquis de Torcy, French Foreign Minister, 1696-1715.

10. "A Bridle for the French King." William III sits secure on the pedestal, while Louis XIV below, recoiling in terror, says "what I stole I will refund," while female figures attempt to slip a bridle over his head. (British Museum.)

11. William III of England. (British Museum.)

12. Louis XIV receiving James II of England at Saint-Germain-en-Laye. (British Museum.)

13. Simon Fraser, Lord Lovat, in his prime.

14. "Jacobite Hopes Dashed." The Stuart Pretender, "Perkin" is shown being drawn by monsters named "popery," "tyranny," and "slavery," over the prostrate bodies of "toleration," "liberty," "moderation," and "property." Perkin Warbeck was a pretender to the English throne. His dubious claims had been espoused by King James IV of Scotland with an invasion in 1496 of England. (British Museum.)

15. Colberts: from left to right, top to bottom: Jean-Baptiste, founder of the family fortunes; his brother Charles, Marquis de Croissy; his son, Marquis de Seignelay, and Croissy's son, the Marquis de Torcy.

PROLOGUE

In the winter of 1717, in a house on the corner of the rue de Richelieu and the rue Neuve St. Augustine in the city of Paris, François de Callières was dying. It was a very fine house, not as grand as the hôtels of the upper nobility but there was a coach and four in the stable and a staff of twelve. It was not far from the Louvre where the French Academy had its headquarters. Callières was a member of that body, elected in 1689 without a dissenting vote. He had taken his seat on the same day as his close friend Eusèbe Renaudot, editor of the *Gazette de France*, the propaganda organ of the court, who lived next door.

In the last weeks of his life Callières altered his will to name Renaudot as his executor, leaving him his "books, manuscripts, and *memoires*," state papers addressed to the King rather than reminiscences, carefully preserved for posterity. They are still scattered anonymously among Renaudot's papers in the Bibliothèque Nationale. The nineteenth century archivist who compiled the catalogue cannot be blamed for failing to recognize the distinctive handwriting, or the reference in one of them to "my brother who is Governor General in Canada."

We have the inventory of the furnishings of the house, room by room, because Renaudot sold them off at auction in accordance with Callières's instructions.[1] He had never married and he had no direct heir. With the exception of small bequests to a nephew and a sister back in Normandy, all the proceeds went to the Hôtel-Dieu. The house itself is long gone, but the careful records the auctioneers made of each transaction would allow its interior to be reconstructed down to the last detail by a film company with deep pockets.

The dying man was a connoisseur of fine art, and he was an accomplished draftsman himself. Throughout the house there were paintings, some 150 in all: old masters, Rubens, Veronese, several Breughels – some originals, others copies, some with religious motifs, others with scenes of nymphs and satyrs. There were portraits of the great men Callières had known: of Louis XIV who had died a little over a year before; of the young Duke de Longueville, who died in battle in 1672 as Callières was on the verge of obtaining his election as King of Poland, or so

---

[1] *Legs universel de François de Callières au profit de l'Hôtel-Dieu*, and *Inventaire après le décès de M. de Callières*, from the *Archives de l'Assistance Publique*, published in *Documents pour servir à l'histoire de l'Hôtel-Dieu de Paris*, IV, 131-46, M. Brièle, Paris, imprimerie Nationale, 1887. See also Waquet, *François de Callières*, 71.

he later maintained; of Jan Sobieski, who as King John III rode to the rescue of the Hapsburgs at Vienna in 1683, and whose election in 1674 Callières had attended though he supported another candidate. In the bedroom under the eyes of the dying man there was a copy of Hans Holbein's famous portrait of the martyred Thomas More, whose last words on the block Callières would have known: "I am the King's good servant, but God's first." Among the books in his extensive collection were editions of La Fontaine, Rabelais, Molière, and Corneille. 'Loque', an unfamiliar name, must have puzzled the auctioneer's clerk when it was dictated – John Locke's *Essay on Human Understanding* was first published in French translation in 1700.

It was the house of a lifelong bachelor, however pious, and there were also four erotic drawings 'representing nudity and indecent postures.' Even in the lax days of the Regency of Philip of Orleans they could not be put on sale without giving offense to public decency, and they were burned in the presence of witnesses – or so the auctioneers declared.

A prominent physician named François Picoté de Belestre, who received 300 francs from his estate, attended Callières. Belestre must have been a man of parts since he left his extensive library to the Faculté de Medicine in Paris. Did the two men talk books? The Picoté de Belestre family had a Canadian branch, so perhaps there was a connection to Callières's younger brother Louis-Hector, the Governor General, who had died in Canada of fever in 1703. Callières would have been bled and the other useless and cruel remedies of the time applied but it was a relatively short illness. His last attendance at the Academy is recorded on November 9, and he died on March 5.

It was known in the city that Callières was dying. In a letter to the powerful Duke de Noailles, one J. B. Henri de Valincour, the royal historian and a colleague at the Academy, wrote to solicit his lucrative post. Valincour told the Duke that he thought he could do as good a job of drafting letters as anyone.[2] Instead the Regent gave the position and its revenues to his principal minister, the unscrupulous Cardinal Dubois.[3] It is fair to assume that Callières would not have approved.

In addition to the memorial service at the Franciscan monastery of Les Cordeliers organized by his colleagues at the Academy, there was a funeral at Saint-Eustache, the church near Les Halles where Jean-Baptiste Colbert is buried along with Richelieu, Molière, and other notables. It cost a total of 277 francs, a considerable sum. Bells were rung (15 francs), eight

---

[2] *Les Correspondants du Duke de Noailles, lettres inédites de Le Verrier, Renaudot, et Valincour*, 153.
[3] S/S VI, 163.

priests carried the lead casket (24 francs), and a total of 63 priests and 6 choir boys were there to sing the mass (66 francs). Callières was buried in the church floor which had to be taken up (52 francs), but there is no longer any trace of him above ground. There was once an inscription on a pillar near the Chapel of the Angels, where the Archangel Michael still casts the fallen angels down after their revolt, directly across from Charles Antoine Coysevox's magnificent baroque sculpture of Jean-Baptiste Colbert. It read:

> François de Callières, Seigneur of La Rochellay and Gigny, Counselor to the King in his Councils, Secretary of Cabinet to His Majesty, formerly Ambassador Plenipotentiary of France at the negotiation of Ryswick and Envoy Extraordinary to Lorraine, who died on March 5, 1717 at the age of seventy-one years. He left all his property to the poor of the Hôtel-Dieu of Paris, and founded a Mass in perpetuity in this church.

That Mass was to be sung in the Chapel of the Angels – Callières made a donation to Saint-Eustache of 10,000 francs to endow it – but perpetuity is a long time.

Friends, including Renaudot, would have been in attendance at Callières' deathbed, but at a certain point his thoughts would have turned to the consolations of religion. He would have sought the demanding good death of the time, in accordance with the stoic Jansenist code, which required a renunciation of all worldly attachments at the last, alone with a confessor. Given his strength of character and will it is probable that he managed it.Wealthy and full of honors, as he lay dying Callières would have cast his mind back over a long life in which he had risen from provincial obscurity to a seat at the right hand of power.

NORMAN ORIGINS

His origin would perhaps be better known if it been less illustrious.
– Jean-Aimar Piganiol de La Force on Jacques de Callières

François de Callières was baptised on May 14, 1645, in the Norman village of Thorigny, to a family in the service of the Matignons, hereditary rulers of Lower Normandy. His father, Jacques, was a professional army officer who held a royal commission with the senior rank of *maréchal de bataille*, roughly equivalent to colonel or brigadier general. Jacques's marriage to Madeleine Pothier de Courcy, a noble but penniless girl, had been arranged by the Matignons the year before, and François was their first child, named after François Goyon de Matignon, Count de Thorigny, his godfather.

Figure 1. Images from the Le Monde illustré, 1890, Montréal, of the parents of François de Callières. The originals, miniatures once in the Museum at Cherbourg, are lost. We have included them here, in spite of their quality, since they are the only pictures of Callières' parents. (Bibliothèque et Archives Nationales, Québec)

Grainy likenesses of his parents Jacques and Madeleine have survived across the centuries in the pages of an illustrated Montreal magazine—the originals, miniatures once in the municipal museum at Cherbourg, appear to have been destroyed during the allied invasion of Normandy. They show a smiling couple, with kindly faces.

In 1645, Louis XIV was a child of seven. France was ruled by his mother Anne of Austria, the daughter of King Philip III of Spain, and Cardinal Jules Mazarin, an Italian cleric rumored (probably falsely) to be her lover. When elements of the nobility and magistrate class rebelled against Mazarin and the Queen in the series of marches and counter-marches known as the Fronde (1648-1651), the Matignons reluctantly took up arms, prodded by their traditional ally the Duke de Longueville, hereditary Governor of Normandy. The leaders of the insurrection were his brilliant and charismatic wife the Duchess de Longueville and her brother Louis II de Bourbon-Condé, the celebrated general known as Monsieur le Prince.

Jacques fought with his Matignon patrons at the inglorious siege of the Norman town of Valognes in 1649, against royalist forces. (Both sides claimed to be acting in defense of the young King.) A loyalist garrison of some 300 in the walled city held out for weeks against an overwhelmingly superior Matignon force, though Jacques is said to have "spared no effort" as commander of the Matignon artillery.[1] After the outnumbered garrison finally surrendered, he appears to have taken over the town and governed it for the Matignons, since in a 1653 document in the Matignon archives he is described as the "Lieutenant of the Vicounty of Valognes."[2] He subsequently became Governor of the town and fortress of Cherbourg, and he held that office under the Matignons until his death in 1662.

Jacques's loyalties were uncomfortably divided during the Fronde, and when Mazarin negotiated a settlement with Spain in 1659 that allowed the return of Monsieur le Prince to France from exile, his relief is evident from a poem dedicated to Mme de Longueville, published at Saint-Lô in

---

[1] *La Fronde en Normandie*, Paul Logié, "chez l'auteur," 20 rue du Four, Amiens, 1951 and 1952. Tome II contains an account of the inglorious affair at Valognes, 126 and following.

[2] *AN, Fonds Matignon, Série J 84, 403: conseiller du Roi, Sieur des Noëlles et lieutenant en la vicomté de Valognes.* The document contains a detailed inventory of the arms in the castle: "In the arms room, about a thousand musket balls, a box full of clay grenades and eight iron grenades," etc. The Matignons declare formally that the arms in the Château had been used only in the King's service, and they turn the keys over to Jacques. This may have been part of the arrangement after the Fronde by which the King's representatives took effective control of Normandy from Longueville and the Matignons, perhaps a face-saving compromise, since Jacques was both a royal officer and a Matignon client.

1660. Jacques assigned a convenient degree of collective responsibility for the rebellion: "France forgot its duty." In his "ancient fortress by the sea," the poet is informed by two Tritons who leap implausibly out of the waves that Monsieur le Prince is returning from exile, and he rejoices that the battle laurels of the ever-victorious general will again merge again with the royal lilies of France. His friend the Paris critic Jean Chapelain pointed out to him that the verses didn't always scan, but the Longuevilles were Chapelain's patrons too, and Chapelain told Jacques that he thought the ode would please Monsieur le Prince. Perhaps that great captain read it with an amused smile in a distracted moment. It was not a poem that would have found favor at court in Paris where statues of the young Louis XIV with his foot on the neck of a monster representing the Fronde were more the fashion.

For Jacques was not just a professional soldier, he was also a humanist and a writer, and his duties at Cherbourg left him with time to indulge these habits, particularly after the risk of an invasion by Spain or Cromwell's England had subsided. His first book was published in 1657, a treatise on proper conduct in the genre of works about the perfect courtier.[3] It was a bestseller thanks to the patronage of the so-called "Grande Mademoiselle," Duchess de Montpensier, the King's cousin and the richest heiress in Europe; many of its themes would reverberate his son's writings a generation later. Like his son, he expressed a preference for practical "knowledge of the world" over the "knowledge of pedants," and his writings reflect the fashionable Jansenist pose of "scorn for the world" and "vulgar conquerors" that was a favorite of his son as well.[4] In his dedication of the work to the Duke de Longueville, Jacques wrote that what he admired in the Duke was not his genealogy but his virtue. He suggested that it was difficult to gain fame as a soldier without high rank: "I have known men who have committed extraordinary acts of bravery unknown to anyone outside their own company." Was he perhaps thinking of his own military career?

Judging from his writings, Jacques was a moderate and tolerant man. Like his son, he admired the Protestant Dutch and their fight for liberty against Spain. He was a member of the Academy of Letters of Caen

---

[3] *De la Fortune des Gens de Qualité*. Several other editions followed and the book was pirated and translated into various languages. Forty years later, François found that it was still for sale at booksellers all over Europe *Letters*, 209, 210.

[4] Both father and son were fond of an anecdote from Plutarch which they had by way of Montaigne. King Pyrrhus outlines his plan for world conquest to his counsellor and Ambassador Cineas, who continues to ask the King what will come next. Having run out of lands to conquer, Pyrrhus tells his friend that "we will then sit together and laugh and talk at our ease". "That's fine", says Cineas, "but what keeps us from doing that now?"

that included many Protestants in the days before the revocation of the Edict of Nantes, and in his otherwise hagiographic biography of the 16th century Duke de Joyeuse, a Matignon ancestor and founder of the family's fortunes, he suggested that the Duke's responsibility for episodes of butchery during the 16th century wars of religion was to be regretted. Of the massacre of Protestants at La Rochelle he wrote:

> If I were permitted to express my own opinion, I would say that such an ill-considered zeal comes from the weakness of our judgment. ... There is no doubt that God wants us to die rather than to deny our faith; but he does not command us to exterminate, or even to hate, those who do not believe what we believe.[5]

Scorn for the world notwithstanding, to both of his sons Jacques transmitted the idea that upward mobility was possible and ambition legitimate – a rare perspective in a society in which status was fixed at birth. He wrote that an able young gentleman should leave his native province and seek to rise in the great world by his own talent, and that there is nothing that touches a father so much as the love of his children and the hope that their renown will spread to "the most unknown climes." He would have been pleased had he lived to see one son rise to the position of principal secretary to the Sun King, while the other became Governor General of New France.

Jacques's own origins contain a mystery that may explain much about the career of his eldest son.[6] He is said to have been born in 1619 in the Loire valley, at the Château of La Roche, a manor house in the village of Cheillé near Azay-le-Rideau that still exists. If so, this would make him very young indeed in 1635, when on the evidence of his own writings he was fighting in Holland with a French expeditionary force against the Spanish.[7] In *On the Fortune of Men of Birth*, Jacques writes, obviously from personal experience, of the long apprenticeship required to gain experience in warfare, including the use of artillery in sieges, trenches, engineering, reconnaissance and the rest, but by 1644 he was already a senior officer in the service of the Matignons. This is scarcely credible if he was really born in 1619. In his biography of the 16th century Maréchal

---

[5] *Le Courtisan prédestiné*, 388.
[6] The definitive account of the genealogy of the Callières family is Leibel, *La Famille Du Chevalier De Callières*.
[7] In *De la Fortune des Gens de Qualité*, Jacques writes that "I saw a mastiff make his fortune in Holland ... when he somehow recognized the Prince of Orange and would not leave his tent." In 1635, Cardinal Richelieu sent a French force to the assistance of the Prince of Orange; it is difficult otherwise to account for the presence of a French officer near the Dutch commander's tent.

de Matignon[8] who was the founder of the family's fortunes, an expensively bound and illustrated work which is preserved at Chantilly, Jacques writes that no pleasure from a mistress can equal that of the victorious general who "thinks of his coming fame while he tramples proudly over the dead, their muskets abandoned, their pikes broken, their standards torn on the bloody field of battle, while captives implore his mercy." It is an image he can only have derived from an extensive experience of war predating his arrival in Lower Normandy.[9]

Adding to the puzzle, it appears that Jacques, who held a royal military commission, could not lay claim to the four quarters of nobility that conferred the right to bear arms, and that his putative father Hector was not himself of noble birth. Indeed, it appears that the coat of arms that François and his brother would later use was concocted out of whole cloth.[10] Despite this, it is clear that Jacques received a particularly expensive and careful education in both the arts of peace and the arts of war, at a time when even the best-born young men of the nobility pursued either one path or the other, not both.

One plausible explanation for this set of facts is that Jacques was an illegitimate Matignon, or even a Longueville. It is difficult otherwise to account for his rise in military rank and his translation from the relative obscurity of a manor house in Touraine to the palace of the Matignons at Thorigny. The author of a guidebook to Paris who had known François hinted at this when he wrote that the ancestry of Jacques would "perhaps be better known if it had been less illustrious" – a clear suggestion that Jacques was the illegitimate offspring of a member of the upper nobility.

What is certain is that François inherited his father's view that virtue was more important than noble birth, and that all his life he was extremely sensitive about these matters. At the risk of alienating his noble patrons, including the Marquise d'Huxelles, he wrote with an acid pen of "gentlemen with grand genealogies who easily persuade themselves that they are cut from a different rank than other men."[11] It is probably not a coincidence that neither François nor his younger brother Louis-Hector ever married, even though from Jacques's writings it appears that the marriage of their own parents was a happy one. (Weighing the merits of a

---

[8] *Histoire du Maréschal de Matignon.* This contains an extensive fold-out genealogy of the Matignons, now the royal family of Monaco.

[9] In *Le Courtisan prédestiné* Jacques is critical of his hero for the "horrible butchery" of Huguenots at La Rochelle and other excesses. There is a Calvinist echo in the French title.

[10] This is clear from the meticulously researched genealogy in Leibel, *La Famille Du Chevalier De Callières.*

[11] *Letters,* 175.

marriage for money against a marriage for love, he comes down squarely in favor of the latter.) Was this because an equal union in the nobility would have required the documentation of their spurious coat of arms, and it would not have survived close examination by any notary?

What is certain is that the Matignon and Longueville connection was central to the later career of François. In the next chapter, we will see where ambition took him in the service of the Longuevilles.

FIRST MISSION TO POLAND

A young negotiator is usually presumptuous, vain, flighty, and indiscreet. There is a risk in entrusting a matter of consequence to him unless he is a person of singular merit whose native genius has furnished him at a young age with the advantages usually attained by age and experience.
– Francois de Callieres, *On Negotiating with Sovereigns*

His father's death left Callières with only the family connection to the Matignons and the Longuevilles to sustain him. Years later he wrote to Mme d'Huxelles that among the great men who had befriended him was Jacques-Auguste de Thou, the proprietor of a library of some 13,000 volumes that was open to the public, and that in de Thou's library he had met the austere Duke de Montausier, tutor to the Dauphin. His father's friend Chapelain would have been a useful contact in the Longueville household for the young man. Jacques's biography of the Duke de Joyeuse, the companion of Henri IV and general turned monk, contains a stamp of theological approval from Thomas Fortin, Principal of the Collège d'Harcourt on the Boulevard Saint-Michel – the ancestor of the Lycée Saint-Louis, which stands on the same spot today. This suggests strongly that Callières was a student at Harcourt, which was in any case where young Norman gentlemen were generally sent to study.[1] It was an establishment of anti-Jesuit and pro-Jansenist views, and Callières was profoundly influenced all his life by the austerity of Jansenist thought.

But it is clear that his youth in the precincts of the Latin Quarter was not solely that of a grave scholar. His first book, published in 1668 at the tender age of 23, and probably composed earlier as a schoolboy lark, was entitled *A Lover's Logic.*[2] It was a send-up of an influential Jansenist text, the *Port Royal Logic* of Pierre Nicole and Antoine Arnauld, and it was dedicated to Charles-Paris d'Orléans, Count de Saint-Paul – the son of Madame de Longueville, and the last and best hope of that noble house. In the book's dedication, Callières promised to serve the Longuevilles with

---

[1] See *l'Ancien college d'Harcourt.*
[2] *La logique des amans, ou l'amour logicien*, Monsieur de Caillières le fils. (Like his father, François still spelled the name *Caillières* with an extra "i".)

the same fidelity as his father before him. Occasionally amusing, the little tome bordered on the obscene in some passages, and it would have been an embarrassment to the grave royal counselor that Callières became in later years, in the ascendancy of Mme de Maintenon at Versailles. A sample passage:

> After the face comes the neck, the arms, and the hands, and what some rakes call the little goose ....[3] Few hearts can resist the call of a fair bosom when it allows itself to be glimpsed. With its pleasant apples, it awakens desire in the most insensible of hearts, for these two fruits are so lovely that one longs to taste them with one's mouth, and one feels an agreeable emotion though one merely gathers them by hand.

Or this, by way of a satire of scholastic logic:

> Major premise: Without wealth, one cannot be happy in love.
>
> Minor premise: Old Amaryllis is rich.
>
> Conclusion: One must be in love with her.

The book had a modest success and there was even an English translation thanks to the contemporary prestige of all things French and gallant. But the principal audience Callières had in mind was Saint-Paul, the book's dedicatee. A handsome young *preux chevalier* who set hearts fluttering everywhere, Saint-Paul was widely believed to have a brilliant future. Half the great ladies of Paris were in love with him, and Callières was determined to attach his own modest car to the Prince's chariot.

SAINT-PAUL AND THE POLISH CROWN

At the library at Chantilly, the former palace of the princes of Bourbon-Condé, a visiting researcher may consult a folio in red leather containing mostly deciphered correspondence from a variety of conspirators with code names.[4] One of them is an undercover agent identified only as "Monsieur de Large," but he has a widowed mother in Saint-Lô, a "Madame de C." – and so we know, from this and other evidence as well as from his own later testimony, that Callières set off in the spring of 1670 at the age of 25 on an undercover mission to Poland to establish Saint-Paul on the throne of Poland. Strange as it may seem, the enterprise had a reasonable prospect of success.

---

[3] *La petite oye*, literally the giblets, was a coy synonym for "a lady's penultimate charms."

[4] *Chantilly, Bibliothèque et archives du musée Condé, "papiers de Condé": Série R, XIV, correspondences relatives à la candidature du comte de Saint Pol au trône de Pologne, 1670-1671.*

The covert war between Austria and France for supremacy in Poland was the "great affair" of the early days of the reign of Louis XIV. The Polish-Lithuanian federation, while diminished as a result of the depredations of its neighbors, still ruled vast territories, from the great trading port of Gdansk at the mouth of the Vistula to the thriving cities of Krakow and Warsaw. A contemporary Irish traveler, Bernard Connor who was the King's physician, has left an account in which he describes Poland as a country "not so contemptible as we in the Western parts of Europe have imagined." Had the country's abundant natural resources been properly exploited, Connor suggested. It would "doubtless have been able to vie with any kingdom in Europe, of which the King of France and other princes are now sensible having spent great sums on Polish elections."[5]

Poland was a unique political construction, a Confederated Republic with a constitution and ancient institutions to which the Polish and Lithuanian gentry were deeply attached.[6] Polish Kings derived their powers not from divine right of birth as in Western Europe, but from the free vote of the Assembly of the Nobility, the *szlachta*, numbering up to 11,000 persons representing fifteen provinces and the Grand Duchy of Lithuania, often elected themselves by local assemblies.[7] The nobility was profoundly jealous of its privileges, and after 1652 each Polish elector acquired the right to block an election by a single vote – the *liberum veto*.

---

[5] Connor, *The History of Poland*, 239.

[6] The American founding fathers were well aware of the Polish precedent. Jefferson cited it as a precedent for unwelcome foreign interference in American elections, writing to John Adams in 1787 during the drafting of the Constitution that "[The] President seems a bad edition of a Polish King. He may be elected from four years to four years, for life. Reason and experience prove to us, that a chief magistrate, so continuable, is an office for life. When one or two generations shall have proved that this is an office for life, it becomes, on every occasion, worthy of intrigue, of bribery, of force, and even of foreign interference. It will be of great consequence to France and England to have America governed by a Galloman or Angloman." Hamilton on the other hand cited the Polish federation with approval as an example of a state of roughly the size of the thirteen colonies that had managed the election of its chief of state, but he also warned against the Polish model of a weak federation: "If more direct examples were wanting, Poland, as a government over local sovereigns, might not improperly be taken notice of. Nor could any proof more striking be given of the calamities flowing from such institutions. Equally unfit for self-government and self-defense, it has long been at the mercy of its powerful neighbors; who have lately had the mercy to disburden it of one third of its people and territories." *The Federalist Papers* 19.

[7] A Polish scholar, Jan Dziegielewski, has counted 11,271 present and voting at the election of King Michael Wisniowiecki in 1669, while at the 1674 election of Jan Sobieski he believes there were a third of that number. (These figures are courtesy of Professor Stephania Ochmann-Stansziewka of the University of Wroclaw.)

The result was a weakened political system inviting foreign intervention, since the votes of the nobility were often for sale to the highest bidder.[8]

French interest in the Polish throne dated to the 16th century, when in 1573 the cross-dressing Duke d'Anjou, a son of Catherine de Médicis, had briefly served as King in Warsaw before returning to France to occupy the French throne as Henri III. Cardinal Mazarin had mediated the 1661 Peace of Oliva ending the war with Sweden, sending a French Queen to the Poles in the person of Marie-Louise de Gonzague, Duchess de Nevers, and increasing French influence to the point that one resentful Pole complained that "there are more Frenchmen in Warsaw than there are devils in hell."

Figure 2. Jan Andrasz Morsztyn, Grand Treasurer of the Polish Republic, and his wife Lady Mary Catherine Gordon of Huntley, Callières's patrons and friends from their first meeting in Poland in 1670 to the end of their lives in France. (Czartoryski Museum, Krakow.)

In 1670, the principal leaders of the French party were Jan Sobieski, commander of the Army and Grand Marshal of the Nobility, and Jan Andrasz Morsztyn, the Grand Treasurer of the Republic, a canny survivor of the rough and tumble of Polish politics. Both men had married penniless girls who had gone to Poland as ladies-in-waiting to the Queen. Sobieski's wife was Marie de la Grange d'Arquien, an ambitious woman from a prominent but impecunious French family. For his part, Morsztyn had married a noblewoman from the clan Gordon, Lady Mary Catherine

---

[8] A contemporary French observer wrote that "Poland is now properly a Republic, and it is by that name that the Polanders call it, looking upon their King as no more than the head of their Commonwealth .... But they do not consider that while they design to shun so great an evil, they fall into another that is worse, since their neighbors, who are all of them their enemies, finding the country open, easily invade it," Hauteville, *Rélation historique de la Pologne*, 79.

Gordon, a daughter of the Marquis of Huntley. Their preferred French candidates for the Polish throne were either Monsieur le Prince or his son the Duke d'Enghien, and when King Jan Casimir declared his intention to abdicate,[9] the French Ambassador, a handsome bishop named Bonzy, intrigued in support of Condé with Morsztyn, Sobieski, and the two Marys, who appear from their correspondence to have been rivals for his affections.[10]

In 1667, Louis XIV had promised Morsztyn, come to Versailles as an envoy of the Republic, that he would send Condé through Germany at the head of an expeditionary force of 9,000 men to assume the throne as soon as Jan Casimir abdicated. But by the next year, Louis had cooled to the idea, among other reasons because he was preparing for war with Holland and could not easily spare the troops and the considerable expense. To the disappointment of Morsztyn and Sobieski, Louis promised instead to support a German prince with a strategic seat on the Rhine for the Polish throne, the Duke of Neuburg, and the King extracted from Condé a written promise to stand down.[11]

With Condé declared off limits by Louis XIV, the election of 1669 resulted in the compromise choice of Michael Wisniowiecki. He was an impoverished Polish gentleman with good Vasa bloodlines but little else to recommend him. In their disgust at this turn of events, Sobieski and

---

[9] His tomb is in the church, which remains from the former Abbey, and a bas-relief there shows him handing down his sword and scepter. Morsztyn was the executor of his estate, leading to a lawsuit lasting some twenty years against Morsztyn by the Condé family with Morsztyn's estate finally sentenced to pay the estate of Condé 400,000 francs in compensation. (Both of the principals were dead by that time.) The dossier is in the Polish Library in Paris.

[10] See Waliszewski, *Marysienka*.

[11] The Polish Library in Paris contains a collection of documents marked *extrait des archives du royaume* that appeared to have been prepared in 1688 for a lawsuit filed by Morsztyn. They include a letter from Condé to Lionne, the French Foreign Minister, written in Condé's aristocratic scrawl: "The King has told me that I must desist from the crown of Poland, to which I have reluctantly agreed. Now my son informs me that I must refuse to accept the crown even if it is offered. This is dishonorable, and if I were not suffering from an attack of gout I would go to the King myself. You must convey this for me, I have agreed to everything else he has asked." Instead, Lionne sent Neuburg a copy of the letter the King had forced Condé to write, apologizing that it was not a more explicit refusal to accept the crown under any circumstances. In an effort to persuade the understandably suspicious Neuburg of French good faith, the Foreign Minister described a turbulent meeting during which Condé had accused the King of seeking to "attach his body to his chariot in triumph." "I can hardly tell you the things the Prince said to me yesterday," Lionne wrote, and "if I did you would pity me." He told Neuburg that Bonzy in Warsaw had been instructed by the King to make any use of the letter Neuburg directed, "which Monsieur le Prince does not know, and will never know."

Morsztyn resolved to force Michael's abdication in favor of the Count de Saint-Paul.

It is not always possible discern with clarity the intentions of Louis XIV towards the candidacy of Saint-Paul from the available records. He clearly blew hot and cold, worried about upsetting the relationship with Austria, and there appears to have been an attempt after the fact to remove compromising documents from the archives that could be used in the lawsuits that followed. It is clear from his instructions to the French Resident in Danzig, Antoine Baluze, that the King's Secretary of State for Foreign Affairs, Hugues de Lionne disapproved of the candidacy of the person he referred to derisively as *mon soi-disant sieur de Saint Pol*, an allusion to Saint-Paul's illegitimacy as La Rochefoucauld's natural son.[12] Lionne was at pains to preserve Austrian neutrality with the invasion of Holland in prospect; at the same time the King does not appear to have resisted the temptation to steal a march on the Austrians on the sly. If Saint-Paul could be installed in Poland it would create a military alliance between France and Poland against the Hapsburgs, and an element of duplicity was present from the beginning. It was essential that the French hand be hidden as much as possible in order to preserve a measure of plausible deniability.

'MONSIEUR DE LARGE'

Callières later suggested to the Marquise d'Huxelles that he had been in charge of the Longueville delegation. In fact, at the age of twenty-five he was its most junior member, and when he left France for the Polish border in the spring of 1670, there were already two conspirators on the ground ahead of him, both with extensive experience of political work abroad. The head of the clandestine team was a shadowy cleric named Jean de Courthonne, Abbé de Paulmiers, codenamed "monsieur du Bourg," and he was already well-established at the gateway port of Gdansk, down the Vistula from Warsaw. A second conspirator, Roger Akakia du Fresne who had been a secretary to the French Ambassador to the Ottoman Sultan, had left earlier, arriving on June 2 in Hamburg. He had traveled overland in the jump seat of a post chaise from Paris to Hamburg without much sleep, he wrote, obliged to hold on for fear of falling under the carriage wheels, and there under the transparently French code name of "Monsieur le Lis" he waited impatiently for Callières. Their correspondent in Paris was Pierre de Tourmont, the chief clerk to Lionne, and they addressed him as "Monsieur de Saint-Pierre, merchant in Paris."

---

[12] *CP Pologne* 38, Lionne to Baluze, April 11, 1670.

Their mission was a delicate one, and they were aware that at any moment the King might pull the rug out from under them. If this happened, Akakia wrote to Tourmont, it should be sooner rather than later, "before our friends are committed." Without the King's backing the road ahead would be a hard one, and "the expense of it will be greater, not to say infinite."[13]

On arrival in Hamburg, Callières sent two letters to Tourmont to be forwarded to his mother and his friend with a return address of Coutances in Normandy – unopened so that Tourmont could see for himself that he was not compromising the operation. The young Callières justified the breach of security on the grounds that a friend might come looking for him, drawing attention to his absence. He wasn't as worried about his mother – he had taken the precaution of lying to her, he told Tourmont – but there was a risk that she might try to track him down, drawing unwanted attention to his absence from Paris.[14]

Unlike Akakia, Callières had traveled in some state, using the name of "Monsieur de Large" and pretending to be a Baron from the independent Duchy of Lorraine, an Austrian ally at the time; his cover would have been destroyed if he had run into anyone from Lorraine in his travels. His route went through territory in which Austrian agents could operate freely, and there was real danger of discovery and compromise.

By early September, Callières had made his way to Königsberg on the Baltic, present-day Kaliningrad, a day's sail from Gdansk, and there he established contact with Paulmier. The young operative was understandably worried about his cover. He wrote to Tourmont that "people are trying to discover our mission here, and we are in a country where we would run the risk of having an ill turn done to us if it were known what we are about." He did not want to linger. He had fired a domestic who had been overly curious. Tourmont should stop writing to him in care of the Formont banking house, which was too well-known as a French front.[15]

In Gdansk, Paulmier grew impatient with the nervous young undercover agent who had been foisted on him, and he suggested to Tourmont that someone with more experience might be better suited to the delicate task at hand. He noted that the expense of keeping up Callières's cover was considerable. Callières was pressing him to pay for his horse and carriage, even as the Abbé himself, his superior, contented himself with a "monkish" existence, or so Paulmier wrote. By October, the Abbé was suggesting outright to Tourmont that it would save money to recall

---

[13] *Chantilly*, Le Lis to Saint Pierre, June 2, 1670.
[14] *Chantilly*, de Large to Saint-Pierre, July 28, 1670.
[15] *Chantilly*, de Large to Saint-Pierre, September 5, 1670.

Callières[16] but Paulmier eventually found a task for him that he thought might be suited to his talents as the handler of the Grand Treasurer, Jan Andrasz Morsztyn.

Morsztyn was hard-pressed at the time by pro-Austrian elements in the Polish Senate to account for coded correspondence that had been seized from a confederate, the Castellan of Posnania. Under surveillance and unable to travel himself, he sent his Scottish wife Lady Mary to make contact with Paulmier.[17] The Abbé did not fully trust Morsztyn, suspecting him of playing a double game, and instead of going to meet Mme Morsztyn himself, he sent her a cipher for use in corresponding with him, and he instructed Callières to handle the contact as she was "in his neighborhood."[18]

The handsome Mme Morsztyn was to all intents French, and born to high politics she was a full participant in her husband's affairs.[19] She would have been in a disturbed emotional state when Callières made contact with her. Earlier in the summer she had lost a two year old son to illness.[20] Moreover, she was understandably anxious for reassurance with regard to the strength of the French commitment. Callières's initial meeting with her near Königsberg established the close connection to the Morsztyns that would endure until their deaths in prosperous exile in France many years later.

Paulmier soon became convinced that instead of managing the Morsztyns and threatening them as ordered with dire consequences, Callières was taking their side, and he came to regret the errand he had given to his young assistant. By October, the Abbé was complaining to Tourmont that Callières was keeping him in the dark:

> M. de Large sends me neither a copy nor any extract of what Mme Morsztyn has written to him. I don't know what the subject of this pourparler is, so I sent him a long mémoire on the state of the negotiations and all the four points her husband raises. If she raises other matters, he is to listen as they

---

[16] *Chantilly*, du Bourg to Saint-Pierre, letters of October 18 and October 22, 1670.

[17] A key confederate of the French party, the Castellan of Posnania had been badly beaten to force him to reveal the contents of a letter in cipher. Writing much later to the Marquise d'Huxelles, Callières cited this incident as an indication of the perilous nature of his mission, *Letters*, 94. It is highly unlikely that the intercepted letter was from Callières, as he implies with the careful phrase "on my behalf." Callières had not arrived in Hamburg when the incident occurred.

[18] See their miniatures in the illustrations.

[19] Lady Mary was the great grandmother of the last King of Poland, Stanislaus Augustus Poniatowski, as well as an ancestor of Lord Byron. See Bulloch, *The Gay Gordons*, 44-8.

[20] *AAE, CP Pologne* 37, reports of Desnoyers, August 2, 1670.

say in Germany ad referendum, without making any other commitment – apart from one to keep me informed.[21]

By November, Paulmier had completely lost control of the Morsztyn channel to Callières, writing to Tourmont that

I now learn that instead of going back to Königsberg he has stayed with Monsieur and Madame Morsztyn to be, or so he thinks, closer to the news. But the news that comes through this channel will always be suspicious as far as I am concerned. Partly because of the trick he (Morsztyn) played on our friends with regard to the Crown from Krakow, people have little confidence in him and hide their intentions from him.[22]

Preparing to leave Gdansk for the Polish interior, Paulmier told Tourmont that he would not be able to take the carriage Callières had bought, "partly because it is too large, and partly because I can't get it," since Callières had gone off with it. He complained that Callières's departure had deprived him of the use of a French valet, leaving him only with a German secretary who knew no Polish. When Callières reported to Paulmier that Morsztyn had admitted to him that he had no avenue of retreat, Paulmier instructed him to reinforce his isolation by telling Morsztyn that if the venture failed "all our friends would blame him as the author of their misfortunes and feed off his corpse."[23] It is unlikely that Callières complied. By this time, he was clearly playing both ends against the middle.

By November as the Poles continued to procrastinate and the business dragged on without result, Saint-Paul concluded that his mother's money and his own inheritance were being spent to no purpose. In a peremptory scrawl to Tourmont, he ordered that there be no further expense, "affairs having advanced so little." It was clear that the Poles would not offer a crown "unless a purse is first opened." He ordered Tourmont to draw up an instruction recalling the mission and make a copy for him so that he could approve it: "I will speak tomorrow to Monsieur de Lionne. Burn this letter as soon as you have read it."[24] Playing for time, and appealing to the honor of the young Prince, Tourmont responded that it would be wrong for Saint-Paul to pull the rug out after giving Paulmier had raised funds on the strength of his written commitment. If the effort was to be abandoned, he argued, it should be the Poles who made the decision. He

[21] *Chantilly*, du Bourg to Saint Pierre, October 25, 1670.
[22] *Chantilly*, du Bourg to Saint-Pierre, November 12, 1670. Morsztyn had taken the crown from the Treasury in Cracow where the crown jewels were kept, *AAE CP Pologne* 37, reports of Desnoyers, November 1670.
[23] *Chantilly*, Du Bourg to Saint-Pierre, November 12, 1670.
[24] *Chantilly*, Saint-Paul to Tourmont, November 13 or 14, 1670. Tourmont obviously failed to follow these instructions.

promised Saint-Paul that no more money would be spent in any case, and he argued that a final decision should await the return of Callières "who knows more of the affair than I do." Lionne's clerk seems to have hoped that Callières might be able to bring Saint-Paul around.[25]

In the meantime, disaster struck when Akakia was unmasked as a French agent. Furious, Lionne ordered Akakia to return immediately but he dragged his feet, arguing that that it would be wrong to abandon the affair just when it was on the brink of success. He told Lionne that given his appetite for food and drink King Michael wouldn't last long in any case, and that Morsztyn had told him that Saint-Paul's election was a certainty. Both Morsztyn and Sobieski were deeply committed, Akakia argued. This was an affair for which the "great men of this country have put at risk their fortunes, their honor, and their life."[26] But Akakia's pleas fell on deaf ears. When he finally returned, a furious Louis XIV clapped him in the Bastille.

Ordered to return to Paris himself, though he had not been exposed as a member of the undercover team, Callières was in no hurry to comply either. On December 19, he wrote to Tourmont from Stettin, present-day Szczecin, that he had received two letters addressed to Paulmier, absent in the Polish interior where he had gone to meet with Sobieski. He had thought it right in Paulmier's absence to open these letters to his superior "in part to ease the dilemma I am in, and in case they should require a response." He recommended that a final decision to withdraw the mission not be made before Paulmier had seen Sobieski. That meeting would decide the fate of the entire negotiation. As for him, "having conferred with Monsieur du Bourg (Paulmier), if he believes my presence here is no longer useful for the service of His Highness (Saint-Paul), I will return immediately." Morsztyn had promised him a full report on the state of affairs in Warsaw, he told Tourmont, and he wanted to stay long enough to receive it so that on his return to France he could give a "full account of what can be hoped for."[27]

Saint-Paul, meanwhile, responding to reports from Paulmier casting doubt on Morsztyn's good faith, wrote to Tourmont that while Morsztyn might be playing a double game as Paulmier clearly believed, care should be taken not to say anything to him that might suggest that the French were suspicious.[28] Siding with Callières against Paulmier in a way that suggests that Callières was writing to him behind Paulmier's back,

[25] *Chantilly*, Tourmont to Saint-Paul, ca. October or November 1670.
[26] *BnF, Ms fr* 21103, *Fonds Clairambault*, 103-105.
[27] *Chantilly*, de Large to Saint-Pierre, December 19, 1670.
[28] *Chantilly*, undated letter from Saint-Paul to 'Monsieur Aubert'.

Saint-Paul argued that Sobieski was the principal problem and that Morsztyn's conduct appeared to him to be straightforward. With regard to Akakia, and his imprisonment, Saint-Paul promised Tourmont he would speak to Lionne and urge his release from close confinement on the grounds that "the comedy has lasted long enough, without adding cruelties that would only torment him without being useful for the affair in question." Lionne promised Saint-Paul that he would take the matter up with the King, but Akakia stayed in the Bastille.

On his return, Callières composed a report to Saint-Paul entitled *"Recommendations with regard to certain matters which it may please His Highness the Count de Saint-Paul to consider."*[29] The report is drafted as if from Paulmier, but it is in Callières's handwriting, and in plain text, which could hardly be the case if it had really come from Paulmier in the Polish interior.

The report recommended that before Saint-Paul left to rejoin the Army, letters should be prepared for him to sign and address in his own hand to his principal supporters in Poland to thank them for their past support. Saint-Paul should lobby the King to pay Morsztyn's back subsidies, and work for Akakia's release from prison, since his continued detention which was confusing the Poles about French intentions. Despite Akakia's arrest and the King's order to cease and desist, Callières suggested that Saint-Paul should continue to plan what he would do "if you are called to Poland." He should plan to take along military engineers since these were lacking in Poland, but not many other French military officers since the proud Poles were generally unwilling to serve under foreigners. It concluded with the following passage, which was clearly the central point at hand:

Monsieur de Callières in my view could well be included in the entourage of His Highness. His remarkable memory and his hard work in the short time he was here enabled him to learn enough German to pass as a native (*passer pays*) and to carry on a conversation (*jargonner*). His zeal has been amply demonstrated, and his ability shown by the contacts he has made. He demonstrated discretion and skill in handling the tasks he was given, and managed Mme Morsztyn and through her the Grand Treasurer so well that he contributed greatly to keeping this important man on the right side. I admit that I would have been less well suited to bringing him back to our side since we [that is Paulmier and Morsztyn] had been at odds behind the scenes, and this had left some awkwardness between us, which M. de Callières was able

---

[29] *Chantilly, mémoire de diverses choses sur lesquelles il plaira à Monseigneur le Comte de Saint-Paul de faire consideration.* This is the last document in the Chantilly volume.

to overcome. By his entire conduct he has shown that for the nobly-born soul, virtue is not a matter of age.

This last phrase is lifted from Corneille's *Le Cid*, where it is used by the eponymous hero Don Rodrigue of himself.[30] Perhaps Callières included the reference as an inside joke between the two young men. Saint-Paul would have known the play, perhaps the most famous one of the time, and the familiar line is still known to French schoolchildren. It was in any case a remarkable display of cheek. The sole accomplishment Callières could cite was that he had managed to smooth over Paulmier's strained relations with the Morsztyns, and learned some German – though there is no evidence of this in his subsequent career. Saint-Paul may well have wondered whether this justified the expense of his mission.

In the summer of 1671, disaffected Cossacks and Tartars urged on by the Ottomans poured into Poland's Eastern provinces, and at the end of the year the Ottomans formally declared war. Sobieski finally took to the field, reluctantly accepting a sword from King Michael's hands. In Paris, meanwhile, Lionne had died, replaced as the dominant voice in the King's council by François-Michel le Tellier, Marquis de Louvois, the aggressive Secretary of State for War who was preparing for the invasion of Holland.

With this change in the European balance and the prospect of inevitable conflict with Austria, Louis XIV reversed course and gave Paulmier who had remained in Poland full powers to support Saint-Paul's election. The French files appear to have been purged of the incriminating evidence, but proof of this has survived in Poland in the form of a document signed by the King and countersigned by Louvois, dated December 6, 1671. It gave full powers to Paulmier to make commitments on his behalf in support of the election of the Duke de Longueville, the title Saint-Paul had been allowed by the King to assume earlier in the year.[31]

---

[30] *Monsieur de Callières ... a dans toute sa conduite ici montré qu'aux âmes bien nées la vertu n'attend pas le nombre des années.* In *Le Cid* Don Rodrigue says:
Je suis jeune, il est vrai; mais aux âmes bien nées
La valeur n'attend point le nombre des années.

[31] *Listy*, 84, from a copy in the Polish archives unearthed by K. Waliszewski. The commitment is an explicit one. There is no copy of this document in the *correspondence politique*, but it is clearly genuine. Both Sobieski and Morsztyn later sought reimbursement for the considerable expenses they had incurred in support of Longueville on the strength of this commitment by Louis XIV. Recriminations continued for years, and Morsztyn was still seeking repayment from Longueville's heirs in 1693. The Chantilly files also contain an August 1670 letter from Paulmier to Tourmont in which he says "you did well to follow the advice of M. Akakia with regard to sending the full powers of His Majesty the King in the cover of a book," suggesting that there may have been an earlier document as well. In the aftermath of the election of Sobieski as King in 1674, the French Ambassador, Forbin-Janson, reviewed the evidence and urged that Morsztyn be compensated, convinced that
(continued)

King Michael still refused to abdicate, stiffened in his resolve by his Austrian Queen who was the Emperor's sister, but by July 1 the great men of the Kingdom, including the Primate, Sobieski, and Morsztyn, had all put their signatures to a formal *pacta conventa*, a state of formal insurrection provided for by the Polish constitution.[32] The stage was set for Michael's removal – by force if necessary.

Sometime in early 1672 after this renewed support for the conspiracy from Louis XIV Longueville sent Callières back to Poland. There is no contemporary documentation, but there is no reason to doubt the essentials of his later account to the Marquise d'Huxelles, even though as usual he exaggerated his role. He wrote that he had arranged for Longueville to make his way incognito across Germany to Lübeck, where he had commissioned and equipped a vessel to convey him to Poland: "you may judge, Madame, the joy I would have had from the elevation of such a Prince, who loved me and esteemed me enough to entrust me with his full powers though I was only twenty-two at the time, with the order to give me all the money I asked for ...."[33]

These hopes were dashed when on the way back to France carrying the news of Longueville's impending election, Callières learned that the young Prince was dead.

"NO QUARTER!"

Figure 3 shows a detail from Van der Meulen's famous painting of the battle of Tolhuis on June 12, 1672 – one of the most celebrated feats of arms of the age of Louis XIV. Longueville is visible on a charger prancing under the eye of the King, who is portrayed as directing the action, with Longueville's uncle Monsieur le Prince off to the side.[34] With a group of young nobles eager to show off their courage in the presence of the King, including Condé's son, the Duke d'Enghien, Longueville had made his way

---

Paulmier had been authorized to make commitments to reimburse him on behalf of Louis XIV. The issue became an irritant in the relations between Sobieski after he became King in 1674 and France, and it contributed to souring him on French good faith.

[32] The July 1 date is in Waliszewski, *Marysienka*, p. 245. See also the *Cambridge History of Poland*, I, 534.

[33] *Letters*, 99-100. Callières has subtracted five years from his age. He was twenty-seven in 1672, not twenty-two. It is probably not a coincidence that he was courting a younger woman who was a friend of Mme d'Huxelles at the time.

[34] Of the many accounts of this river crossing under fire, the most vivid is perhaps one Louis XIV is said to have composed himself, presumably dictated to a secretary. The King's account is in Rousset, *Histoire de Louvois*, 527-8.

Figure 3. Detail from "Crossing of the Rhine," Adam Frans van der Meulen. The Duke de Longueville is prancing on a charger before the King. (Réunion des Musées Nationaux / Art Resource, NY.)

across the river in a small boat, his charger swimming alongside, while Dutch troops in trenches waited on the opposite bank and prepared to surrender to the superior French force. The experienced Condé tried to restrain the impetuous young men from riding hell for leather into the fortified Dutch positions, but before he could stop them they charged, shouting "no quarter," leaving the Dutch with no alternative but to resist. Longueville was killed instantly.

His body was transported back across the Rhine in the same small boat in which he had crossed, covered with his grieving uncle's cloak. When the news reached Paris it caused shock waves. Mme de Sévigné has left a famous and moving account of the reaction of Mme de Longueville to the news of her son's death. To her own daughter, she wrote that "all Holland is not worth such a prince." She also recorded with her usual malicious wit that the Marquise d'Huxelles had taken to her bed, and that there was something ridiculous in this excessive grief of Paris ladies of a certain age.

As for Callières, his dejection was still fresh in a letter to Huxelles a quarter century later: "It was such a bitter blow that I lost all taste for the glories of mankind, and it taught me the vanity of all human endeavors."[35]

Could Longueville really have been occupied the Polish throne if he had not been killed on the Rhine? It seems unlikely, though far from impossible. Morsztyn and Sobieski both argued in subsequent correspondence with Louis XIV that he would have, but they were

---

[35] *Letters*, 100.

interested parties seeking to recover the money they had spent on the strength of the full powers granted by Louis XIV to Paulmier.[36] Moving Longueville incognito in the face of Austrian opposition through German territory for Lübeck where he could take ship for Gdansk and travel up the Vistula to Warsaw would not have been easy. It appears that the Poles were requiring that Louis XIV send troops and money with Longueville as a condition of his election, and whether Louis XIV could have managed this in the midst of the fighting in Holland is open to question. There would still have been the unpredictable and xenophobic Polish electors to deal with. They might well have defied the pro-French magnates as they had done in 1669 with the election of Michael, wary of an absolute monarch on the French model who could threaten their liberties.

In this regard, the contemporary assessment of the Grande Mademoiselle is relevant. She was the great lady to whom Jacques de Callières had dedicated his book on court manners. In her memoirs, she recalled that Mme de Longueville had argued for her marriage to her son the prince on the grounds that some day he would be King of Poland. The Grande Mademoiselle had her doubts, as she made clear in telling the tale: "She (Mme de Longueville) launched into the Polish business.[37] A gentleman from Normandy named Calières who was involved in the negotiation told me subsequently that when Longueville died the affair was a sure thing – from the Polish point of view. But although the King is said to have allowed the negotiation, I'm not sure he would have been pleased if it had succeeded, and he might have prevented it in the end. He never liked M. de Longueville."[38]

Longueville's death eliminated a patron with a brilliant future, but Callières was resilient and as ambitious as ever, determined to exploit his connection to Morsztyn and the knowledge he had gained of Polish affairs

---

[36] On July 12, probably soon after news of Longueville's death reached Poland, Paulmier had signed a promissory note pledging to reimburse Sobieski a total of 93,000 francs he had expended to buy support for Longueville. A notation in the margin indicates that of these sums "32,000 has been reimbursed by the Republic" suggesting that state funds were diverted for the purpose. Morsztyn had also spent heavily, later claiming to have advanced 300,000 francs from his own funds. These were enormous sums of money in the Polish (or indeed in any other) context, and were in addition to the 160,000 francs Longueville had borrowed from his own estate. It was a very expensive failure, *CP Pologne 38, copie de la promesse de l'abbé Paulmier*, July 12, 1672. After Sobieski's election, Forbin-Janson told Pomponne that Sobieski had shown him a copy, and he urged that the King settle this debt.

[37] *Elle s'embarqua à l'affaire de Pologne.*

[38] *Mémoires*, 385-6. It is noteworthy that Mlle de Montpensier, who was punctilious about matters of birth, refers to Callières as a Norman gentleman, without the noble *de*. She refers to Jacques in the same way.

When a little over a year later King Michael died, unlamented, he seized on the occasion to commend himself as an undercover operative to Poland once again – this time directly to Louis XIV himself.

BACK TO THE VISTULA

If we examine the true duties of Bishops, we shall find that they are not very compatible with embassies, and that it ill suits them to travel around the world, instead of taking care of their primary occupations.
– Francois de Callieres, *On Negotiating with Sovereigns*

Figure 4. Jan Sobieski as Grand Marshal of the Crown.

In the aftermath of Longueville's death, Sobieski reluctantly came to terms with Michael, taking the field against the Ottomans and eventually regaining enough ground to gain a peace, negotiated by Morsztyn, which the Polish Diet indignantly refused to ratify. By the "shameful" Treaty of Buczacz (October 12, 1672) Podolia and Ukraine were ceded to the Ottomans and their Cossack allies, and Poland agreed to pay a yearly tribute to the Sultan. The following year, however, Sobieski resumed the offensive, and on November 11 of 1673 he decisively defeated an Ottoman army at Chocim. Michael having died of a stomach complaint on November 10, the stage was set for the election of a successor.

When the news of Michael's death reached Paris, the ambitious young Callières drafted a detailed set of recommendations on Polish affairs directly to Louis XIV.[1] It is undated, but based on the context it must have been composed in December of 1673. The paper was notable for its overuse of the first person – its brash author was only 28 – and he conveys a measure of exasperation that he is not being listened to. An addendum at the top of the first page notes that Callières has already "informed His Majesty by repeated *mémoires* through M. de Pomponne as to what I know of the situation in Poland," and that he had decided to write again, this time directly to the King. The clear implication was that Pomponne had failed to adequately convey his views.

Callières argued that the absence of an active French envoy on the ground was allowing the Austrians to have their own way by default. The Austrian candidate to succeed Michael was the Duke of Lorraine, one of the leaders of the anti-French coalition formed since the French invasion of Holland, while France was still pledged to the son of the Duke of Neuburg, a neutral German prince. This created the risk of a stalemate, and to avoid a civil war the Poles could well turn to a compromise candidate as had happened with the election of Michael. Thus, Callières argued, there was an urgent need for a fallback to the preferred French candidate if France were to stay in the game.

In the time-honored manner of the servants of princes everywhere, Callières outlined three options designed to lead the King to the middle course he favored. The first option would to promote the candidacy of the Prince de Conti, then all of eight years old. As a French prince of the blood he would have the support of Sobieski but he was a little young for the job Callières admitted. (Conti would be a French candidate for the Polish throne some twenty-two years later.) At the other end of the age spectrum, Callières suggested, was Henri de la Tour d'Auverge, Viscount de Turenne, Louis's leading general. His military experience might incite the jealousy of Sobieski – "though I am informed that this could be overcome," Callières wrote. At the same time, the elderly Turenne was unlikely to appeal as a husband to Michael's Austrian widow, the Emperor's sister Eleanor.

---

[1] *Mémoire pour Sa Majesté sur les affaires de Pologne*, BnF, NAF 21103, Fonds Clairambault, 105-107. A translation is at Annex A.

Having bracketed these unlikely alternatives, Callières marshaled the arguments in favor of his candidate, the young Count de Soissons, known as Prince Thomas of Savoy-Carignan. Thomas was neither a French prince of the blood nor a great general, but at 17 he was the right age to marry the Austrian queen, and since he was not quite French there might be less opposition to him from the Austrians, particularly if he were to marry Queen Eleanor.

It was imperative in any case that the right man be sent to Poland immediately in order to prepare the way for the King's Ambassador, Callières told the King. The ideal candidate, he argued, would be someone who was close to Morsztyn – someone who knew Poland and the principal Polish personalities, and who could come and go without being recognized as a French agent. And as it happened, he had the ideal candidate in mind: "During my previous stay in this country I was careful not to be known as what I was to anyone but a few of the principal men of the French party, whose trust I acquired. Having worked with some success on the affair that was entrusted to me, and as I am particularly well-informed with regard to the manner of dealing with these gentlemen in order to advance His Majesty's interests, I flatter myself that I can render good service to His Majesty in this country should His Majesty see fit to send me there immediately." Callières warned the King against the damage that would be done if Louis XIV failed to follow his advice: "The slightest delay in giving this order would cause notable damage to His Majesty's interests and benefit those of his enemies."

ENVOY OF THE DUKE OF SAVOY

In the event, Louis XIV ignored this warning and the peremptory invitation to send Callières to Poland as an undercover advance man for his Ambassador, but Callières nevertheless managed to secure a commission to attend the upcoming election. Once again, his mission to Poland was financed by a great lady with ambitions for her son – the imperious and headstrong Olympia Mancini, Countess de Soissons, Cardinal Mazarin's niece.

Olympia had been the playmate if not more of the young Louis XIV during his adolescence, though it was with her sister Maria that the young Louis fell in love. Her uncle the Cardinal had arranged her marriage to the noble but impecunious Count, a grandson of the Duke of Savoy who was related to half the crowned heads of Europe. Unable to come to terms with the new order and her changed relations with the mature Louis, Olympia had been caught spying on his love affairs and been sent away in disgrace from the court. Her husband had commanded the prestigious Swiss

Regiment, and when he had died suddenly in the field in October of 1673 there were persistent rumors in Turin that she had poisoned him.

The Count's death and their mother's lack of favor at court left their two young sons without prospects. Thomas was the elder at sixteen, and the younger boy, Eugene, a shy and reticent child of ten, was destined for a career in the church. Their uncle Charles Emmanuel II, the sovereign Duke of Savoy was a key ally who supplied France with four regiments of troops, and Louis XIV was reluctant to say no to the candidacy of his nephew. From the Duke's perspective, sending an envoy to the Polish election would be an occasion to promote Savoy as a major player in European politics, and with the wealthy Olympia paying expenses, there was little to lose. She provided Callières with a draft on the Fromont brothers in Gdansk for 60,000 francs.

Callières's remarkably detailed report on this mission has survived in the Polish Library in Paris, some fifty pages in manuscript.[2] The light it sheds on this second mission to Poland is not always flattering to Callières and his veracity when it is contrasted with the contemporaneous reports of the French Ambassador, the Bishop of Marseilles, Toussaint de Forbin-Janson.[3]

---

[2] *Bibliothèque polonaise de Paris*, manuscript 13, 311-60. This document in Callières' hand is entitled *Relation de mon voyage en Pologne en qualité d'envoyé extraordinaire de S.A.R. en l'année 1674*. It is not bound but tied together with string, on good paper, carefully written with only a few alterations in the text, generally well-preserved. The Bishop's detailed instructions, his reports, as well as Callières' letters to Pomponne are in the Archives des Affaires Etrangères, *CP Pologne 40*. In the *BnF, ms. Fr Clairambault 501*, 35-66, there are what appear to be copies of some of his reports to the Duke, the last in July of 1674 when he reports on a fire in Warsaw that damaged Morsztyn's palace.

[3] The circumstances suggest strongly that Mme de Sévigné had a hand in the Bishop's appointment. She was a close friend of Arnauld de Pomponne, who had replaced Lionne as Foreign Secretary, and Pomponne's writ included the former papal territory of Avignon in Provence, where her son-in-law the Marquis de Grignan was the King's Lieutenant-General. Forbin-Janson was a defender of the power of the local clans against Grignan, and Grignan's assignment was to assert royal authority. In this quarrel, Mme de Sévigné assured her daughter that Pomponne, the King's minister after all, took their side. At about the time the decision was made to send Forbin-Janson to far-off Poland, we know from her letters that she spent an hour with Pomponne discussing the affairs of Provence. The appointment of a Bishop as Ambassador on the occasion of Polish elections was usual, since under the Polish Constitution the chief of state during an interregnum was the Archbishop of Gniezno. The previous French Ambassador, Bonzy, had been rewarded with the red hat of a Cardinal which was in the gift of the Polish King. It was in any event convenient for Mme de Sévigné and the Grignans to get Forbin-Janson out of the way, and he was anxious in Poland to get back to Provence as soon as possible. Sévigné's name for him was *la grêle*: "sleet and freezing rain."

Figure 5. Toussaint de Forbin-Janson, Bishop of Marseille, later Cardinal de Janson, who recommended against employing Callières as the French Resident in Poland.

Forbin-Janson's instructions spelled out the King's intentions clearly, anticipating the contingencies Forbin-Janson might confront in Warsaw without constraining his freedom to act as circumstances might require. His primary and overriding goal must be to block the election of the Austrian candidate, the Duke of Lorraine; if absolutely necessary to defeat the Duke, he was authorized as a fallback to support Thomas as a compromise candidate. He could promise Sobieski and Morsztyn the considerable sum of 400,000 francs, payable after the election, and he was authorized to reiterate his earlier promise to grant Sobieski the title of 'Marshal of France' among other dignities. The Poles to whom Louis XIV had previously promised pensions, including Morsztyn, could be left to hope they would be finally paid, with a bonus payment of a back year as a goodwill gesture.[4]

Callières helped prepare the Ambassador for his departure – at least the dossier that was assembled for Forbin-Janson contains several documents in his distinctive hand. They include a background piece on the parlous financial situation of the French family of Sobieski's ambitious

---

[4] *CP Pologne* 40, March 30, 1674.

wife, Marie d'Arquien, and what appears to be a draft for Forbin-Janson of an address to the Polish Senate.[5]

Anticipating delays that might prevent the Ambassador from arriving in Poland in time for the election if he took the land route through Austrian-controlled territory, Louis XIV secured the agreement of Charles II of England, a recipient of French subsidies, to supply his envoy with a small but elegant 'yacht' to carry Forbin-Janson and his entourage as far as Hamburg.[6] The party included the young "Envoy Extraordinary" of the Duke of Savoy, and it left Paris on the last day of March, 1674, boarding the yacht in Calais. However, violent winds blew them back almost to the Thames estuary, and on April 10, Forbin-Janson wrote to Pomponne that he was stuck there. It was April 17 before the delegation finally made landfall in Hamburg.

Two weeks together in close quarters on board the small yacht did not improve the relationship between the two envoys. Callières shared his secret instructions from the Duke of Savoy with the Ambassador and promised to disregard them if they were troublesome, but the lordly Bishop of Marseilles clearly did not take to his ambitious young colleague. As soon as the English yacht docked in Hamburg, he sent Callières off to proceed by himself overland via Berlin while he continued by sea to Gdansk. To Arnauld de Pomponne, who had successed Lionne as Foreign Minister, the Bishop wrote that he wanted to avoid the appearance of collusion with Callières, since they were supporting different candidates. With a sniff of disdain, he told Pomponne that in addition to the 60,000 francs the Countess de Soissons had authorized, drawn on the same banking house of Formont that had financed the Longueville mission, Callières "flatters himself" that the Duke of Savoy would go up to a million in exchange for his nephew's election. [7] Since Forbin-Janson's own spending limit from Louis XIV was 500,000 francs, itself a small fortune, it was extremely unwise of Callières to boast that he was empowered to outspend the Sun King himself.

---

[5] *BnF, MS fr Clairambault 21103*, 101-5, contains this part of the dossier compiled for Forbin-Janson.

[6] Yachts were among the favorite playthings of the nautical Charles. He had admired the luxuriously appointed vessel the Dutch East India Company had given him to sail to England when he was restored to the throne, and he commissioned the building of several others on the same lines by the naval architect Sir Christopher Pett for his own use. They were comfortable, with elaborately carved woodwork; Samuel Pepys felt that they surpassed the Dutch models, Pepys, *Diary*, V, 306, n. 3. Callières does not name the yacht, nor does the Ambassador in his dispatches, but since Charles II is unlikely to have sent anything but his best to Louis XIV it may have been the 'Royal Catherine', launched in 1664.

[7] *CP Pologne* 40, Forbin-Janson to Pomponne, April 17, 1674.

In his own report to the Duke, Callières put the matter differently. Without quite saying so, he implied that he had decided himself to part with Forbin-Janson in order to make better speed, since the Ambassador was making a "slow progress." Callières traveled "day and night" by post chaise from Hamburg to Berlin, from Berlin to Stettin, on to Gdansk, and up the Vistula to Warsaw where the Diet was already in session in preparation for the election of a successor to Michael, arriving on May 5.

What Callières did not tell the Duke, however, was that before leaving Hamburg he had sent an obsequious letter to Pomponne offering his services, again expressing willingness to disregard his instructions if they caused any difficulty for France. It was sent in plain text since Callières did not have a French cipher, incurring the risk of interception by postal officials en route, and the experienced Pomponne would have wondered at Callières eagerness to be on with a new master before he was off with the old. By writing to Pomponne behind Forbin-Janson's back as he would continue to do throughout his time in Poland, the ambitious Callières risked jeopardizing his relationship with Forbin-Janson even as he betrayed the trust of the Duke of Savoy:

> Having confided in the Ambassador," Callières wrote, "I thought it my duty to write to you, though I have no cipher. I shall rule my conduct so as to derive the glorious advantage I so passionately seek, which is to make known to His Majesty the greatness of my zeal and my entire loyalty to his interests in every respect, which is ever my sole object in all my travels. I will conform myself precisely to the Ambassador's orders and keep him completely informed without allowing it to appear that we are acting in concert. He will tell you My Lord that in showing him my credentials I offered to disregard them if they caused the slightest difficulty to him, and I give the same assurance to you. I will pass as the subject of the prince who employs me, but I will follow the ambassador's orders in everything. I beg for the honor of a good word from you to His Majesty, which you have had the kindness to lead me to believe I might hope for ....

In a postscript, Callières added: "I gave the Ambassador a copy of a letter from Morsztyn. I would have sent it to you directly except that I agreed with him that we would take separate roads and I would travel through Stettin and Berlin."[8]

While Callières proceeded overland, the Bishop continued his stately progress to Gdansk. He arrived in Gdansk on May 1, none too soon, and when told that the election could take place as early as May 11, he rushed off to Warsaw on such short notice that he left much of his considerable suite behind.

---

[8] *CP Pologne* 40, Callières to Pomponne, from Hamburg, April 18, 1674.

From Besançon where the French Army was camped, Pomponne told Forbin-Janson that "the King to whom I read your letter of April 17 entirely approved of your decision to send Monsieur de Callières separately because of the bad impression that might be created with regard to interests which are not those principally supported by the King."[9] He did not say that Callières had written to him directly offering to work for France. Perhaps he thought it was unnecessary to mention.

EXCESSIVE ZEAL

Arriving in Warsaw before Forbin-Janson, Callières went to work with his customary diligence and energy. He reported to his master the Duke of Savoy that there were two principal factions, one pro-Austrian and the other pro-French. The French party headed by Sobieski and Morsztyn was much stronger than the Austrian faction headed by the powerful Michal Kazimierz Pac, Grand Chancellor of Lithuania, Callières thought, and buoyed by his victory over the Turks at Chocim Sobieski was the popular favorite. This was an accurate reading of the situation. But Callières also maintained, less plausibly, that if the two sides could not agree there would be a risk of civil war and the breakup of the federation. In that case, the door might be open to Prince Thomas as a compromise candidate.

Paying an initial courtesy call on Sobieski, Callières delivered a letter to him from the Duke of Savoy, and went from there to see Morsztyn, reporting to the Duke that "I gained his support, having prepared the way with letters and taking advantage of the close friendship I made with him almost five years ago."[10] He told the Duke that Morsztyn, the "finest mind in the Kingdom," had agreed to work with him to form a party for Thomas. This was an overstatement at best. Morsztyn was a strong ally of Sobieski and France, and on the French payroll. It is much more likely that Callières and Morsztyn reached agreement that Olympia Mancini's money could usefully be spent on mutually agreed objectives, and that Morsztyn had agreed not to be openly hostile to the unlikely candidacy of the young Thomas.

Callières wove a tangled web of intrigue in Warsaw, and his report to the Duke contains a careful mixture of fact and fiction. He knew that Sobieski's ambitious French wife Marie d'Arquien was determined to see

---

[9] *CP Pologne* 40, Pomponne to Forbin-Janson, May 6 and May 8, 1674.

[10] In fact, Callières's connection to the Morsztyns dated to the late summer of 1670, less than four years earlier, when Paulmier had sent him out from Königsberg to meet Madame Morsztyn. This potted chronology may be intended to suggest to the Duke that Callières had last gone to Poland for the election of King Michael in 1669, rather than as a clandestine operative for the Longueville interest in 1670-2.

her husband elevated to the throne, and he was also convinced that Sobieski was quite prepared to entertain the idea of the throne, despite his vehement public denials. He nevertheless argued to Sobieski ("who listened readily," he told the Duke) that only the election of Thomas could avoid a civil war, and that he had persuaded Sobieski after several meetings to promise that he would prefer Prince Thomas over all other foreign princes "for the security of which I drew up a written agreement with which the Grand Marshal appeared entirely satisfied." In fact, as Callières well knew, Sobieski had no intention of placing his sword and his Army at the disposal of any foreign prince.

Having taken these measures with Sobieski, and having worked to make himself "agreeable to his principal friends" – a euphemism for bribes – the resourceful Callières made an indirect approach to the opposing faction through the French wife of Chancellor Pac of Lithuania, lady-in-waiting to Queen Eleanor. Meeting with her in secret at the castle, Callières gave her a miniature of Thomas that he persuaded her to take to the Queen, and he reported to the Duke that Queen Eleanor had been so taken by it that she kept it for three days, asking to have it back again so that she could show it to her friends.

With regard to Chancellor Pac himself, Callières made clear that the Lithuanian leader was a tough nut to crack. Pac objected (as well he might) that Thomas was too young. Poland needed a strong and experienced leader to command its armies and marry the Queen. Callières fell back on the line he had taken with Sobieski: if the choice were to come down to Neuburg or Thomas, could the Chancellor not agree to prefer Thomas? This Pac promised through his French wife Mme de Mailly, Callières reported, and to seal the deal he drew up a document involving a considerable sum to be paid to Pac – after the election. As he had done with Sobieski, Callières "assured himself" (as he puts it) of the support of well-placed informants in Pac's entourage. The effect of all this clandestine maneuvering was to undermine Neuburg, the French candidate.

Before presenting his credentials as the Duke's envoy to the Bishop of Krakow, in his capacity as acting chief of state, Callières first extracted the Bishop's agreement that his master the Duke would be referred to as a "Royal Highness." This was not an mere matter of protocol by any means. The Duke sought every opportunity to establish the precedent that he was an independent sovereign rather than an Austrian dependent, and it may have been largely to establish this precedent at an important European gathering that Callières had been sent in the first place, given the long shot nature of the candicacy of Thomas. The Bishop readily agreed that the Duke would be referred to as *sua regia majestas cypri*, his Royal Majesty of Cyprus, an empty hereditary title held by the Duke that conveyed sovereignty, and he repeated the phrase several times much to Callières's satisfaction.

The ceremony at which Callières presented his credentials went well, or so he reported. The principal men of the Senate, Morsztyn included, had risen to their feet on his arrival, given him the place of honor at a long table, and heard out his speech on the virtues of the ancient House of Savoy with every appearance of close attention. Callières argued to the Senate that as a relation of the principal ruling houses of Europe, including both Austria and France, Thomas had been divinely sent to heal the divisions of the Polish Republic. What the grave magnates of Poland and Lithuania really thought of the young French envoy's eloquence is open to question, but Callières told the Duke that they had listened with great attention. Chancellor Pac did ask what could be expected in concrete terms from the Duke of Savoy if Prince Thomas were elected, and Callières avoided a direct response.

By the time the Bishop of Marseilles arrived in Warsaw he may have repented of his decision to send Callières on ahead. Forbin-Janson was displeased by what he considered to be Callières's excessive zeal on behalf of Thomas, and in a dismissive footnote to a long dispatch to Pomponne, he wrote that

> Monsieur de Soissons [as he called Prince Thomas] has sent Monsieur de Callières here with his credentials. He is bustling about on behalf of Soissons and intriguing inside the Pac household, and he has spoken to Madame the Grand Marshal, a bit too strongly in fact, but he has not found any readiness on either side.

Apparently undiscouraged by the lack of a response to his previous letters, Callières sent Pomponne his own independent report on the situation, bypassing the Ambassador. Forbin-Janson's anger had he known of this can be imagined. Callières reported that Forbin-Janson had succeeded in gaining Sobieski's agreement to the exclusion of the Duke of Lorraine and that "all should go in accordance with His Majesty's wishes, I hope so with all my heart, and I hope that I will someday have the opportunity to demonstrate my zeal, respect, and veneration." He made no mention of his feverish activity in support of Thomas, but he painted a picture of potential stalemate and a "double election" with the risk of civil war, laying the basis for a possible resort to Thomas as a compromise.[11]

Callières also reported that Sobieski had sent troops (interestingly, he says they were "Milanese dressed as janissaries," with Turkish drums

---

[11] *CP Pologne* 40, May of 1674. Callières and Forbin-Janson's letters are juxtaposed in the file.

and flutes, testimony to Ottoman influence) to take up positions at the wooden bridge over the Vistula that connected Warsaw to the polling ground outside the city, refusing to allow Lithuanian forces loyal to Pac to share control of the strategic bridge. In the event of a contested election he thought that Sobieski would have the upper hand, but that to overcome the Lithuanians he would need French support. He described the magnificent arrival of Forbin-Janson and his suite, signing himself "le Sieur de Callières" in the high style of an Envoy Extraordinary.

Meanwhile Forbin-Janson got on with the serious business of carrying out his instructions to block the election of the Duke of Lorraine. He quickly concluded that Neuburg could not overcome Lithuanian objections. As for "Monsieur de Soissons," he knew that Sobieski would not agree to serve a untried youth who would inevitably become the creature of the Austrians, and that left only Sobieski himself. On the eve of the election, Forbin-Janson wrote to the King that he had decided "to disburse 150,000 francs to Sobieski, as the election is tomorrow," and with that sum "he claims he can debauch almost half of Lithuania."[12] It was a brave decision, and it would have been heavily criticized if it had failed, but Forbin-Janson had calculated his last-minute intervention well.

The following day Sobieski headed for the election ground with a large retinue, telling Forbin-Janson with a confident smile that if Pac continued to oppose him he would "let the saber decide." The *szlachta* gathered, and Callières and the other foreign envoys took up their prescribed places, while across the river the merchants of Warsaw boarded up their shops in anticipation of potential violence. The Palatine of Russia, a Sobieski ally, put the name of the victor of Chocim into nomination, urging him to accept the crown he had saved in so many battles. The Grand Marshal's modest show of declining the honor fooled no one, and soon all of the Polish delegation had been won over for Sobieski, leaving only Pac and his Lithuanians as holdouts. The Poles demanded that the Bishop of Krakow as acting head of state proclaim Sobieski's election – but led by Chancellor Pac the 600-700 nobles of the Grand Duchy of Lithuania, perhaps a quarter of the electorate present, walked out.

This left open the possibility of the "double election" Callières had hoped for as the only possibility for Thomas to emerge as a compromise, and during the night of May 19-20 he continued to intrigue in ways that would have been annoying to Forbin-Janson, by now fully committed to Sobieski. Pac offered through intermediaries to abandon the Duke of

---

[12] *CP Pologne* 40, Forbin-Janson to the King, May 18, 1674.

Lorraine in favor of Thomas, or so Callières claimed, but Forbin-Janson declined this gambit, and through Sobieski he advanced another 100,000 francs to the general commanding the Lithuanian Army. Thereupon he broke ranks with the Lithuanian Chancellor, leaving Pac to negotiate the best deal he could get in return for an agreement to make the election unanimous. Sobieski consented to a day's face-saving delay, and after one last meeting with Forbin-Janson to assure himself of French support, on May 21 he was elected by acclamation King John III of Poland.

"LESS SUITED THAN BALUZE"

It was a triumph for both Sobieski and Forbin-Janson whose timely intervention had broken the stalemate. Callières reported to the Duke that Sobieski had shed tears of gratitude when he was addressed as Your Majesty for the first time by Forbin-Janson. One refractory gentleman from the provinces threatened to exercise his right of *liberum veto* to block the election, fleeing to a neighboring jurisdiction to file a formal protest and requiring one last payoff. Callières called on Sobieski to congratulate him, reporting to the Duke that at a state banquet the newly-elected King had invited him to drink from his own cup. Callières, for his part, had managed to irritate Forbin-Janson to no purpose, playing a weak hand well past the point of diminishing returns.

Before the week was out, Callières was offering to switch his allegiance from Savoy to France, and he wrote to Pomponne to ask for appointment as the permanent French Resident in Poland. He said he had asked Forbin-Janson to recommend him for the job, and that "with the best grace in the world" the Ambassador had promised to do so. It was true, Callières allowed, that Forbin-Janson had also told him that he had already recommended someone else, "but in a manner that had committed him only to be guided by your choice." As the French Resident, Callières thought he could be in a position "to do significant service to His Majesty in this country where I have many important friends with whom I have acquired considerable credit." For example, as a young and active man in good health, he could accompany Sobieski to the front in Ukraine, where he might be able "given my special knowledge of his character and inclinations, to insinuate matters that would work to advantage in the service of His Majesty." This was intended as a hint that he might be able to keep Sobieski from campaigning too enthusiastically against the Turks.[13]

---

[13] *CP Pologne* 40. Callières to Pomponne, May 28, 1674.

Forbin-Janson, for his part, had no desire to prolong his stay in "this cold country," as he wrote to Pomponne, and with his rivalry with the Grigans in mind, he asked for leave to return to sunny Provence in time for the fall assembly of the nobility, urging Pomponne to reinforce his request by telling the King that he was needed urgently back in Avignon. He reviewed the two principal candidates for the job of permanent Resident: the first was the current incumbent, Antoine Baluze, and the second was none other than Roger de Fresne Akakia, "Monsieur le Lis," back again in Poland apparently none the worse for his year in the Bastille, the very personification of French bad faith. Forbin-Janson noted that Baluze was on bad terms with the Lithuanian Chancellor, and he thought that Akakia was the more capable of the two. As for the third candidate, Forbin-Janson added a curt postscript: "Monsieur de Callières has asked to be Resident as well and that I write to you on his behalf. I believe he is less suited for the job than Baluze."[14]

Louis XIV was justifiably impressed by Forbin-Janson's admirable performance in Poland. The Bishop's last-minute decision to buy off the Lithuanians had been perfectly timed to win Sobieski's gratitude, and it had put a pro-French candidate across the finish line. Forbin-Janson went on to win a Cardinal's red hat and to serve as the French envoy to the Vatican among other posts in a long and successful diplomatic career. Thus there may be some score-settling when in *On Negotiating with Sovereigns* Callières suggests that Bishops make poor ambassadors: "A state must be sadly lacking in subjects from other professions who are suited to these employments for a Prince to be obliged to remove a Bishop from the bosom of his church ...."[15]

On June 1, the unsuspecting Callières, unaware of Forbin-Janson's "anyone but Callières" recommendation, sent a second note to Pomponne by a different channel, a copy of the first, with a postscript: "Send me word through M. de Tourmont if there is any hope you will employ me."[16] He dallied in Poland for four long months until it was clear that there was no hope of his appointment as the French Resident, and he justified this by telling his master the Duke that he had used the time to "make known the grandeur of the Royal House of Savoy." Among the friends he had acquired for the Duke, he wrote, was Morsztyn – "one of the greatest statesmen in Europe." Finally on October 2, after waiting in vain for word from Pomponne, the Envoy Extraordinary left on a leisurely progress in the

---

[14] *CP Pologne* 40, Forbin-Janson to Pomponne, May 29, 1674. Baluze, who had the support of Forbin-Janson's predecessor Bishop Bonzy, eventually got the job.

[15] Chapter XXI, 'On the choice of negotiators'.

[16] *CP Pologne* 40, Callières to Pomponne, June 1, 1674.

general direction of Turin to claim the reward for his faithful service. Although the Polish connection recurs regularly throughout his later career, he was never to return to the banks of the Vistula.

IN THE COURTS OF POWERFUL WOMEN

> I had the great misfortune of losing a great and powerful protector in the late Electress of Bavaria, having had the good fortune to enjoy her esteem and confidence while I was an Envoy Extraordinary at her court.
> – François de Callières to the Marquise d'Huxelles

Throughout his career Callières had a knock of acquiring powerful women as patrons. Mme de Longueville and the Countess de Soissons had financed his missions to Poland. Later, the Marquise d'Huxelles would be a powerful backer. As he set out on the long road from Warsaw to Turin to claim his reward for having obtained the coveted *trattamente reale* for Charles Emmanuel II from the Poles, Callières was mindful that his employer's sister Henriette-Adelaïde was married to the Elector of Bavaria. Passionately pro-French, she was hoping for a French marriage for her daughter. It was worth a stopover at her court in Munich.

HENRIETTE-ADELAÏDE IN MUNICH

Leaving Warsaw on October 2, the Envoy Extraordinary made a leisurely progress, with stops at the principal German courts on the long road to Turin. Crossing Bohemia, Silesia, and the Marquisat of Luzace he stopped over in Breslau (Wroclaw) and in Dresden, capital of the Elector of Saxony, visiting the Elector's magnificent Treasury. In his report to the Duke, he noted that a gallery with portraits of the ancestors of Saxon Kings contained "several handsome gifts" presented to Electors of Saxony by the Dukes of Savoy. In Leipzig, the great trade fair held on the feast of Michaelmas was underway, and he called on the Electoral Prince and his wife, the sister of the King of Denmark, reporting that the Prince and his wife "received me with great courtesy." He visited Weimar and the fortress of the Elector of Bavaria on the Danube at Ingolstadt, and after a month on the road he arrived in Munich on November 1 with a new commission from the Duke of Savoy – one he almost certainly had solicited himself.[1]

---

[1] Waquet, *François de Callières*, 47-8.

Like the other princely German states, Bavaria was torn between Austria and France, and there were rival factions at the electoral court. The French Ambassador was François Marie de l'Hôpital, Duke de Vitry, an experienced and capable envoy. His mission was to keep the Austrians from quartering troops in Bavaria or allowing them passage through Bavarian territory. The Elector had been persuaded to keep the Austrians out by a generous French subsidy, but he was at pains to remain outwardly neutral, and he kept a careful balance between the Austrian and French factions at his court. His chancellor was pro-Austrian, but his wife the Electress Henriette-Adelaïde plotted with Vitry to establish a French alliance, keeping the Ambassador closely informed about the inner deliberations of the state council.

The arrival in Munich of Callières, a French subject with credentials of a sort from Henriette-Adelaïde's brother, presented Vitry with a dilemma. Callières was a French subject, but he was also the envoy of a foreign prince. How should the French Ambassador to the Elector treat him? There could be a problem if Callières had high-level protection and he failed to treat him with due regard. On the other hand, Callières might also be a parvenu or even an impostor, and his pretentions seemed excessive to Vitry.

Writing to Louis XIV on November 7, at the end of a long dispatch, Vitry took the precaution of raising the problem directly:

> I saw immediately that there would be some difficulty with regard to his treatment, since his status as envoy here did not appear to be particularly well established in his credentials, and it was from the Electress herself that I heard of his arrival. The next day they readied for him the apartment beneath mine, where only envoys are lodged, and I resolved to send a gentleman to the Electress to tell her that I was concerned that I might be embarrassed with regard to the Sieur de Callières. I didn't know whether he was really the envoy of the Duke of Savoy, he being French and Your Majesty's subject, and that unsure as to how to deal with him I would follow her orders blindly in the matter.

The Electress having responded that she would be grateful if Vitry were to treat Callières with courtesy as an envoy of the Duke of Savoy, Vitry reported to Louis that that he had done so "solely to please her. I would not have done it if I hadn't been following the custom of this court, and if I hadn't known that envoys don't represent" – in other words, that unlike Ambassadors envoys were not treated in protocol terms as heads of state.

Vitry closed with a fervent justification of his conduct, obviously worried that the King might be displeased.[2]

Oblivious of the Ambassador's dilemma, Callières stayed on in Munich for a month, and while he was there he wrote again to the French Foreign Minister to solicit employment, stressing to Pomponne how hard he was working to advance French interests. Describing his initial meeting with the Elector, he told Pomponne that he had argued that Sobieski would be soon in a position to defy Austria as soon as Ottoman pressure on Poland was relieved, and would then move his forces to the border of Prussia, with "other arguments, too long to recount here, advantageous to His Majesty." Callières told Pomponne that he had stressed to Baron Reichberg, the pro-Austrian Chancellor to the Elector, that the Austrians "wanted to place Bavaria under their heel". He reported proudly that the Chancellor had "called on me at the residence for Ambassadors where I am treated magnificently and lodged at the expense of the Elector, who renders me all imaginable honors, to which the Electress adds a thousand marks of her esteem, enabling me to have long conversations with her." She always had a portrait of Louis XIV at her breast, said Callières, and for her he was always *the* King. In response to the "passionate" desire of the Duke of Savoy to reward him, he told Pomponne that he would be leaving soon for Turin via Innsbruck and Milan. If Pomponne should wish to ask him to carry out some task en route he would be honored to do so. His most fervent wish was that someday he could prove his zeal for the King and for France. The Duke of Savoy had asked him to come to Turin so that he could reward him for his service in Poland, Callières wrote, and Pomponne could reach him there with any orders he might have for him.[3]

Callières appears to have won the confidence of Henriette-Adelaïde, but he did not quite tell Pomponne everything about his long talks with the Electress. The Foreign Minister would not have approved, and Louis XIV would have been furious, had they known about the highly secret matter of state in which he had he had chosen to involve himself: Henriette-Adelaïde's dream was that one day her daughter might marry the eldest son of Louis XIV, the Dauphin of France. To put it mildly, the King would not have taken kindly to Callières's meddling in these sensitive family matters. Later, Callières boasted to the Marquise d'Huxelles that he had continued to receive regular letters from the Electress about the marriage after his return to Paris – one every eight days, full of "esteem and

---

[2] Vitry's dispatches, and the letter from Callières dated November 7 to Pomponne, are in the AEE, *CP Bavière* 19, *négociations de Vitry*, 98.

[3] *CP Bavière* 17, Callières to Pomponne, November 14, 1674.

kindness" he told the Marquise with probable exaggeration.[4] The marriage between Henriette-Adelaïde's daughter and the Dauphin did eventually take place, but it was negotiated some four years later by Colbert de Croissy, who had replaced Arnauld de Pomponne as Foreign Secretary. By that time Henriette-Adelaïde had died, depriving Callières of yet another influential patron.

Callières also failed to tell Pomponne that he continued to promote the improbable notion that Thomas of Savoy might still become King of Poland despite the election of Sobieski, who had still not been crowned. Despite her attachment to her native Savoy, even the Electress was sceptical about this, writing to Vitry that "it will not be as easy to raise this prince [Thomas] to the throne of Poland as the Sieur de Callières would have you believe. The cause is his lack of experience" – the lack of experience of Callières that is, rather than Thomas. She nevertheless hoped that the King would do something for Thomas and Eugene, the two young sons of Olympia Mancini, "given the faithful services their father the Count has rendered, and in consideration of the House of Savoy as well as that of Bavaria ...."[5]

For some time, this improbable notion appears to have been maintained on life support by Callières in his correspondence with the Electress, until Vitry, now back in Paris, wrote to her husband the Elector to put an end to it once and for all. He told the Elector that "I have not failed, Monseigneur, to explain to the King the desire Your Royal Highness would have to see Prince Thomas of Savoy on the throne of Poland, and to express your hope to the King that His Majesty might be willing to help with this when the time comes. Speaking in all honesty His Majesty believes that this time is very far off." With heavy sarcasm, Vitry told the Elector that "His Majesty can only admire the facility with which the Seigneur de Callières flatters all those who are interested in the elevation of this Prince, despite the King's certainty with regard to the robust and solid health of the King of Poland."[6] Allowing for some venom on the part of Vitry, who clearly had little time for Callières, it appears from this that Louis XIV took a skeptical view of the young Envoy Extraordinary of Savoy.

---

[4] *Letters*, 101.
[5] She still hoped that the King would do something for the young princes of Soissons "given the faithful services their father the Count has rendered, and in consideration of the House of Savoy as well as that of Bavaria ...," *AAE, CP Bavière* 22, Henriette-Adelaïde to Vitry, March 2, 1675.
[6] *CP Bavière* 22, Vitry to the Elector of Bavaria, ca. September 15, 1675.

Marie Jeanne Baptiste De Savoye
Duchesse de Savoye, Princesse de Piemont, Reyne de
Chypre &c. Tutrice, et Regente &c.

Figure 6. Marie Jeanne Baptiste de Savoie-Nemours, Madame Royale.

MADAME ROYALE IN SAVOY

At the end of November, Callières left Munich for Turin and the court of Charles Emmanuel II to receive the reward for his faithful service, traveling via the Tyrol to Venice, where he spent several days. Charles Emmanuel was a great builder, and Callières took pains to note in his report to the

Duke that he had visited and admired his castle at Vercelli, "one of the strongest and most beautiful fortresses of Europe."[7]

The Savoyard court in Turin was an elegant one, with entertainments and court ballets, balls and elaborate hunting parties, all in imitation of the French model, and here Callières found still another powerful patron with close ties to France, Marie Jeanne Baptiste de Savoie-Nemours, the wife of the Duke – known to her contemporaries as *Madama Reale*, or *Madame Royale*.[8] The arrival of a young Norman gentleman who took himself very seriously indeed inevitably aroused jealousies at the little court. The Marquis de Saint-Thomas was the Duke's principal minister, and he had already received reports on Callières from his agent in Munich, one La Pérouse, who wrote that Callières had been held up to ridicule by Vitry. "He is what we would call in good Italian a *ciarlone* and nothing more," La Pérouse wrote – literally a "chatterbox," or perhaps better in modern terms, a "lightweight."[9]

The 78 year old French representative at Savoy, Ennemond de Servien, who had been kept far too long at his post, took little notice of Callières's arrival. In a letter to Pomponne on October 6 containing his only reference to Callières, Servien reported:

> The Duke of Savoy having congratulated the King of Poland on his election, he responded with a very polite letter in which I am assured that he is given the title of Royal Highness, which his predecessor had always declined to use. They say that it is a Frenchman who managed the whole business, and even that he is being brought here to be given a position.[10]

Callières had little to say later about his time at the Court of Savoy, though he remained in Turin for a prolonged period, from December of 1674 until the following summer. It was embarrassing to admit at a later stage in his career that in his younger days that he had served a foreign prince. Callières did later tell the Marquise d'Huxelles that the Duke had commissioned him to "negotiate an agreement with the King to renew hostilities in Italy against the Republic of Genoa, which would have been a useful diversion for the King, then engaged in a war against the House of Austria, and that was in 1675." This is more or less confirmed by a commission to Callières from Madame Royale, who became the effective ruler of Savoy following her husband's death in June of 1675. On July 18 she wrote to Pomponne commending Callières as her representative. She wrote that he had served

---

[7] It would withstand a prolonged French siege in 1704.

[8] Oresko, 'Maria Giovanna Battista'.

[9] Waquet, *François de Callières*, 49.

[10] *CP Sardaigne* 64, Servien to Pomponne, October 6, 1674.

her late husband the Duke well on "several important occasions," and that he enjoyed her full confidence. Callières would speak to Pomponne about unspecified "matters concerning us," with regard to which she hoped that Pomponne would use his good offices with the King.[11] It appears that Callières was to hold out the prospect that Savoy, already a de facto French client, might intervene on the French side in the war with Holland in exchange for a French subsidy.[12] It was a delicate business for a French subject to be involved with without any authority from the King, and in the end nothing came of it. Perhaps the price Madame Royale set was too high.

Remarkably, Callières eventually received a commission from Madame Royale sending him to England as her representative, but again nothing came of it. In an effort to reduce her exclusive dependence on France and to gain some freedom of maneuver for her vulnerable principality, the Duchess was contemplating an exchange of resident envoys with the Court of Saint James.[13] The commission, probably drafted by Callières himself, specified that he was being sent "in light of the knowledge he has of the genius of this nation and the dispositions of its commerce in this region"— despite the fact that there is no indication that Callières spoke any English at all, or that he had any expertise with regard to commerce. It specified that he was to promote the use of the Duchy's port of Villefranche on the Mediterranean by English shipping, and that as he had done so successfully in Poland he was to obtain the "royal treatment" for the Duke from England. Callières would certainly have been at pains to assure Pomponne that he would serve French interests in England, but he did not cross the Channel. Louis XIV was determined to keep Madame Royale from branching out in ways that might reduce her dependency on him, and France would not have favored her efforts to diversify her relations.

Callières did continue to act as an agent in France for Madame Royale for a time, attempting to sell the Duchy d'Aumale since she was hard pressed for cash, but the deal never went through.[14] Perhaps the King quietly blocked the transaction in order to keep her dependent on his subsidies. In letters to Saint Thomas in Turin, Callières also solicited a position as an envoy of Savoy to the European Peace Congress that would convene at Nijmegen in 1677, but nothing came of it, and eventually his once promising relationship with Madame Royale dwindled away to

---

[11] *CP Sardaigne* 64, July 18, 1674.
[12] *Quelque profit assuré*. Waquet, *François de Callières*, 48.
[13] Oresko, '*Maria Giovanna Battista*', 33.
[14] Waquet, *François de Callières*, 50.

nothing. He could not continue to represent her in political matters in France without giving rise to a charge of divided loyalties.

It was the end of his time as an emissary of Savoy. In later years as a high official at Versailles, when Savoy was often allied to the enemies of France, Callières was careful to obscure the fact that he had once represented a foreign state. Saint-Simon does not appear to have known of it, although he was aware of the first Longueville mission, nor did Callières mention his mission to Poland for the Duke of Savoy in the letters to the Marquise d'Huxelles in which he reviewed his early career. He maintained instead that he had always served French interests, which was perhaps true, at least in part.[15] Like his scandalous first book, his time in the service of Savoy was best forgotten.

---

[15] *Letters*, 94: "*moi, qui ai toujours travaillé pour nos princes ....*"

IN SEARCH OF PATRONS

One of the most important and often neglected tasks of a minister is to
select those who will work under his direction for the service of the state.
– François de Callières, *De la science du monde*

Back in France in the summer of 1675, Callières could not have
contemplated the future with much optimism. A year had passed since he
sailed for Poland with the French Ambassador in the King of England's
yacht, and his prospects for preferment were dim. Like Elizabeth I of
England, the Sun King took the view that his dog should wear only his own
collar, and Callières's employment by a foreign power, even a friendly one,
was not in his favor. The Duke de Vitry is not an objective source, but his
report to the Bavarian Elector that Louis XIV had ridiculed Callières's
claims that Thomas might still become King of Poland is telling. Nor can
Callières's repeated expressions to Arnauld de Pomponne of his eagerness
to betray the trust of Savoy have done him much good, suggesting to that
powerful and sensible minister that Callières might be too ready to acquire
one master while he was still serving another. His pretentions as an Envoy
of Savoy had annoyed Forbin-Janson and Vitry, powerful ambassadors and
courtiers. Callières had gained experience and knowledge of the courts of
Europe, but at the age of thirty-one he seemed to have little prospect of
joining the ranks of those the King trusted with the management of his
foreign affairs.

MORSZTYN'S MAN OF BUSINESS

The one bright spot was his connection to the man he had described to the
Duke of Savoy as one of Europe's greatest statesmen, Jan Andrasz
Morsztyn, Grand Treasurer of the Polish Republic. The close connection
Callières had established with Morsztyn and Lady Mary during his two
trips to Poland would endure to the end of their lives in prosperous exile in
France. Morsztyn traveled to France as a Polish emissary in 1679-80, and
he was granted French nationality by Louis XIV as a recognition of his
services, and he used Callières in this period as both a trusted man of
business in France and as his political agent. To Forbin-Janson Morsztyn
wrote that Callières would call on the Bishop with a paper having to do

with his unreimbursed expenses in connection with the Longueville affair: "I beg of Your Excellency to think from time to time of my interests, and to re-read the paper that you gave to me once and that will be shown to you by Monsieur de Callières." (The reference is probably to the full powers granted by Louis XIV to Paulmiers and countersigned by Louvois.) Morsztyn wrote to a correspondent in 1682 that Callières had "entered the ministry," meaning that he had taken a government office of some sort, but there is no other evidence of this, and on balance a formal position seems unlikely.[1]

By 1683, as Sobieski tired of unkept French promises and the winds shifted in Warsaw in an Austrian direction, the pro-French Morsztyn came under increasing political pressure. While over French objections, Sobieski rode into history with of the Polish cavalry to the lift the Ottoman siege at Vienna, cementing his alliance with the Hapsburgs, Morsztyn was detained and accused by Sobieski of conniving with the French Ambassador – a younger brother of the Duke de Vitry who had treated Callières with such condescension at Munich. The Grand Treasurer managed to flee to France with much of the Polish Treasury, and he lived out the remainder of his days as the Count de Châteauvillain, an estate outside Paris Callières acquired for him – ironically from the Vitry family, which had fallen on hard times, probably as partial payment of loans he had made to the Ambassador in Poland. For a time, Callières took up residence with the Morsztyns at their *hôtel particulier* on the corner of the rue des Saints Pères on the Quai Malaquais in Paris – a lugubrious house with an air of a prison according to one source, and he was still using that house as a forwarding address for correspondence on his return from Holland in 1698, although by that time he had acquired property of his own.[2]

The Morsztyn connection also led Callières to the Duke de Chevreuse, head of one of the first families in France. Saint-Simon, who was close to Chevreuse, records that Callières was Morsztyn's agent for the negotiations with Chevreuse over the marriage of his daughter to Morsztyn's son. According to Saint-Simon, who was in a position to know, Chevreuse was influenced by the "irresistible logic of those without the means for a dowry." Notwithstanding Morsztyn's reputation for keeping a close hold on his purse, a bargain was struck quickly, and it was in the

---

[1] *Listy*, 104-9, 120, 355.

[2] *BnF* NAF *1663*, *"négotiations de Riswick"* dated December 20, 1697. Callières advises a Baron de Suffig in Koblenz that Louis XIV has granted him an annual pension of 4000 francs a year, probably for secret services rendered during the Ryswick talks, and that the Baron should contact Callières at the Morsztyn hôtel on the Quai Malaquais where he would be staying.

course of these negotiations, again according to Saint-Simon, that Callières gained the esteem of Chevreuse, a moderate who was to become one of the most influential men at Versailles. Morsztyn dies in 1692, and when his entirely French son was killed in 1695 at one of the several sieges of Namur, Callières helped look after his widow and their two daughters.[3]

THE MARQUISE D'HUXELLES

Prominent among the other patrons Callières acquired was Marie le Bailleul, Marquise d'Huxelles (1626-1712). At her house on the rue Sainte Anne across from a re-education center for Protestant girls with the Orwellian name of *les nouvelles catholiques*, the political elite could meet outside the sterile and formal confines of the court, and Callières found himself very much at home by her fireside and at her table.

The Marquise was a woman of considerable power and influence. This is clear from Callières's letters to her as well as from other sources. Saint-Simon's portrait is notably respectful, although he does not appear to have known her well himself. It conveys the sense that she was something of an arbiter in matters of both taste and politics:

> She was a woman of great intelligence, who had been beautiful and fashionable, who had been of the highest society all her life – not at all of the court. She was imperious, and she had acquired a right to authority. Men of wit and letters and gentlemen from the old court assembled at her house, where she presided over a sort of quite decisive tribunal. She kept her friends and the respect of the world until the end."[4]

Although earlier Paris salons have received all the scholarly attention, during the latter part of the long reign of Louis XIV, the house of the Marquise had become an important political gathering place and watering hole. In sending her a present of game, for example, Achille de Harlay, President of the Parlement of Paris, wrote in 1696 that "I hope it will be worthy ... to take its place on that delicate table to which all of Europe sends its politicians to decide its fate, and to predict for us by an unfailing prophecy whether we shall have the misfortunes of war, or the blessings of

---

[3] Chevreuse himself was married to a daughter of Jean-Baptiste Colbert, and in later years he was closely allied to the Duke de Beauvillier who had also married a Colbert daughter. Both men became an increasingly powerful advisors to Louis XIV in the later years of his reign. They would be central to Callières's later career at court.
[4] *S/S* IV, 486.

peace.[5] There is certainly some flattery here, but to be effective flattery must contain a kernel of truth.

Huxelles was from a distinguished family of magistrates with roots in Normandy. Her father Nicolas had been ambassador to Savoy, ending his career in 1643 as *surintendant des finances*. Thanks to these connections and a substantial dowry, she had married into the nobility of the sword. She first acquired a widow's freedom from male authority when her first husband, the Marquis de Nangis, died at the siege of the town of Gravelines in Flanders after only a few months of marriage, in 1644. The following year she remarried to Louis-Chalon de Blé, Marquis d'Huxelles – losing this second husband to a death in battle some fourteen years later at a siege of the same strategic town.

Given the disparity in age and rank, there was no question of a romantic relationship between Callières and the Marquise, but they became close friends and allies, united by a common passion for politics. Her set included diplomats, both French and foreign, as well as the great and good of French society: Arnauld de Pomponne himself, after his return to royal favor; the Count de Briord, Ambassador in Savoy and Holland; Abbé Rizzini, the long-serving envoy of the Duchy of Modena; Michel Amelot, Ambassador to Venice, Portugal, and Spain; and the powerful d'Estrées clan, including Cardinal César, descended from the favorite of Henri IV Gabrielle d'Estrées. Among her intimates were soldiers like the Marquis de Rouville who had been envoy to England, as well as Boufflers, Villars and Tallard, Marshals of France, all of whom served in diplomatic capacities as well. Regulars at her table included Toussaint Rose, the principal private secretary to the King whom Callières would replace in 1701. Mme de Sévigné was an intimate friend from their early days together at court, when both women had been compromised by the downfall of the powerful *Surintendant* Nicolas Foucquet.[6] For over thirty years, Huxelles distilled the news she gathered at her salon in weekly letters to Antoine Escalins des Aimars (or Adhémar), Marquis de La Garde, the neighbor and first cousin of Mme de Sévigné's son-in-law, the Marquis de Grignan, Lieutenant General in Provence.[7]

---

[5] Quoted in Barthélemy, *La Marquise d'Huxelles et ses amis*, 112. In addition to Callières, her correspondents included Louvois, Arnauld de Pomponne, Forbin-Janson, Cardinal d'Estrées, and Mme de Maintenon among many others.

[6] The first letter in the collected letters of Sévigné is one in Italian to Huxelles, about an amorous assignation.

[7] These reports to La Garde of the political and military news and the doings at court are a neglected source for the history of the much-chronicled age of Louis XIV. Huxelles wrote faithfully to him until the very end of her life in 1712, and she was astonishingly well informed, often deriving her information from those directly involved, including Callières. *(continued)*

On the evidence of Callières's letters to Huxelles – hers have not survived, but judging from his replies they were equally warm– their relationship was a close one, based on a shared passion for politics, the "public good," and it is clear that promoted his political career with the influential people in her circle. Not the least of the bonds between them was the memory of the young Longueville and his untimely death on the Rhine. The Grande Mademoiselle records in her memoirs that Mme d'Huxelles had even talked at one point of going to Poland with Longueville if he were elected King.[8]

THE ABBÉ RENAUDOT

A second connection was with Eusèbe Renaudot (1647-1720), an Abbé in minor orders who was intimately connected through his long life to Callières. The two men probably first met at the Collège d'Harcourt, where Renaudot was awarded a degree of master of arts in Greek and Latin philosophy in 1664 at the tender age of sixteen. His father, also named Eusèbe, had been the Dauphin's principal physician, and his grandfather Théophraste, a revered physician to the poor, had founded the *Gazette de France,* a weekly newspaper controlled by the court, as well as the *Bureau d'adresses,* an office open to the public where information was posted about tradesmen, offers of employment, publications and the like. (The literary *Prix Renaudot* is awarded in his name.) These monopolies and a royal pension provided Renaudot with a comfortable revenue stream, and Callières and Renaudot became close political allies and friends.

She was far better informed as to political developments than Mme de Sévigné, and her letters to la Garde were intended for Mme de Grignan and her husband as well as La Garde. Unlike Sévigné's letters which exist mainly in the form of eighteenth century copies, many of the original letters Huxelles wrote to La Garde are still extant. The story of their provenance and survival is too long to tell here. Voltaire drew on them for his histories, as did André Boislisle, who cited them regularly for context in his great nineteenth century edition of Saint-Simon's memoirs during periods when the Dangeau court chronicles were silent. In 1925 eight volumes were bought at auction by the John Rylands Library of the University of Manchester in England where they remain. Of the remaining four volumes of the correspondence, three went to the Musée Calvet in Avignon and are now in the municipal library of that city. A fourth was added in 1975, the gift of an unidentified French diplomat to the Foreign Ministry, making a total of four volumes in the Avignon library. There in Manchester and Avignon they languish, unknown, uncatalogued, unread, and virtually forgotten, in the twenty-first century. See Fawtier, "The Correspondence of the Marquise d'Huxelles and the Marquis de La Garde."
[8] *Mémoires,* 386.

Figure 7. Eusèbe Renaudot, at the time of his election with Callières to the Académie Française. (Musée des Chateaux de Versailles et de Trianon, Versailles.)

Renaudot was a polymath and a protean figure – orientalist, codebreaker, theologian, propagandist, and political operative. Even if we discount the claim that he spoke and wrote seventeen languages fluently, it is clear that he was a considerable linguist, with a working knowledge of Hebrew, Arabic, Chinese, and a variety of other languages – including English. An anti-Jesuit controversialist and a fierce defender of the Gallican principles giving the King primacy over the Pope with regard to ecclesiastical appointments in France, Renaudot was complex man, the bitter enemy of the skeptic Pierre Bayle, but also a friend of John Locke.[9]

Evidence for Callières's political activities in this period comes largely from letters written from Rome to Renaudot from 1682-85 by Abbé Claude Bernou, Renaudot's deputy at the Gazette, in nearly all of which Callières is mentioned, some 800 pages in manuscript.[10] From this

---

[9] For background on Renaudot, see Burger, 'Renaudot'.

[10] *BnF*, NAF 7487, hereafter *Bernou*. The Bernou letters have often been mined by Canadian and American historians in connection with the La Salle expedition, but they are also an important and neglected source for the intellectual life of the time. Bernou was busy with the acquisition of Chinese manuscripts for the royal library from the Vatican as well as with the contentious relationship between France and the Papacy, and he wrote anonymous *(continued)*

correspondence it is clear that Callières was among the leaders of a shadowy group Bernou calls variously the "Society of the rue des Victoires," which was the street where the Naval and colonial offices were located; sometimes the "Society Royal of brothers," an ironic reference to the newly created Royal Society in England; and sometimes the Society *des Bons Enfants*, after a street in Paris in the same neighborhood. It appears to have been an interlocking client-patron network of intellectuals and officials rooted in the service of the Colberts, Jean-Baptiste and after his death his son and heir the Marquis de Seignelay.

A GRAND AMERICAN DESIGN

The principal though by no means exclusive focus of this network was American affairs. Bernou was one of the leading geographers of his time, a tireless propagandist and cartographer, and it is clear that looked to Callières and Renaudot for political direction. He appears to have had a very expansive idea of Callières's influence, though this may be partly flattery, since the letters he wrote from Rome as he makes clear were intended for both Callières and Renaudot. When Seignelay assumed charge of the naval and colonial ministry after the death of his father Jean-Baptiste Colbert in 1683, Bernou worried that Seignelay as head of the Colbert family would lose ground to the rival faction at court led by the Letelliers and the powerful ministry of war, the Marquis de Louvois. The brilliant Seignelay had a reputation for burning the candle at both ends, and Bernou suggested that Callières's influence over Seignelay was considerable. He wrote to Renaudot that "the advice of M. de Callières would be useful to M. de Seignelay in light of this change, to persuade him to apply himself more and not to give rise to complaint."[11] In 1679 Seignelay had married

---

propaganda tracts, at least one of which was praised by Louis XIV. After the revocation of the Edict of Nantes in 1685, he deplored the negative attitude of the Curia and the Pope, who had ridiculed the "jackbooted conversions" of Protestants in France. He and Renaudot debated the problem of "chronology" that preoccupied the intellectuals of the time: how could the Biblical account of the Flood be squared with Chinese and Egyptian dynastic accounts that suggested that civilization was much older? Bernou was much preoccupied with an attempt to arrange the marriage of a French prince to the Portuguese Infanta while in Rome, and Callières and Renaudot were involved in this as well, though the details are not clear. Nothing came of it.

[11] *Bernou*, September 28, 1683. Among its members were the senior administrators of the naval and colonial ministry under Seignelay: Morel de Boustiroux who was replaced at the Navy ministry on his death in 1685 by Pierre de Clairambault the younger; Cartigny, the Naval *intendant*; Bellinzani, Seignelay's principal assistant before his disgrace and imprisonment for peculation; François de Bretcuil, Counselor of State; and Jean-Louis Bergeret, the principal clerk for the Foreign Secretary Colbert de Croissy, whose office as *(continued)*

into the upper nobility in the person of the beautiful Catherine de Matignon, and this Matignon connection would have helped Callières introduce himself as a trusted retainer and counselor in the Seignelay household.

It was a network that favored what Bernou called "our great design"[12]: a plan to extend French control of the American continent from the Gulf of Mexico to the St. Lawrence and the interior, even at the risk of conflict with England and Spain. Callières and his friends allied in this with Louis de Buade, Count de Frontenac, who as governor for a decade from 1672 to 1682 had promoted colonial expansion and the restless schemes of the explorer Robert-René Cavelier de La Salle. Their strategy of colonial expansion was opposed by the Jesuit order, which had helped to engineer Frontenac's removal.

When in 1682 La Salle returned to France to seek financing for an expedition to found a colony at the mouth of the Mississippi, Callières and Renaudot lobbied the court on his behalf, and there is considerable evidence from the Bernou letters of Callières's influence over La Salle's last disastrous expedition to the Mississpppi in 1684. On February 1, 1684, for example, in making various suggestions for about how to gain ministerial approval for the expedition, Bernou wrote to Renaudot that he was submitting his ideas" to the censorship of M. de Callières, La Salle, and you." On February 15, he wrote to Renaudot that "you and M. de Callières are doing better for him (La Salle) than I could," and "can manage this business better than I can." He was delighted to hear that a meeting between La Salle and Seignelay had gone so well "thanks to you and M. de Callières." On April 4, 1684, as La Salle was obtaining final permission and financing for his expedition, Bernou asked Renaudot "in what form M. de Callières has proposed it." Worried about a map he had given to La Salle, which he feared would be compromised, Bernou asked that it be left with Callières, "the promoter of the affair" whose discretion was not in question and who might need it in the future.[13] On May 9, having learned

secretary to the King Callières would assume many years later. The network provided the government with a sort of brain trust of orientalists and experts in exotic languages and places: François Pétis de la Croix, father and son, referred to as *petit pater* and *grand pater* in the Bernou letters, both Arabic translators at the court; Barthélemy d'Herbelot, author of the *Dictionnaire orientale*, a digest of Arab and Persian authors; and Melchisadech Thévenot, "Melek" to Bernou and Renaudot, named director of the Royal Library to Renaudot's chagrin in 1684 since it was a post Renaudot believed he had been promised by Jean-Baptiste Colbert. There were men of action as well, whom the Bernou refers to as his "godchildren," or *fillots*: Pierre-Paul Tarin de Cussy, sent in 1683 to govern the French colony at Santo Domingo, as well as Callières's own brother Louis-Hector.

[12] *Bernou*, January 25, 1684.
[13] *Bernou*, April 18, 1684.

that Callières's younger brother, Louis-Hector had been appointed to command at Montreal, the avuncular Bernou expressed his delight that that "M. de Callières has now become doubly the protector of my godchildren." When a competitor for backing at court arose in the enigmatic and romantic person of the Don Diego Dionsio, Count de Peñalosa, a well-born refugee from a Creole family in Peru and Mexico, it was Callières who negotiated a truce between La Salle and Don Diego, who was lobbying for a self-financing attack on Mexico to be paid for from the seized mining revenues as an alternative to La Salle's more expensive proposal. Callières brokered a meeting between La Salle and Peñalosa in which the two men agreed to work together. but La Salle declined to share authority and eventually Peñalosa faded from view.

In the event, La Salle's expedition foundered some 400 miles from the Mississippi delta, and the explorer was murdered by his own mutinous men.[14] News of this disaster took some time to reach France, and Callières continued to cling to the hope that the explorer would somehow make his way back. In October of 1687, from Châteauvillain, the estate outside Paris he had acquired for Morsztyn, Callières wrote to an unidentified correspondent in Paris who is probably Renaudot: "There was still no word of La Salle in Quebec as of July 18, which is a very bad sign for him.

---

[14] The historiography of the last La Salle expedition has been contentious since excerpts from the Bernou letters were transcribed by the French archivist, Pierre Margyry, in the nineteenth century and used by Francis Parkman in his histories of North America. Historians have struggled to account for the fact that La Salle went so far astray. Parkman was the first to imply on the basis of the excerpts from the Bernou letters as transcribed by Pierre Margyry that Bernou and Renaudot had deliberately conflated the non-existent Rio Bravo in Mexico with the Mississippi in order to encourage the idea of an attack on Mexico along the lines of the Peñalosa proposal, and he argued that La Salle's "overwrought brain" accounted for his otherwise inexplicable pursuit of this "chimera." (Parkman's colorful and dramatic account is in his *La Salle and the Discovery of the Great West*, vol. I, 713ff.) The high-water mark of this hypothesis is an account by a Jesuit scholar who cast La Salle as the innocent victim of a nefarious plot: "He cast his lot in with two theory-spinning abbés who meant him no good. They concocted a madcap enterprise, they assigned him the role of a pawn, which he accepted, they got him moved into a desperate position, they abandoned him to his fate," Delanglez, *Some La Salle Journeys*, 99. This is nonsense. La Salle was nobody's pawn, and in locating the mouth of the Mississippi well to the west of its actual location, Bernou based his opinion on the best cartography of the time. He had no intention of misleading La Salle, and he would have had no motive whatsoever for doing so. The principal cause of the disaster, in addition to the arrogance of La Salle, was the technology of the time, which made it impossible to establish longitude with precision. For a more sensible account, see Wood, 'La Salle'. Wood concludes that La Salle's ruin had more to do with navigational error than conspiracy. See also Weddle, *The Wreck of the Belle and the Ruin of La Salle*, for a readable account of the disaster, which however incorporates Parkman's fanciful notion of a clerical plot led by Bernou from Rome of all places.

Please inform the Abbé Bernou, as the matter relates to his department."[15] The letter is evidence of his deep involvement in this period in American affairs, probably based in part on regular reports from Louis-Hector in Montreal, and the reference to Bernou's "department" suggests that he was presiding over a relatively structured network in the naval and colonial ministry, although there is no trace of this to be found in the naval and colonial archives. In the same letter, Callières also writes chillingly that of the some 200 Iroquois captured, not counting the women and children, only sixty would be found to be fit for the galleys and sent to France. One of them, the "chief of the Aignez nation," was an important spy. A Jesuit, Father Lambreville, had managed to escape from the Iroquois, which was just as well as otherwise he would have filled their cooking pot "notwithstanding the little liking they have acquired for the flesh of Black Robes."

'RADISHES AND GOOSEBERRY'

As an advisor to Seignelay in this period, Callières also managed the affair of two celebrated Canadian adventurers and explorers of Hudson's Bay, the brothers-in-law, Pierre Radisson and Médart de Chouart, Sieur des Groseilliers – known to generations of Canadian schoolchildren as "radishes and gooseberry."[16] Searching for the Northwest Passage, Groseilliers and Radisson had discovered that in the summer Hudson's Bay could be used as a lucrative trading post to obtain beaver pelts and other furs from the indigenous peoples, and they offered their services to England and France, depending on the circumstances. After many vicissitudes, the two were given a sort of commission by Colbert's clerk, Bellinzani, returning to Hudson's Bay in 1682 where they raided the English post of Port Nelson and seized the furs of the traders.[17]

England and France were at peace at the time, and the English Ambassador, Lord Preston, a shareholder in the newly formed Hudson's Bay Company like his master James II, took a dim view of these escapades. Preston made repeated representations to Colbert de Croissy, the foreign secretary, as well as to Seignelay, and the latter turned to Callières in order

---

[15] *BnF, Fonds Clairambault* 1016, 483.

[16] This is a very old joke. In a letter to Renaudot of April 24, 1685, Bernou complains that "I don't know this Signor Gooseberry you refer to – unless you are maliciously translating his name into English, which I don't understand."

[17] For a lively account in English of the adventures of Radisson and Groseilliers see Nute, *Caesars of the Wilderness.* Radisson would end his days as a pensioner of the Hudson's Bay Company, and Bellinzani was later imprisoned for corruption. For a definitive biographical sketch of Radisson, correcting Nute, see Warkentin, 'Radisson'.

to deflect the Ambassador's pressure. Convoking Radisson on Seignelay's authority, Callières dictated an order for them to return to Hudson's Bay with a passport provided by the English company and dismantle the French trading post.[18] The order allowed for eighteen months for this to be accomplished, however, leaving French traders in possession of "Fort Bourbon" in the meantime, and instead of complying, Radisson chose to offer his services to England. Inconclusive negotiations over the dispute continued between France and England after the accession to the English throne of James II – who as Duke of York had been the Governor of the Hudson's Bay Company – but in the meantime, France remained in possession of the fort and its lucrative fur trade.

There is a footnote. Years later, as the nine year War of the League of Augsburg drew to a negotiated conclusion at Ryswick in September of 1697, the principal drafter for France of the Ryswick Treaty was François de Callières. The Treaty provided that the forts in James and Hudson's Bay were to be divided between the two countries and the *status quo ante* restored, but the relevant articles were worded to the advantage of France. French rights to places taken before and during the war were explicitly confirmed, but there was no equivalent recognition of English rights in the area, and disputes were to be adjudicated by a joint commission, that never convened.[19] Reporting to the King on the signing, Callières proudly told Louis XIV that "We obtained the restoration of the *status quo* in the colonies, including the return of Fort Bourbon in Hudson's Bay and reparation for its capitulation when it was seized by the English last year."[20] "The fort remained in French hands until it was ceded back to Great Britain by the Treaty of Utrecht in 1713.

---

[18] Quoted in Nute, *Caesars of the Wilderness*, 344-6, from the Public Records Office, America and West Indies, Volume 359: "In the years one thousand six hundred eighty three he came from Canada to Paris by order of Monsr. Colbert who soon after Dyed. And this deponent being at Paris was there informed that the Lord Preston Ambassador of the King of England had given in a Memoriall to the Ministers of His Most Christian Majesty's court against the action of this deponent at Port Nelson & after this deponent had been several times with the Marquis de Seignelay and Monsr. Callière (now one of the Plenipotentiaries for His Most Christian Majesty at the Treaty of Peace) on the Occasion aforesaid & this deponent then found that the French had quitted All pretenses to Hudson Bay & thereupon He this Deponent in Paris In the Month of April in the year One thousand six hundred Eighty four In the chamber of the Sd. Monsr. Callière he this deponent with his own proper hand but of the Special Direction of the Sd. Monsr. Callière did write the paper hereunto annexed ...."

[19] Ryswick Treaty, article 7: "But the possession of those places which were taken by the French, *both in times of peace as well as during the late war*, and were retaken by the English during the war, shall be left to the French ...." (emphasis added).

[20] *BnF, Fonds Clairambault* 1125, folio 144.

LOUIS-HECTOR AND THE INVASION OF NEW YORK

While La Salle was making his final preparations at La Rochelle, Callières's younger brother Louis-Hector sailed in the summer of 1684 for Quebec to take command of the frontier post at Montreal with the somewhat grand title of Governor General. A career Army officer then thirty-five years old, four years younger than François, known as the "Chevalier de Callières," he had already spent twenty years in the King's service, joining the Army at the age of fifteen soon after the his father's death of their father, and rising to the rank of Captain in the Piedmont regiment. Since 1679, he had served in the regiment of Navarre as an inspector and troop commander[21], but the way to further promotion seemed blocked. A regiment was expensive, and François was connected to the Colberts rather than to Louvois who controlled preferment in the Army. In deciding that Louis-Hector should go to Canada, he and his older brother must have concluded that the grand design of a French empire in the new world offered a better opportunity for an ambitious Army officer. Having observed at first hand at La Rochelle the tensions between the naval officer commanding the expedition and the imperious La Salle, Louis-Hector wisely decided not to travel with the expedition.[22]

Louis-Hector is well known to the historians of French Canada – the historical museum in Montreal at Pointe-à-Callières is located on the site of the property he left on his death in 1703 to François, and its exhibits incorporate their spurious coat of arms. His entry in the dictionary of Canadian biography describes him as a tough leader who was respected if not loved, and it concludes that "in the history of the colony there probably never was an abler and more devoted servant of the French monarchy."[23]

From his rude frontier post, Louis-Hector lost no time in advancing the "grand design," sending a long and strongly worded *mémoire* to Seignelay entitled the "Usurpations of the English on the French colonies

---

[21] See his petition to Seignelay for the appointment at Montreal, *BAC*, MIKAN 3049329.

[22] The naval officer in command of the expedition, Beaujeu, wrote to Bernou's rival geographer Cabart de Villermont (*BnF*, Clairambault 22799, fols 103-5) that "*j'avais prévenu ce que vous me mandez au sujet de M. le chevalier de Callières, il ne passe pas avec nous.*" It appears that Beaujeu was suspicious of Louis-Hector, and that having observed at first hand a quarrel between La Salle and Beaujeu over precedence, Louis-Hector wisely decided to travel to Quebec with the French fleet instead. Differences between Beaujeu and La Salle contributed to the failure of the expedition.

[23] The article in the *Dictionary of Canadian Biography* is by Yves F. Zoltvany.

of America."[24] A learned paper that drew extensively on the history of French colonization of the continent to show that French claims were better founded than English ones, it can only have been drafted in Paris with the help of the network presided over by François. Tracing French claims back to the arrival of Norman and Breton sailors during the reign of François I, Louis-Hector argued that "New England was always part of New France, having been taken possession of in the name of our Kings before the English ever thought of going there."

Louis-Hector complained that Governor Thomas Dongan of New York – a Catholic who had fought under French arms, which made him particularly dangerous, argued Louis-Hector – was "taking advantage of the war that Monsieur de La Barre declared last year on the Iroquois," an implicit criticism of his superior in Quebec. Governor Dongan had taken the Iroquois under his protection, claiming all of the lands north of the Kennebec River, including large parts of French Acadia, for England, and he was attacking French possessions in Hudson's Bay, exploiting the defection of Radisson and Groseilliers: "These enterprises and usurpations of the English are the more dangerous in they may cause in the future the ruin of our colonies in New France."

From the frontier at Montreal, Louis-Hector continued to promote an aggressive policy against the English colonists, sending *mémoire* after *mémoire* to Versailles, but Louis XIV and his ministers were at pains to preserve a fragile peace with James II, and there was no response.[25] Finally in 1688, with war between England and France on the horizon, he obtained permission to come back in person to press the case for an invasion of New York. It is safe to assume that the two brothers worked together at court to advance the plan to take the offensive against the English. It would be the last time they would meet face to face.

It was a bold plan, to put it mildly. Had it succeeded, the course of Canadian and American history might have run in a somewhat different direction, at least for a time. Louis-Hector argued that with an additional 450 troops to bring the garrison in Canada up to its authorized complement of 1750, he could descend the Hudson by stealth and take the lightly defended fort of *Manatte* (as he called it) from the rear. Leaving three hundred regulars behind to guard the principal forts in the colony, he would

---

[24] *BAC*, MIKAN 248700, *Mémoire pour monseigneur le marquis de Seignelay touchant les usurpations des anglais sur les colonies françaises de l'Amérique, joint à la lettre du Sieur de Callières du 25 février 1685.*

[25] Louis-Hector's *mémoires* are collected in Roy, *Le projet*. The need to make peace with the Iroquois was always the central factor in his analysis, and the elimination of English influence was a means to this end.

lead the remaining men to Lake Champlain on the pretext of launching an offensive against the Iroquois, proceeding instead by canoe to Orange, present-day Albany, living off the land by seizing supplies along the way. Entering Orange, if necessary "sword in hand," and enlisting any French renegades he found there, he would descend the Hudson to the fort of *Manatte* before the English garrison there could react. Only four companies of infantry and three of cavalry defended *Manatte*, he argued, and the little fort at the end of the island could easily be taken with the artillery he would seize in Orange.

To ensure success and prevent the English from sending reinforcements, Louis-Hector wrote, he would need two frigates to blockade offshore, and they could be drawn from the fleet that was sent annually to convoy fishing vessels to Acadia. They would proceed off *Manatte* and await his order attack the fort with their guns. Having taken the town, Louis-Hector would winter there with most of his troops. With *Manatte* in French hands, *Baston* would not resist for long, and the Iroquois would be easy to deal with, deprived of the support of their English allies. There was no time to lose, he argued, sounding as insistent as his brother, as such a favorable occasion might not come again. His proposal to the King closed with a dire warning as prescient as it was premature: if the opportunity to take control of New York and New England were lost, then "we must expect that by intrigues with the Iroquois and other savages they will soon cause Canada to perish."[26]

On June 7, 1689 in an instruction to Frontenac who was to return to the colony with Louis-Hector as his military deputy, and at war with England, the King finally gave his agreement to the "proposition made by the Sr. Chevalier de Callières, Governor of Montreal, to carry out an attack on New York with the troops that His Majesty has in Canada and a number of *habitants* of that country." But by that time it was too too late. By the time they reached Quebec late in the year, Callières and Frontenac found that there was clearly no question of stripping its defenses in order to take the offensive against the English. The colony was in a state of near-panic. In August, a band of Iroquois encouraged by the English had attacked the outpost of La Chine on the upper end of Montreal island – named in ironic reference to the search for the Northwest Passage – massacring many of its nearly 400 inhabitants. The two frigates wandered back to France.[27]

---

[26] Roy, *Le projet*, 34.
[27] The King's instruction to Frontenac and Louis-Hector, as well as the self-justifying report to Seignelay of the captain of one of the frigates, *La Caffinière*, on his return, are in the *AN, Archives de la Marine*, B4, 107-18.

Louis-Hector continued to argue for the New York enterprise throughout late 1689 and 1690, but it was the English who took the offensive. In 1690, Nova Scotia fell to a New England fleet, and Quebec itself was hard pressed. Finally in April of 1691, an instruction from the King to Frontenac written "in camp, before Mons" put an end to the business once and for all. France was contending against a sea of enemies in Europe in the War of the League of Augsburg, and the "state of His Majesty's affairs" did not permit him to envision the enterprise proposed against New York and New England. Frontenac could continue to plan, but he should consult before undertaking any offensive action. In the meantime, the colony should look to the fortifications of Quebec and Montreal and seek peace with the Iroquois.[28]

When Frontenac died in Quebec in November of 1698, Louis-Hector was one of two candidates to succeed him, the other being the Marquis de Vaudreuil. From Montreal, Louis-Hector prepared a letter putting forward his claim, entrusting it to his aide Augustin Le Gardeur de Courtemanche, and sending him down the Hudson through the back door to France by way of New York. Vaudreuil who had family connections to the powerful Navy Minister, Pontchartrain, fearing just such a "Norman trick," sent his own emissary to Paris from Quebec, who managed to hire a ship at Pentagoët, present-day Castine, in Maine, and nearly caught up to Courtemanche at Versailles. According to one contemporary account, when Pontchartrain went to see the Louis XIV on Vaudreuil's behalf, Louis informed him that he was too late – he had already promised his secretary François de Callières that he would give Louis-Hector the position.[29]

François was deeply proud of Louis-Hector, and although they were physically separated for most of the lives, the two brothers, both unmarried, were very close.[30] When Louis-Hector lay dying of fever in Quebec in 1703, in a will he was too ill too sign with a trembling hand, he

---

[28] Roy, *Le projet*, 74-5.

[29] The sole source for this often repeated story is the anonymous *Recueil de ce qui s'est passé au sujet de la guerre, tant des anglais que des Iroquois, depuis l'année 1682*, pp 57-8, from *Manuscrits de Paris publiés sous la direction de la société littéraire et historique de Québec*, Montreal, 1871. There was undoubtedly more to the King's decision, but this is clearly the version that was accepted in Quebec at the time. François is referred to in this account as the "*comte de Callières.*" See also the entry for Courtemanche in the *Dictionary of Canadian Biography*. Louis-Hector rewarded Courtmanche on his return by making him Captain of his personal guard.

[30] See *BnF, Fonds Renaudot* 7487, 407-13, the draft of a letter from François to the Duke de Beauvillier in which he celebrates the "great peace" Louis-Hector negotiated between France and the Iroquois in 1702, as well as the references to Louis-Hector in his letters to the Marquise d'Huxelles, *Letters*, 123, 137, 287.

asked that after his death his heart be separated from his body and "preserved in a casket of lead or silver until his brother, the Marquis de Callières, should make known his wishes."[31] When the news reached Callières of the death from fever of Louis-Hector at the governor's residence in Quebec, at the age of 54, it would have been a hard blow.

---

[31] Godefroy's 'Testament De Louis-Hector De Callières', contains a transcript of the will. Louis-Hector left his property to François, and he also commended their sister Anne's son, the "Chevalier de Courcy," to François, "having known him to have nothing but good intentions," suggesting that Courcy needed his intercession. The reference to Callières as a "Marquis" in this document is notable. As we will see below, others referred to him by this title as well in this period, reflecting his prominent position at court. He never claimed the title himself.

CLIMBING PARNASSUS

> A man of letters is much better suited to make a good negotiator than a man of no learning.
> – François de Callières *On Negotiating with Sovereigns*

The *Académie française*, the celebrated body of forty immortals which continues to exist today, uniforms, swords, cocked hats and all, with the mission of protecting the purity of the French language, had been established in 1635 by Cardinal Richelieu, and it was an ornament of the Sun King's long reign. In theory, it was a self-perpetuating body, and the Academy's members elected their own successors whenever a vacancy occurred. Three votes were taken: the first to choose a candidate; a second to send the nomination to the King; and the third to elect the candidate after the King had agreed.

In fact, like everything in the age of Louis XIV, a seat in the Academy was in the gift of the King and senior members of the court. When a flatterer proposed that Louis's illegitimate son the 15-year old Duke de Maine be admitted, the Academy complied with embarrassing alacrity, leaving it to the King to reverse the decision when he heard of it. Literary merit was irrelevant. The King's brother, Monsieur, obtained a place for his daughter's tutor, Abbé Têtu, while Jean-Louis Bergeret, Colbert de Croissy's assistant at the Foreign Ministry, was made a member, even though neither man ever published anything at all. Saint-Simon tells the story of the King's decision to place the pompous Bishop of Noyon on the Academy as a joke.[1] When Callières and Renaudot were elected to the Academy in the same session in February of 1689, Renaudot had published nothing with the exception of the *Gazette de France*.[2] (Callières's scandalous *Lover's Logic* was best forgotten in the devout age of Mme de Maintenon.)

Callières had, however, taken prudent steps to establish minimal literary credentials in preparation for election. In 1687, he composed an

---

[1] See Rouxel, *Chroniques*. For the Noyon story see *S/S*, I, 192-6.
[2] The *Gazette* was a propaganda platform for the régime, with articles of any military or political sensitivity vetted by Ministers prior to publication and sometimes inspired by the King himself.

Epistle to the King, had it privately printed, and presented it at Versailles, on the occasion of the King's recovery from a successful operation for an anal fistula, which Louis XIV had borne with considerable fortitude. [3] The poem contained judicious flattery of Seignelay, a "zealous, firm, active, and diligent minister," but the King was its subject, the great monarch who had tamed the hydra of heresy with his revocation of the Edict of Nantes, and the universal monarch who submitted all of Europe to his will: "To other sovereigns, you prescribed laws, and victorious King, you were the master of Kings."[4] There was a second poem in similar bombastic style, dedicated to the Dauphine, the daughter of Henriette-Adelaïde, on the baptismal day of her three sons, the Dukes of Burgundy, Anjou, and Berry. Again sounding the note of universal Bourbon monarchy that appalled the rest of Europe, Callières proclaimed that by their birth she had given "Kings to the universe." (One of them, Anjou, would go on to rule Spain as Philip V.)

With his election on the horizon, in the fateful year of 1688, Callières drafted an 'Historical Panegyric to the King,' which he obtained permission to read to the Academy in person.[5] In imitation of Pliny the Elder's celebration of the Emperor Trajan, Callières celebrated a Louis the Great whose accomplishments outshone all the heroes of antiquity. He radiated flattery in all directions: to Mme de Maintenon, "a lady illustrious for all the virtues that may make a person of her sex renowned"; to Louvois, the powerful war minister, head of the LeTellier clan; to La Reynie, the Lieutenant of police; to Colbert de Croissy; to François Fénelon, a rising and influential cleric; to Montausier, Chevreuse, and many others. Callières urged – very delicately indeed – that the King visit Paris, a city he had avoided since the Fronde, preferring the splendid isolation of Versailles, Marly, and the other royal residences: "what joy if you should deign to accord a brief visit to Paris." Surely it could be done "without renewing the memory of those sad and unhappy times when France was exposed to the furies of domestic violence." Either Callières's verses had unexpected influence, or far more likely he had inside information about a visit already in the final planning stages, since two days after the presentation of the poem the King was received with pomp

---

[3] *Épitre au roi, présentée à sa majesté le 18 janvier 1687, avec des vers pour Madame la Dauphine, par M. de Calières* (sic), *Pierre Aubouin, Pierre Emery, & Charles Clousier, Quai des Augustins, proche de l'hôtel de Luynes, à l'écu de France et à la Croix d'Or.* The only copy I am aware of is in the *BnF*, Clairambault 501, folios 767-81.

[4] *"Aux autres souverains, tu prescrivis des Lois, Et Roi victorieux, tu fus maître des Rois."*

[5] *Panégyrique historique du roi: à messieurs de l'académie française, Pierre Aubouin, Pierre Emery, & Charles Clousier*, 1688. There is a handsomely bound and handwritten presentation copy in the *BnF*, ms. Fr. 2293, presumably the one given to the King since it is stamped *bibliothecae regiae*.

and circumstance at the Hôtel de Ville, a rare visit to the city where he had been held hostage as a child.

ANCIENTS AND MODERNS

Callières also made a judicious intervention in an angry dispute that had divided the Academy into the warring factions known to history as the "ancients and the moderns." The bitter polemic had been touched off on January 27, 1687 by the reading in the Academy of a poem entitled *The Age of Louis XIV* by Charles Perrault, prepared for the same occasion that had given rise to Callières's *Epître* – the King's recovery from the risky surgery he had endured with remarkable stocism. Exploiting the cover provided by the usual lavish praise of the royal person, Perrault had suggested that "one can compare, without being unjust, the age of Louis, to the age of Augustus"; he went on to argue that modern authors must be as superior to the ancient ones as Louis was to that Roman emperor.[6]

Perrault's provocation was deliberate, and the passion of the classic French *affaire* that followed is difficult to appreciate, unless one considers that what was at stake was the profoundly subversive idea a later age would call progress. The debate would cross the Channel to England in time, taking on a somewhat different form.[7]

Callières's contribution was an attempt to spread calming oil on the waters. His *Poetical History of the Newly Declared War between the Ancients and the Moderns*, published in 1688. It was a clever book, and it took a sensible middle ground, although Callières's pose as a neutral pleased neither side. Cast in the form of a contest for Mount Parnassus between the rival armies of modern and ancient poets and dramatists, the

---

[6] *Histoire poétique de la guerre nouvellement déclarée entre les anciens et les modernes*, Paris, P. Aubouin, 1688. For an excerpt from Callières's contribution, see Fumaroli, *La querelle des anciens et des modernes*, pp 337-60. In his few lines on Callières, Fumaroli describes him as having been as Ambassador to Poland in 1672 and manages to omit any reference to *On Negotiating with Sovereigns* in a list of his books (p. 336). For an older and still useful account, see Rigault, *Histoire de la querelle des anciens et modernes*. An English version of the *Histoire poétique* appeared during the English phase of the quarrel. Wrongly (and probably deliberately) attributed by the translator to Fénelon, it is titled "Characters and criticisms upon the ancient and modern orators, poets, painters, musicians, statuaries, & other arts and sciences: with an heroick poem (in blank verse) intituled 'The age of Lewis the Great,' written originally in French by the Archbishop of Cambray, and made English by J.G.," London, 1714.

[7] During the English phase of the Quarrel, Jonathan Swift was accused of having borrowed from Callières without attribution, since his *Battle of the Books* uses a similar conceit involving an assault on Parnassus, but there is little similarity between Swift's muscular wit and Callières's artful positioning between two fires.

63

book was illustrated by a foldout sketch of the battlefield drawn by Callières himself.[8]

Callières is sometimes said to have taken the side of the ancients, but this is not at all the case, as even a casual reading of the book will show. [9] He celebrated modern technology and discoveries – the telescope, the microscope, circulation of the blood, not to mention gunpowder and artillery – and he had the good sense to imply that both factions were guilty of anachronism. The gardens at Versailles are said to outrival anything in antiquity.[10] The book was learned and well-written, even if the conceit of an assault on Parnassus by rival armies was difficult to sustain. In the last chapter, Apollo renders a solemn and final judgment to which both sides assent. Homer remains the prince of poets, but Corneille and Racine are to be known henceforth as the Sophocles and Euripedes of France – even as Sophocles and Euripedes may be known, Callières adds, tongue firmly in cheek, as the Corneille and Racine of Greece. The prize for comedy goes to Molière, *ex aequo* with Menander and Aristophanes but above Plautus, and Molière's four best plays (listed as *Misanthrope, École des Femmes, Femmes Savantes,Tartuffe*) are described as models of perfection in the comic genre.

In his speech of reception at the Academy, Callières sounded a distinctly political rather than a literary note, asserting that it was only the cabals of his enemies that had forced the peace-loving King of France into the War of the League of Augsburg. In response, François Charpentier, an old retainer of Jean-Baptiste Colbert, mentioned only the Panegyric among Callières's published works, noting in a delicate allusion to the circumstances that he had been elected by a "sort of acclamation" without any sordid lobbying or cabals, without referring to his contribution to the ancients and moderns debate – the divisive subject was perhaps best avoided altogether. As for Callières's friend Renaudot, installed in the same session, in a long declamation that must have left his audience squirming in their seats, he declared that he would have been afraid of being found unworthy had he campaigned for the seat, a way of saying he had been elected without the need to solicit votes. Charpentier praised him for the *Gazette*, that faithful "cradle of truth."[11]

---

[8] The sketch is unsigned, but it is clearly by the same hand as Callières's sketch of the election ground at Warsaw. (See the cover illustration.)

[9] See for example Wilson, *François de Callières*, and Schweizer's, *François de Callières*, which follows Wilson.

[10] See also Call, 'The Battle for Molière's corpse/corpus', 47-59.

[11] The speeches are in the *Recueil des harangues prononcées par messieurs de l'académie française*, Tome 2, Amsterdam, 1709, 142-9.

ACADEMICAL WORKS

Between 1692 and 1694 Callières published the three books he later referred to as his *ouvrages académiques*, meaning works written as an academician, in defense of the French language and proper behavior at court. Their titles can be roughly anglicized as *Newly Fashionable Terms* (1692); its sequel *Good Usage, and How Court Language Differs from that of the Bourgeois* (1694); and *Witticisms and Anecdotes of the Ancients and Moderns* (1692).[12] They are similar in style, and written with an occasional touch of wit, though Callières could never keep himself from over-explaining a joke or an allusion. They were a great success with their intended audience, perhaps not so much the fashionable world of the court and the Academy as the emerging middle class satirized so memorably by Molière. Written in the form of a dialogue, and printed by Claude Barbin in large type, one hundred or so words to the page, the books flatter the reader by introducing him (or her) into the aristocratic salon of a Duchess of a certain age. Its denizens include a young and fashionable Marquise and a grave Commander of the Order of Malta who has spent many years abroad – the stand-in for Callières himself.

Fashionable Terms went through at least three French editions. Criticizing both the affectations of court usage and upwardly mobile bourgeois who ape their betters, Callières argues that infatuation with genealogy and rank should be avoided: "I would prefer that our young men work tirelessly to adorn themselves with their own virtues, rather than seeking to appear adorned with the virtues of their fathers." After all, rank can only be awarded by the King, Callières noted, echoing the same point his father had made in *On the Fortune of Gentlemen of Birth*. To a noble lady who is overly proud of her ancient lineage, the Commander makes the unassailable mathematical point that after a certain number of generations everybody in Europe must be more or less related to everybody else. He ridicules the precious usage that implied that the world revolved around Versailles, as in "today there is ball," or "today is there is toilette," or "it's still night at the King's" when His Majesty arose late in the day. The bourgeois gentleman who thinks it sounds an aristocratic note to refer to his spouse as "Madame so and so" would do better simply to say "my wife."

The book concludes with a poem it would be uncharitable to judge too harshly – the panegyric genre was after all a convention of the time. On the pretext of contrasting the careless manners of young courtiers with those of their elders, Callières lavishes praise in limping alexandrins on the

---

[12] The French titles are listed in the Bibliography.

political figures who would be his principal patrons: Cardinal d'Estrées, and the Dukes de Chevreuse and Beauvillier.[13]

Witticisms and Anecdotes of the Ancients and Moderns makes more interesting reading today. It contains good stories, many about politics, art, and literature, although the reader sometimes wishes Callières would not feel obliged to gloss them at tedious length. One or two of them skirt indecency, given the decorous standards of the times. A few samples freely rendered into English will be enough to give the idea:

> Henry VIII of England, having a bone to pick with François I of France, resolved to send an ambassador with a harsh and threatening message. His choice for this mission was a bishop in whom he had great confidence. The bishop objected that if he were to deliver such a message to the proud King of France his life could well be forfeit. Henry responded that the bishop need not worry. If he lost his head, Henry would cut off the heads of all the Frenchmen in his realm. Replied the Bishop, that's very well Your Majesty, but of all those heads, not one suits my body as well as this one.

> Thomas More, the famous Chancellor imprisoned by Henry VIII, let his hair and beard grow. A barber came to shave him and cut his hair. Never mind that my friend, said Moore, the King and I have a case in law over this head, and until I learn who is to have the use of it I am reluctant to incur the expense.

> Bacon, another English chancellor, was visited by Queen Elizabeth at the country house he had built before he came to court. Why such a small house, Master Bacon, asked the Queen? Replied Bacon, my house was not too small until Your Majesty made me too great for it.

---

[13] A sample:
Beauvillier me présente un autre example illustre,
Qui des mêmes vertus reçoit un si beau lustre,
Qui joint la politesse à la solidité,
La grandeur de courage avec la piété,
Généreux Cardinal, ferme et savant d'Estrées,
Dont la gloire répand par toutes les contrées,
Ton esprit, ton grand Coeur, ton amour pour ton Roi,
Exige dans ces vers des éloges de moi.

The Doge of Genoa, come to Versailles to present his apologies to the King, was asked what he found most extraordinary about the palace. To find myself here, he replied. [14]

The Princess of … having admired a particularly fine painting at the English Ambassador's residence, the Ambassador had it sent to her house. She asked her husband the Prince what he thought of it. Thoughtfully he replied: Madame, either the Ambassador is your dupe, or I am.

Several ladies were talking about childbirth and comparing their suffering. One said she had no more pain in giving birth than she had in eating an egg yoke – to which a gentleman said "Madame, you must have a very narrow throat."

Pope Alexander VII contemplated a painting by Le Brun which shows the family of Darius at the feet of Alexander, flanked on either side by masterpieces by Veronese and Raphael. Asked what he thought of the Le Brun, the Pope replied: it is certainly very fine, but its neighbors are unkind to it.

When Molière died, an indifferent poet composed his epitaph in verse and brought it to a Prince. If only Molière had brought me yours, said the Prince.

The late Quinault was explaining a play of his to a courtier. It takes place in Cappadocia, said Quinault, and you must transport yourself to that place in order to fully appreciate it. Perhaps it would be better performed on location, replied the courtier. [15]

And finally, this anecdote, which was a great favorite with Callières. He recounts it with little variation in a letter to Madame d'Huxelles as well as in *On Negotiating with Sovereigns*:

A visiting Venetian called on the Grand Duke of Tuscany at Florence. The Grand Duke complained that the Venetian Ambassador to Tuscany was a fool. Your Highness shouldn't be surprised at that, replied the Venetian, unfortunately we have many fools in Venice. We have fools in Florence too, the Grand Duke replied, but we never send them abroad to deal with public affairs. [16]

---

[14] The Doge's humiliation took place in 1685 following the savage bombing of Genoa by a fleet under the personal command of Seignelay. It is commemorated by the painting by Claude-Guy Hallé that hangs in the Hall of Mirrors.

[15] Professor William S. Brooks notes that there is no play by Quinault set in Cappadocia. See his *Philippe Quinault, Dramatist*. Callières had taken Quinault's seat in the Academy.

[16] Emphasis in the original.

ON COURT WIT

The last book Callières published during this period was different in tone from the *ouvrages académiques* and more ambitious. Written in a moralizing and ponderous style, *On court wit* sank almost without a trace on its publication in 1695.[17] It is a curious book, an attack on the frivolity of the court and court wit, *le bel esprit*, which is contrasted with good sense, *le bon esprit*. There are attempts at philosophical rigor, and traces of Locke's empiricism: "That which we call our good, and our ill, is commonly only good or bad because we imagine it to be so. Thus it is that so and so is unhappy with that which would make another man happy. It is generally imagination that gives form to things."[18]

In sharp contrast to the prescriptive and theoretical approach of *On Negotiating with Sovereigns*, Callières argues in *On Court Wit* for the purest political pragmatism. He contends that while art and science have principles that can be discerned, political life is the domain of chance and entirely conjectural, with no underlying rules, and that political actors are the sole judge of what is to be done in a given situation: "Its principles are given the lie every time there is a change in circumstances, so that it has no more solid foundation than the prudence and skill of its practitioners. They pay less attention to its maxims than to the changing times and to present circumstances, and adapt rules to affairs, rather than dealing with affairs in accordance with rules."[19] A man of ability is simply someone who can bring his conduct into accord with the times, he writes. The contrast with the prescriptive counsels of *On Negotiating with Sovereigns* could hardly be sharper, and one suspects that this counsel of utilitarian pragmatism is closer to Callières real view of politics and diplomacy.

In one passage in particular, his jealousy of more successful courtiers is palpable:

> I know that everyone doesn't follow the same course, and that each must follow his own way, but the most bizarre way appears to me to be that which some people follow when their presumption brings them to parade at the court of the Prince, where they try to pass for something rare. Believing themselves to be extraordinary, they believe they must take extraordinary measures, and they are sure that the King will overturn all order so as to raise them from the crowd. Bel esprit always believes that it is fated to be the favorite of the Prince and the principal object of his favors. Goods, honors, fortune, everything is owed to it. A few verses, a bad book, some treatise, written or read, a pompous epistle as the preface to a bad translation, all

---

[17] *Du bel esprit.*

[18] *Du bel esprit*, 325.

[19] *Du bel esprit*, 335.

confer the right to the rewards of the Prince, which are no more than its due. If its hopes are disappointed, it blames the King and his ministers for its misfortunes.[20]

Is it reading too much into these lines to suggest that Callières protests too much?

POLAND AGAIN

Literary preoccupations aside, Callières's dominant passion continued to be politics, and once again he lobbied the King to send him to Poland. His '*Mémoire* on the present state of affairs' in Poland addressed to Louis XIV is undated, but the circumstances are those of late 1691 or early 1692.[21] The occasion was the expulsion from Warsaw of the unofficial French representative there, the Marquis de Béthune, the Polish Queen's brother-in-law, forced as a result of heavy Austrian pressure to leave the country. Callières proposed that an envoy be sent to fill the void in French representation left by Béthune's departure, and he provided a recommended outline of the envoy's instructions.

The principal task of the envoy would be to break the Polish alliance with the Hapsburgs by playing on Sobieski's fears of abandonment by Austria and by encouraging a separate peace between Poland and the Ottoman Empire. That the effect of this might be to open Central Europe to a renewed Ottoman invasion – memories of the siege of Vienna were still fresh, after all – clearly troubled Callières not at all. Without quite offering to mediate, since France could not openly be neutral between the Ottomans and Christendom, the envoy of Louis XIV at the Porte would persuade the Ottoman Sultan to agree to the evacuation of Kamieniec, a frontier fortress commanding the approaches across the Dniestr, while the envoy in Poland would urge a peace agreement with the Ottomans The French Queen, Marie d'Arquien, might be a problem with her "pretensions and passions," Callières allowed, but he saw an opening, believing that Sobieski was increasingly suspicious of his Austrian allies.

To implement this new strategy, Callières recommended that letters from Louis XIV be prepared for the principal Polish and Lithuanian leaders. Béthune's replacement could gain Sobieski's confidence by giving him "little presents" in a country where this practice was much observed – for example he could lose small sums to Sobieski at cards, "as "Cardinal de Janson used to do regularly." (This peculiar diplomatic tactic of

---

[20] *Du bel esprit*, 346.

[21] *BnF, Fonds Renaudot*, NAF 7492, 32 and following, *mémoire sur les affaires présentes.*

deliberately losing at cards is recommended in *On Negotiating with Sovereigns* as well as by Jacques de Callières in *On the Fortune of Gentlemen of Birth*.) Since Sobieski was a great reader, the envoy could ingratiate himself by giving the Polish King news of "the latest books and literary works, as well as of various novelties and curiosities that are (his) habitual diversions." In other words, Callières argued, the ideal candidate would have a literary bent as well as experience of Polish affairs. There was one person who fit this bill perfectly – but once again Louis XIV declined to take up the implied offer of Callières's services.

CHAPTER SEVEN

'M. DE GIGNY' GOES TO HOLLAND

There are occasions in which it is advantageous and even necessary to
send to the same place or to the same country several able ministers, hard
working and serious .... In this case, it is well to choose persons who are
friends, and of a compatible temper, so as to avoid jealousies and
divisions that could damage their master's interests, which happens only
too often.
– François de Callières, *On Negotiating with Sovereigns*

Approaching the climacteric of 50 years of age, Callières was still
unmarried. This was as unusual then for a man of his social position as it
would be today. His financial circumstances appear to have been
prosperous enough, thanks to his relationship with Morsztyn and
Chevreuse, his pension as an academician, and perhaps even income from
the sale of his books, though like many an author before and since he
complained that most of the profits went to the publisher.[1] He was now a
man of property, with a Paris house on the rue des Cléry where his
neighbors included Étienne Pavillon, a fellow member of the Academy.[2]
While negotiating in Holland, he would rent it to the Count de Marsan, a
disreputable scion of the house of Lorraine who had married Seignelay's
widow Catherine de Matignon in 1696, and a leitmotif of his letters to the
Marquise d'Huxelles is his effort to prevail on the profligate Marsan to pay
him the back rent he owed.[3]

Although he was reasonably secure financially and membership in
the Academy gave him a prominent social position, from a political point of
view he was still a marginal figure. His dreams of serving as a French
envoy seemed remote. The premature death of the brilliant Seignelay in
1690 – from a combination of overwork and dissipation, it was said – had
deprived him of an important source of patronage, leaving only Jean-
Baptiste Colbert's younger brother the Marquis de Croissy, Foreign
Secretary since 1679, as a representative of the Colbert clan in the higher
councils of state. The Dukes of Beauvillier and Chevreuse who had both

[1] See the preface to Callières, *Des bons mots et des bons contes.*
[2] Pradel, *Livre Commode des addresses de Paris pour 1692*, 293-4.
[3] *Letters*, 45, 49, etc. In the end it was Marsan's father-in-law Matignon who paid Callières.

married Colbert daughters were influential, but they held no ministerial office. When an opportunity arose to insert himself into negotiations to end the War of the League of Augsburg, Callières exploited the opening.

A SITUATION RIPE FOR PEACE

By 1694, this conflict between France and the principal European powers, including England, Spain, and Holland, was entering its sixth year as a virtual stalemate, and a strong peace party took shape at Versailles, led by the moderate and sensible Beauvillier and Chevreuse. The harvests of 1692 and 1693 had been disastrous – it was still the time of what has been called the little ice age in Europe – and in the summer of 1693, Beauvillier had drawn up a memorandum for the King stressing the urgent necessity of peace. Beauvillier was the Governor of the King's children and an admirer of their tutor, the cleric François de Salignac de la Mothe-Fénelon, who had composed a famous letter to the King in late 1693 or early 1694. Fénelon wrote that "France is one great poorhouse, desolate and ill-kept," and that the policies of the King's ministers had made the name of France "odious to all our neighbors." He urged the King to negotiate in good faith, relinquishing the territories and forts he had acquired by force or imposed by treaty in exchange for a negotiated peace.

It is unlikely that Louis ever saw this courageous private letter that would have landed a men with fewer protectors in the Bastille, but peace feelers were initiated soon after it was written, and negotiations between Louis XIV and William III proceeded in fits and starts until the signing of a general European peace treaty at Ryswick in Holland in September of 1697 that required painful territorial concessions by France. Callières played a key role in these negotiations from beginning to end: first as a shadowy cutout, intermediary to another intermediary; then as deputy to a more senior envoy, still not fully trusted by the King; as an incognito envoy sent alone to deal with the representatives of William III; and finally as Ambassador Extraordinary and Plenipotentiary, though still the junior of the three signatories for France of the Ryswick Treaty.

The ups and downs of the complicated talks that finally led in September of 1697 to the signing of the Treaty of Ryswick would be as tedious to relate as to read, and it would be easy to drown in the details.[4]

---

[4] See Legelle, *Notes et documents sur la paix de Ryswick*, for extensive but very selective excerpts from Callières's dispatches. Legrelle's thesis is that the Ryswick negotiations were a success for Louis XIV, thanks in part to Callières and his "devoted skill," and Legrelle omits anything which would conflict with this thesis. He has been followed in this by subsequent writers. The facts, as the reader will see, are more complicated.

Suffice it to say that there were essentially two separate but related issues to be resolved between the representatives of Louis XIV and William III of England, who was also *stathouder* or military ruler of the Dutch Republic. The first, arguably the easiest, was the amount of territory to be surrendered by France. The allies wanted the basis for the negotiation to be the restoration of the territorial *status quo* before the 1678 Treaty of Nijmegen. The Dutch were determined to establish a barrier of forts in Flanders and along their border as a hedge against renewed French aggression, and to this end they sought the surrender by France of the great fortresses of Luxembourg and Strasbourg. The second issue, recognition by Louis XIV of William III as King of England, was more difficult, involving as it did ideological and religious considerations as well as the honor of Louis XIV. In the French view, the Protestant champion William was a usurper, the 'Prince of Orange', who had displaced the Catholic James II as the rightful king of England. Since their flight across the Channel in 1688, assisted by French agents, James and his Queen had been the guests of Louis XIV at Saint Germain-en-Laye. There under French protection they had established a Stuart court in exile, and they were treated by France as the legitimate King and Queen of England. To disavow them would be a bitter pill for Louis XIV to swallow. Against this, he must have known that he could hardly hope to make peace with William III while still supporting the claims of rivals to the throne.

Under William's leadership English and Dutch diplomacy was unified, but there were tensions inherent in the differing interests of the two states, and the fundamental French approach to the negotiations was based on the firm conviction, not without some basis in reality, that the commercially-minded Dutch, and especially Amsterdam with its global trading network, could be tempted by commercial concessions into a separate peace. There were also fault lines for the French to exploit in the allied coalition. The Austrian Empire and the German states would have to agree to an eventual settlement if the peace was truly to be a general one, and Austria was determined to humiliate Louis XIV at any cost. Moreover the Duke of Savoy, Victor Amadeus II, Madame Royale's son come of age, was an unpredictable member of the allied coalition, capable of switching sides on a dime if the price was right. While inconclusive negotiations about negotiations dragged on, the two armies sparred for advantage, and the two sides watched each other closely for signs of moral and economic exhaustion.

Callières later gave different accounts to Saint-Simon and Huxelles of how he managed to insert himself into the first direct contacts between the opposing parties. As usual, Saint-Simon highlights the part played by chance and family connection. He writes that Callières ran into an unnamed

Dutch merchant in the streets of Paris, who told him that Holland was ready for peace. Thereupon Callières went to see Chevreuse and Beauvillier, and they took him to see Colbert de Croissy, the foreign secretary who was after all, "the uncle of their wives" – as well as Arnauld de Pomponne, back now at Versailles as Minister of State. As a result, the decision was made by the King to send Callières undercover to Holland. This makes a good story, but it is at considerable variance with the facts.[5]

The version Callières gave to the Marquise d'Huxelles – unwisely, since she would have known better from her own first hand sources – was equally misleading. He omitted any reference to a 'Dutch merchant' or to Chevreuse and Beauvillier, and portrayed himself as the principal protagonist of the drama. Having come to the conclusion that peace was necessary for the King and the state, he wrote to the Marquise, he had communicated "various projects" to Croissy, one of which was a proposal for a secret mission to Savoy.[6] Based on this initiative and on Croissy's recommendation, he told the Marquise, the King had decided to send him alone to make clandestine contact with the Dutch. Croissy, who "honored me with his confidence and his friendship," had said that "if I made progress, the King might send me a colleague. I urged him to do so before my departure, so that he might be witness to my zeal and sincerity, and that he might assist me with his insights, not presuming myself capable of carrying forward such a grand design alone. M. de Croissy reported this to the King, and His Majesty named Monsieur de Harlay."[7]

The archives of the French Foreign Ministry and other documentary sources tell a different tale.[8]

A DUTCH INTERMEDIARY

The 'Dutch merchant' of Saint-Simon's account was Francisco Mollo, the Polish Resident in Amsterdam, a wealthy merchant and a resourceful and tireless go-between who would operate a back channel between the Dutch and the French on and off through the negotiations for the Treaty of Utrecht

---

[5] S-S. I, 546.

[6] For the details of French contacts with Savoy, and an account which stresses the importance of Savoy in the European balance, see Rowlands, 'Louis XIV, Vittorio Amedeo II and French Military Failure in Italy, 1689-96'. The complicated bargaining involved Prince Thomas, Callières's erstwhile candidate in 1674 for the Polish throne, who was at that time still in French service. He would later defect to Austria and be killed in battle in 1701.

[7] *Letters*, 120-1.

[8] *Archives des affaires étrangères, corespondance politique Hollande 159*, and Hein, *Het archief*.

(1713).[9] Mollo may well have been a *marrano*, a Jew converted to Christianity.[10] He was in any case a creative intermediary with close commercial ties to his fellow merchants on the Amsterdam city council, married to a daughter of one of its members. It was Mollo, not Callières, who initiated the first contacts with France, and at first they were with Morsztyn before his death in 1693, rather than with Callières. As early as 1692, Mme d'Huxelles told La Garde that the "Polish Resident in The Hague" was relaying news about the situation in England to Morsztyn.[11] It was this Polish connection with Morsztyn that accounted for Mollo's initial contacts with Callières, not a chance meeting in a Paris street.

Mollo's first visit to Paris as an unofficial go between dated to November of 1693, when a secret agent in Paris for the Dutch Grand Pensionary, Anthonie Heinsius, reported breathlessly that he had come to France to propose a mediation for a separate peace between Holland and France. The anonymous agent thought Mollo was unlikely to succeed, as his "genius is of the lowest order," and he thought that Mollo was acting on behalf of the Amsterdam *bourgmestre* named Hudde, his father-in-law. The agent recommended to Heinsius that Mollo's treasonous correspondence should be seized as evidence. In fact, it seems likely that Heinsius knew all about Mollo's trip from the beginning, and was using it to probe French positions.[12] During this visit, Callières and Mollo formed a partnership to advance a separate negotiation between Holland and France that eventually supplanted all the other channels, including the offficial channel of Swedish mediation through the Count d'Avaux, the French Ambassador in Stockholm.

In February of 1694, after Mollo's return to Amsterdam, Callières wrote that to Mollo to say that he was authorized to offer a commercial inducement to Amsterdam in the form of an elimination of the French tax on Dutch shipping, and the two men continued to correspond on virtually a weekly basis through the spring.[13] Callières warned Mollo that while there might be hardliners in Holland, there were also those at the French court, "powerful and well-connected," who did not want peace. Some at

---

[9] For Mollo's role at Utrecht, see Bély's extraordinary *Espions et ambassadeurs au temps de Louis XIV*.

[10] Bély, *Espions et ambassadeurs au temps de Louis XIV*, 297. Bély does not cite his authority for this. Mollo is described in the *Recueil des instructions* as Swiss, while Legrelle in *Notes et documents sur la paix de Ryswick* says that he was of Italian origin.

[11] *Bibliothèque municipale d'Avignon*, MS 1419, Tome I, letter of May 5, 1692. Callières may well have been her informant. Since there was no Polish Resident in The Hague, the reference is clearly to Mollo in Amsterdam.

[12] Hein, *Het archief*, 48-50.

[13] Hein, *Het archief*, 67-83.

Versailles believed that William III, 'the Prince of Orange', wanted to maintain himself at the head of the wartime coalition at any cost, but Callières wrote that he was not entirely of this view himself. The situation in Europe was not in his favor, with Flanders "entirely undefended," Germany open to French arms, Hungary exposed to the Turks, Spain without weapons or forts, and England restive under his rule, Callières argued to Mollo in an attempt to convince the Dutch to enter a negotiation. Yes, he acknowledged, it was quite true that bread was expensive in Paris and the poor were suffering cruelly, but French armies were still strong, and the Dutch should not be misled by Huguenot propaganda. On May 10, Callières told Mollo – in response to Dutch complaints about economic sanctions – that Croissy had allowed that they had a case, and he blamed Louvois (who had died in 1691) for their imposition. Now the King's council was unified as never before in support of peace on honorable terms with Holland, he maintained. On May 23, Mollo complained that Callières was writing too openly about the alleged divisions between Amsterdam and the other provinces. If these letters fell into the wrong hands, his credit would be destroyed, and he was "entirely Dutch" in his allegiance, "as you know."[14]

The city fathers of Amsterdam were a cosmopolitan and commercially minded group, with a vast multinational network that reached throughout Europe and beyond on which their extraordinary prosperity had been built, and their interests were jeopardized by the war, although whenever possible they continued to trade with all sides. (During the French invasion of 1672, Amsterdam had continued to supply the French Army with munitions.[15]) Mollo was also in touch in this period with Sébastien le Prestre, the future Marshal de Vauban, the great military architect, who received his letters through Callières, but Callières, unlike Vauban was unwilling to entertain the notion of significant territorial concessions, and he told Mollo that if the "good republicans" of Amsterdam wanted peace, they should forget any thought of securing French territory in exchange.[16] More flexible and realistic about the need to relinquish territory as part of a peace treaty, Callières took over as Mollo's principal French contact, forwarding his coded letters to Croissy and the King while Croissy provided instructions for the responses, sometimes along the lines of Callières's recommendations, often not.

---

[14] Hein, *Het archief*, 79.

[15] Barbour, *Capitalism in Amsterdam in the 17th Century*.

[16] Vauban's correspondence with Mollo is in Hein, *Het Archief*, III, 73-7, with several exchanges between Callières and Mollo.

As is often the case before direct contacts take place, both parties held to maximalist positions, and neither side fully trusted the middleman. Mollo claimed to be motivated solely by "the glory of God and the public weal," but his commercial interests were clearly a more immediate concern. He asked Croissy as a political gesture to release his ship taken as a prize, a Polish-flagged vessel called the *Écluse de Pierre*, but Croissy declined.[17] Prompted by the Amsterdam burghers, Mollo probed the French defenses: would France require the destruction of the fortifications of Luxembourg in a final settlement, for example? Could he offer a reduction on the French duty imposed on Dutch ships? Mollo wanted a letter from Croissy empowering him to make commitments on behalf of France, but Croissy refused, and in an effort to enhance his credibility with the French he offered to try to persuade the Amsterdam city council to ban anti-French publications and arrest their authors.[18] Callières endorsed this proposal, arguing that although such "vain writings" were beneath the King's notice, perhaps a polite note of thanks could be sent to the Amsterdam city council through Mollo. Again, Croissy declined.[19]

Invited to continue the negotiation in France, Mollo proposed ingeniously but implausibly that he come representing not Holland but the King of Poland, and he offered to have Sobieski write a letter endorsing him as a mediator. Callières agreed that Poland might be a useful intermediary, and he told Croissy that "the next time I am in Versailles, I will tell you what use we can make of Prince Lubomirski, Grand Treasurer of Poland, in the service of His Majesty." After the wretched harvest of 1693, France was hard-pressed for grain, and Callières told Croissy that he had had correspondents in Poland who would provide grain to France without risk from privateers.[20] Callières did eventually forward a letter to Sobieski for Mollo to send on to Warsaw, but unsurprisingly neither France nor the allies were tempted by this peculiar Polish gambit.[21]

Alleging that the Amsterdam city council was unhappy that the *Écluse de pierre* had not been released, Mollo continued to argue that the release of the ship and its cargo would provide a commercial cover for his trip to France. When a prize court ruling involving the *Écluse* went against him, he complained to Callières that the life of the peacemaker was a thankless one, but he decided to come ahead anyway, commending himself

---

[17] *CP Hollande* 159, Mollo to Callières dated February 24, 1694.
[18] *CP Hollande* 159, Mollo to Callières, letters of Feb. 27, March 1, and March 4.
[19] *CP Hollande* 159, Callières to Croissy, March 9.
[20] *CP Hollande* 159, Callières to Croissy, Ferbruary 24. Callières attached a *mémoire* that has not survived.
[21] *CP Hollande* 159, Callières to Croissy, October 19, 1694.

to the protection of Croissy for his lost "700 pieces of eight."[22] In preparation for the trip, Mollo asked Callières to find him a house. He hoped that Callières would lodge him nearby, and hire the same servants for him he had during his last visit.[23]

By June of 1694, however, Mollo was still in Holland. He was reluctant to leave for Paris without some credentials from the Dutch, and they refused to provide them. Callières presented Croissy with three options: Mollo could be told to stay in Amsterdam until he was empowered to negotiate; he could be told that he could come only to hear French views and report back; or the Dutch could send an official with him, who would wait in Maastricht or Brussels while Mollo came to Paris to negotiate a venue for official talks. Callières favored option three.

In the end Mollo came alone without any official character, arriving in Paris in July of 1694, and he went immediately to see Callières, "my correspondent and my friend" as he wrote to Heinsius, and the two men went together to call on Croissy at Versailles.[24] Mollo suggested that Croissy send an emissary to Louvain, and Croissy responded with a counterproposal that the Dutch send an envoy to Versailles, but at this stage neither side wanted to take the first step and risk being perceived by European opinion as weak.[25]

With his long experience of negotiations, Colbert de Croissy saw that Mollo was playing both sides against the middle, and he appears not to have been so sure about Mollo's great friend Callières either. In February he reprimanded Callières sharply for talking too much, probably because Callières had gone behind Croissy's back to Beauvillier and Chevreuse: "I understand, Sir, that you have not observed secrecy in this little negotiation, and I reserve the right to have a frank discussion about this with you when I see you next." Callières responded with the injured dignity of the professional whose discretion is called unjustly into question: "Monseigneur, I can say that I am no novice in this trade, and that I have never been suspected of having failed to maintain the secrecy of the various affairs that have been entrusted to me by several princes."[26] In the meeting with Mollo, Croissy did confirm that Callières had been authorized to correspond with him on behalf of the court.

On September 27, 1694, with Mollo still lingering in Paris, the Dutch finally sent the blank passports that would allow French envoys to

---

[22] *CP Hollande* 159, Mollo to Callières, May 20, 1694.
[23] *CP Hollande* 159, Mollo to Callières, May 21, 1694.
[24] Hein, *Het archief,* 90.
[25] Hein, *Het archief,* 91.
[26] *CP Hollande* 159, February 8, 1694.

go to Liege to meet Everard van Dijkveld, William III's representative. The lead French envoy chosen by Croissy and the King was not Callières, but a well-connected magistrate who had the King's full confidence, Nicolas-Auguste de Harlay-Bonneuil. Callières was allowed to accompany Harlay-Bonneuil, but Mollo was told to stay in Paris even though Callières lobbied Croissy for him to go along. Mollo had already attracted too much attention to himself, and secrecy was essential for both sides. The Dutch wanted to prevent leaks that would give rise to the suspicion among their allies that they were making a separate peace, and Louis XIV did not want to appear to be suing for peace from weakness by taking the first step. Writing to Sir William Trumbull at the Treasury in London, George Stepney, an English envoy who was cooling his heels in the Hague "till some German business be cut out for me," wrote later that Callières had been brought along only because of the relationship he had established with Mollo, and this seems likely.[27]

UNDERCOVER TO FLANDERS

While they agreed that Callières could go along with Harlay, Croissy and the King took the unusual precaution of drawing up two separate sets of instructions, one for Harlay-Bonneuil with the real French bottom line on withdrawal and recognition, and another, more anodyne, for them both. The preparation of two sets of instructions, one real and the other for show, was a common practice, but this was different, as Harlay's reports to the King make clear. He was instructed to keep Callières in the dark and not to share his reports with his junior colleague – probably because at this stage Callières was suspected of being too ready to make concessions in light of his connections to Beauvillier and Chevreuse, who by this time were in favor of peace at virtually any price. It may also be the case that Louis XIV had not forgotten Callières's prior service to the Duchy of Savoy, by now a member of the anti-French coalition.

The two men left Paris in great secrecy, travelling separately to avoid detection. Even the King's crony and chronicler, the Marquis de Dangeau, was kept in the dark, recording only that Harlay had left for some "secret and important negotiation," destination unknown.[28] Callières had filled his blank passport out in the name of "Monsieur de Gigny" – as in the

---

[27] TNA, SP87/1/1/31, Stepney to Trumbull, October 20, 1696. Stepney refers carefully to "de Harlay," but Callières is always just plain Caliers, Caillière, or Callièrs, always without the noble *de*, even though by that time he was the sole French negotiator. This must have been standard practice for the allies, at least behind his back, and suggests once again that there were lingering questions about his noble status even among his negotiating partners.

[28] Dangeau, *Journal*, entry for October 23, 1694.

79

title to which he laid claim, *Sieur de Gigny et de la Rochechellay* – while Harlay-Bonneuil was "Monsieur de Saint-Germain." Meeting up at Dinant, they traveled down the Meuse to the meeting in Liege with Dijkveld, attempting to avoid detection by Spanish or Austrian officials as they traveled through Flanders.

Almost immediately, the peculiar arrangement of double instructions proved to be unworkable, and Harlay begged to be relieved of it. Callières had access to his rooms, he wrote to Croissy, and it was awkward to have to keep secrets from him. Harlay also complained that Callières was impossible to work with. He would invariably insist on adding his own length appendix to Harlay's reports, and the only remedy was for them to write separate reports, a "bizarre procedure," Harlay acknowledged to Croissy but a necessary one, since otherwise Callières would inevitably insist on making a few additions and they would turn into a disquisition. "I don't have the heart to tell him it's pointless," wrote Harlay. It wasn't a sign of disagreement between the two men, Harlay maintained: "We are as close as night is to day," he wrote, an interesting and possibly revealing choice of words, and he urged the King to allow him to share his instructions with Callières. Croissy finally told Harlay that the King sympathized with his dilemma, and that he had agreed to send the two men common orders so that he would not always have to be on guard against the "scrutiny of your assistant."

It was a difficult and arduous trip. The cover of the two accredited but secret emissaries was threadbare, and the officials they met on the way soon saw through it. Will you bring us the peace we all long for, one of them asked the two traveling gentlemen? On their arrival in Liege there were no lodgings to be had because of a visit by the Bavarian Elector Maximilian Emmanuel – Henriette-Adelaïde's son, now ruler of the Spanish Netherlands – and they were taken in by a banker named Canto, an associate of Mollo for whom they had a letter of exchange. Canto grew nervous and sent their passports to the local Governor, and a squad of soldiers arrived in the middle of the night to inspect the suspicious visitors.

Their host in Flanders was Everard van Dijkveld, who represented William III and the States General of Holland. His cover story – which nobody believed – was that he was in Liege to look for winter quarters for the army. He proposed that the talks be held instead down the Meuse in Maastricht where there would be better security, but leaks continued in the relatively unfettered Dutch press. Back at Versailles the Marquis de Dangeau, still in the dark, recorded a rumor from a Rotterdam gazette that Dijkveld was negotiating with incognito French envoys, but he failed to connect this with Harlay's mysterious departure.[29] Meanwhile crowds gathered in the street whenever the two French envoys appeared in public, their cover well and truly blown.

The negotiations soon bogged down in mutual recriminations, as it became apparent that in his efforts to bring the parties together the absent Mollo had deliberately misrepresented their respective positions. When Harlay declared that he was not empowered to discuss the recognition of William III, Dijkveld was furious, blaming Mollo for having misled the French into thinking that he would agree to talks without French recognition of his master William III. Harlay and Callières responded that if Mollo had suggested they had come prepared to recognize William III, his conduct was inexcusable. William was still in Holland when he received Dijkveld's report, and understandably he reacted badly to this continued French refusal to acknowledge him as King of England. His departure for England on November 26 effectively ended the acrimonious and abortive discussions.

The French negotiators dawdled on the way back to Paris, and Callières urged Harlay to delay in the hope that something would turn up. At the French camp at Namur, they ran into Mollo on his way back to Holland, presumably not by coincidence, and there Callières was stunned to receive a letter addressed to him under his real name from the Marquise d'Huxelles. In his response he abandoned all pretence at secrecy, writing ruefully that "nothing escapes your scrutiny, Madame. You unearth travelers who conceal themselves with care, and you recognize them under their assumed names, despite the silence they have been obliged to maintain and their lack of courtesy in failing to take proper leave of you …."[30]

Her detective work had been persistent and painstaking. When Callières and Harlay both disappeared suddenly from Paris on October 23 she canvassed her sources. On October 31, she wrote to her friend the Marquis de La Garde in Provence that "Callières is still in the country – they say with the Polish princes."[31] On November 5 she asked Mme Harlay where her husband had gone, and the loyal wife, a relative of the Marquise, told her a cover story about a trip to the country. But Huxelles was not fooled, and by November 7 she had picked up the fact that the two men were together and on the same mission. On November 22, having unraveled the whole story, she wrote to La Garde: "M. Dijkveld is coming and going

---

[29] Dangeau, *Journal*, entry for November 5, 1694.
[30] *Letters*, 41.
[31] Sobieski's sons were visiting France at the time, incognito. It is notable that observers in Paris considered that Callières would be the one to take them around.

to sort things out, and he is conferring in Maastricht with M. de Saint Germain and M. de Gigny, the first being M. de Harlay, and the second M. de Callières." On December 12, citing Guiscard de La Bourlie, the commander at Namur who was also a friend of hers, the Marquise told La Garde that Harlay had been ordered by the King to return: "there is no longer any talk of anything but war."[32]

On December 15, angered by continuing leaks in the Dutch press, Louis XIV sent a peremptory order to his two negotiators to return without further foot-dragging: "the good of my service requires that by a prolonged stay on the border you not allow my enemies to put it out that I am seeking peace." [33] It was not a promising beginning.

CALLIÈRES RETURNS

With negotiations suspended, after the usual break for winter quarters the war continued in the fighting season of 1695 on its various fronts, from the German border to Flanders to Spain. The threat of an Anglo-Dutch invasion of France receded with the failure of an attack on the French naval arsenal at Brest, strengthened by Vauban, and elsewhere the French held their own against a sea of enemies. Bad harvests had left France chronically short of grain, despite the success of the privateer Jean Bart in escorting cargoes from the Baltic, and England was beset by financial difficulties and a lack of money to pay the troops – though the creation of the Bank of England in 1694 had helped alleviate currency shortages. (France lacked any equivalent.)

Back in Amsterdam Mollo continued his tireless machinations with a stream of coded letters through Callières. There was no longer any talk of Harlay's participation. The first contacts had been so unproductive that it may have been considered unwise to send a senior envoy again, and Callières could be disavowed more easily if the talks failed to make progress. In any case, the Dutch had asked for him by name. In May, Mollo forwarded passports from the Dutch allowing Callières to travel to Utrecht. Both sides still wanted to preserve an element of secrecy. Callières posed this time as a dealer in paintings named La Roche, reflecting his interest in art, and he was armed with new instructions. Crossing the border at

---

[32] These references to Huxelles's letters are taken from the notes of Louis Delavaud, contained in carton AB XIX 736 at the Archives nationales his unfinished edition of Callières's letters to Huxelles. They appear to have been drawn from letters to which Delavaud had access which are not in either Avignon or Manchester. Delavaud's extensive notes to the first few pages of his planned edition of the Huxelles letters threaten to overwhelm the text.

[33] *CP Hollande* 159, the King to "Saint Germain and Gigny," December 15, 1694.

Courtrai, after unpleasant encounters with disorderly troops he arrived in Utrecht on June 15, 1695, meeting first with Mollo, and then with Everard van Dijkveld.

Despite Mollo's assurances, it soon became apparent that little had changed on either side. In addition to the central question of the recognition of William III, a sticking point continued to be the fortress city of Luxembourg. The allies were demanding that the negotiation be conducted on the basis of a return to the situation before the 1678 Treaty of Nijmegen, when Luxembourg had been part of the Spanish Netherlands. William III was open to the discussion of an alternative to the return of the fortress, but he made clear that his price would be very high – a total of five towns. As instructed, Callières countered with an offer of two, but privately he urged Versailles to sweeten what he regarded himself as an inadequate "equivalent" for Luxembourg. Instead, Louis XIV ordered him to return to Paris, which he did by a circuitous route in order to increase the chances of a change of heart on either side – again to no avail. The talks appeared to be dead in the water.

In August, however, after promises from Mollo of new flexibility on the allied side, Callières returned again to the border at Lille, once more posing as an art dealer – and there he waited for over a month for an invitation to cross into Holland. In the meantime the important French fort at Namur fell to allied troops, and flush with this victory William III was in no mood to improve on his last offer. Callières was ordered by the King to end his ignominious wait on the border and to return to Paris. He asked to report to the King in Versailles in person, but the Marquis de Torcy – Croissy's son who had taken over as Foreign Minister on his father's death – told Callières that the King thought it would be better if he stayed in Paris. There was already too much gossip about negotiations, Torcy said. It must have been a low point.[34]

---

[34] For a detailed account of these comings and goings, see Wilson, *François de Callières*. Wilson's account is followed by Karl W. Schweizer in his biography with the same title.

VAUBAN AND THE KING

A good negotiator should never base the success of his negotiations on false promises and breaches of faith.
– François de Callières, *On Negotiating with Sovereigns*

That 1696 would prove to be decisive in the effort to negotiate the main outlines of a peace treaty was thanks in part to the determination of Callières, though as always the principal strategist was the King himself. The principal stumbling blocks remained the extent of the considerable territorial concessions France would have to make, with the allies demanding the return of both Strasbourg and Luxembourg or their equivalent in towns and forts, as well as the recognition of William III. The court at Versailles was divided, but a peace party led by Chevreuse and Beauvilliers gained strength as the fighting continued without much advantage to either side, and the war entered its eighth year.

Into the early months of 1696, letters in cipher continued to fly back and forth between Mollo and Callières. On March 2, Callières wrote directly to the Dutch leader Heinsius to say that that the King had authorized him to return to the border. He declined Heinsius's suggestion that he meet with other allied representatives, including Austrians. The French were still hoping to exploit faults in the allied front by negotiating a separate deal with the commercially-minded Dutch. Callières told Heinsius that Mollo would supply him with a name and address for the passport, and that Callières would be prepared to continue on to Holland itself for direct talks.[1] It took some time, but when the roads became passable again he set out for Holland, armed by the King with a new offer to return Luxembourg to Spain as the sovereign in the Spanish Netherlands. Although Callières's instruction was delphic its the language particularly tortured, it seemed to say that he could hold out the prospect of recognition as part of a final agreement.[2] He was instructed to dangle the prospect of a separate peace to the Dutch along with the prospect of commercial concessions. It seems

---

[1] Hein, *Het archief*, Callières to Heinsius, March 2, 1696, 205-6.
[2] *CP Hollande* 162, *Mémoire du roi pour servir d'instruction au sieur de Callières*, March 10, 1696.

likely that Callières was sent rather than de Harlay or another more senior figure because he could more easily be disavowed if the negotiation failed to progress. George Stepney, an experienced English envoy, thought that "Callières was chosen (being least considerable and consequently less subject to be taken notice of) for the errand to come into these parts privately."[3] With regard to the recognition of William III, Louis XIV wanted to hold that card until the last, playing it only after he had driven the best deal he could get.

Once again Callières's trip to Holland through the Spanish Netherlands was difficult, though the reports he sent to Croissy and the King are unlikely to have understated its dangers. A party of drunken soldiers stopped him near Ath and charged him with smuggling because his carriage had taken on a few packages en route. Callières showed his passports, threatened them with reprisals, and they allowed him to go on his way. He thought that if one of them had not been French he would have been taken hostage. Outside Ghent he was confronted again by soldiers who held him up for drink money, and he only arrived at the city gate just before it closed for the night. Initially he stayed secretly at Mollo's house in Amsterdam, emerging gradually from the shadows as the negotiations progressed, moving first to Haarlem, and finally to Delft.[4]

On May 3, Callières had his first meeting with Willem Boreel, the Dutch negotiator who had come to supplement the acerbic Everard van Dijkveld, and their conversation marked the beginning of a serious negotiation. Boreel, a former envoy to Paris, was far easier to deal with than Dijkveld, and Callières appears to have played skilfully on the differences in style between the two allied representatives.[5] He presented a draft document with fifteen articles, and Callières commented on each of them orally while Boreel took notes. Pressed for a commitment on the recognition of William III, and asked whether this would be possible as part of the signing of a treaty, Callières responded orally "agreed" (d'accord), thereby exceeding his ambiguously worded instructions. Boreel raised the possibility that the French Huguenots who had been forced by the revocation of the Edict of Nantes to flee to Holland might have their

---

[3] TNA, SP 87/1//1/32, George Stepney to William Trumbull, October 30, 1696.

[4] TNA, SP87/1/1/31, George Stepney to Sir William Trumbull, October 30, 1696.

[5] TNA, SP87/1/1/31: George Stepney wrote that "I suspect there is no very good understanding between him and Mr. Dickveldt because he seems desirous of shifting himself rather to Mr. Boreel ... which proceeding will (I suppose) make Mr. Dickveldt jealous that the business should be taken out of his hands ...." Callières's preference for Boreel also seems to have raised suspicion among the allies of a separate deal with Amsterdam, which suited his purposes well (SP/87/1/1/132).

nationality restored as part of a general peace, and Callières, who may have been privately sympathetic to their cause, promised to seek instructions.

A few days later there was a second meeting, this time with Dijkveld present as well. Boreel pretended that he had not already handed over the document with the 15 articles, and Callières told the King that although some might think the two men had agreed to "act the story of the good soldier and the bad soldier" – good cop, bad cop that is – he thought their differences were real.

The King was displeased by Callieres's report.[6] He told Callières that he should have stuck to his instructions and not have allowed himself to be drawn on the issue of recognition. The notes Boreel had taken on his oral comments could be read to commit France. As for the Huguenots, the King's treatment of his own subjects –former subjects in this case, since he had stripped them of their nationality – was no business of the Dutch. He wanted no reference to them of any kind in an agreement. It was a sharp rebuke. To soften the blow, a sympathetic Croissy told Callières that most of his responses had been fine.

Callières responded to the King's reprimand with considerable moral courage – as well, perhaps, as the knowledge that he was supported at court by the peace party of Chevreuse and Beauvillier. He argued that his instructions clearly said that he was to remove all doubt with regard to the King's readiness to sign a general peace in Europe. If he had not responded in some way on the recognition question, there would be nothing to negotiate. He had put nothing in writing that could come back to embarrass the King. He added "Finally, Sire, I believe that I can see clearly that this negotiation will soon produce peace, if Your Majesty is disposed to allow me to continue it – the more so because it embarrasses those who do not wish peace, and that one could not do them a greater pleasure than to break it off."[7] It was a pointed reminder to the King that negotiation was a two way street, and that his status in Holland as an undeclared emissary was precarious.

Louis XIV took this well, and there is no indication of continuing displeasure in his response. He approved of the way Callières had handled the discussion of a possible truce, and "I am no less pleased with the conduct you have followed up to the present."[8] Callières could tell the Dutch that the King had a high personal regard for William III ('the Prince of Orange') if that would help move things forward.

---

[6] *CP Hollande* 163, Louis XIV to Callières, May 13, 1696.
[7] *CP Hollande* 163, May 22, 1696.
[8] *CP Hollande* 163, June 8, 1696.

As negotiations continued, the Duke of Savoy stunned the allies by defecting to France. A secret deal had been made involving the marriage of his daughter Marie-Adelaïde to the Duke de Bourgogne along with other French concessions, including the return to Savoy of the fortress at Pignerol, and Callières was instructed to make the most of this major setback to the allied cause. The pace of the talks quickened, and on August 19 he reported to the King that he thought peace could be made "before winter."[9] Louis XIV responded that in exchange for a general peace binding all the allies, Callières could say that as soon as peace was made with England he would in the same document recognize William. But the King stressed that he wanted results quickly, as decisions would have to be taken soon with regard to next year's military campaign.

Alertly, acting without instructions, Callières took the initiative to negotiate an informal truce on naval bombardments by both sides, improving the atmosphere for negotiations. The King approved of the truce after the fact, though he declined to sign a formal document.[10] He also sent Callières money for his expenses and gave him the designation "envoy extraordinary and plenipotentiary." Everything seemed to be on track.

When Colbert de Croissy died on July 28 1696, he was replaced immediately as Secretary of State for Foreign Affairs by his son Jean-Baptiste Colbert, Marquis de Torcy, assisted by Arnauld de Pomponne as Minister of State. To avoid any possibility of conflict, Louis XIV took the precaution of sealing their partnership by arranging the marriage of Pomponne's daughter Catherine to Torcy. Callières was at pains to characterize these changes at Versailles as positive for the future of the negotiations. To Heinsius, he wrote that Croissy had been "a great admirer of yours," and that on his deathbed, his only regret had been that he had been unable to bring the great work of peace to fruition. The young Torcy was able and well-qualified, Callières told Heinsius, and Arnauld de Pomponne was "a former Ambassador to Holland who has a particular inclination for this state." Callières had obviously developed a personal relationship with Heinsius, as he asked in the same letter to meet secretly with him: "I have something I must say to you in person, meet me tomorrow in the same village of Oegstgeest."[11] The Austrians had been delaying a response to French proposals, and on September 15, writing from Haarlem, Callières told Heinsius that if they were to meet publicly, Heinsius would soon see that the couriers from Vienna would acquire "the

---

[9] *CP Hollande* 163, Callières to the King, August 19, 1696.
[10] See Delavaud, 'Un arrangement international sur les bombardements', 698-705.
[11] Hein, *Het archief*, 206.

winged feet of Mercury, instead of being as slow as a tortoise."[12] Despite these increasingly promising relations between Callières and the Dutch, storm clouds were gathering at Versailles.

UNDER FIRE AT VERSAILLES

The central issue was Luxembourg, the strategic fortress city guarding the approaches to Champagne and Paris that had been in French hands since 1678. It was understood all along that in a settlement Louis would either have to cede Luxembourg or make other painful territorial concessions to compensate the allies with an "equivalent" number of cities. If Strasbourg were to be ceded as well, France would be badly exposed, and losing strong places that had been won by so much blood and treasure would be a major blow to French defenses. A backlash developed at Versailles, and since the King himself could not be blamed, Callières was a convenient scapegoat. Among his critics, unsurprisingly, was the Marquis de Barbézieux, Louvois's son, who had inherited his father's portfolio as Secretary of State for War although not his genius. Preserved in the bound volume entitled *papiers de Callières* is a note from Barbézieux in his own hand to Torcy:

> I have the honor to return to you ... the *mémoire* sent to you by M. de Callières. Everything said in it by the man in question is true, but it is also true that I have no knowledge of his loyalty. His excuse for not having written to me because he had no cipher is worthless as he said he didn't want one, and we agreed on other channels. I wonder whether it is to be feared that he might deceive with regard to essential matters as I was deceived in the advice I gave to him.[13]

On October 11, Callières wrote with apparent unconcern to the Marquise d'Huxelles about this backbiting at Versailles, thanking her for taking on those at court who were envious of the *plongeon,* or diving duck – her pet name for him because of his habit of disappearing suddenly from view on secret missions:

> You pour scorn[14] (to use your terms) on those who are envious of the plongeon, against whom they are ill-advised to rail, since he has given them no occasion. I hear from the court that there are several of this sort, who have begun to denounce everything that is done, and who would like to be told that they are right, and that the only thing needed is to follow their advice in order to set things right, that according to them will always go badly as long as they aren't involved. I will allow if they like that it has been a mistake not to

---

[12] Hein, *Het archief,* 211.

[13] BnF, *papiers de Callières,* NAF 3298, 114, Dec. 5, 1696.

[14] *"Vous répandez le verjus et le vinaigre,"* Letters, p. 75.

assign them to the task and take advantage of their insights, but is this my fault, and why take after me? You tell me, Madame, that President Rose has mistreated them .... I judge from what you write of what he has said to you that he is still as lively as ever.

Despite the light tone of this banter with Huxelles, and the strong support from Rose, the King's secretary, who was in a position to know that he was only carrying out the King's orders, Callières was deeply worried, warned by his correspondents at Versailles that criticism of him at court was gathering force.[15] Concerned that Rose's defense of him might have the effect of provoking his enemies, he asked the Marquise several times to tell Rose not to overdo it.[16] And on the same day of his letter to the Marquise, he took the unusual step of appealing formally to the King for protection, using the same language about those who denounce "the negotiation and the negotiator" as in his letters to the Marquise, but in a far graver tone. His regular dispatches, while addressed to the King for form's sake, were not necessarily meant to be read personally by Louis XIV. This one was different. Written in a round hand with a formal opening and closing, and sent under a cover note to Torcy, it was intended for the eyes of the King himself:

> I have learned, Sire, that the honor Your Majesty has done me has given rise to many jealous persons in your court, and that they seek by their arguments to denounce both the negotiation and the negotiator. I am quite untroubled as far as I am concerned, for I am certain that Your Majesty, in imitation of God of whom you are the image, will judge me by my works, and not by their passions.[17]

VAUBAN CRIES TREASON

For the problem was not only jealous courtiers whose backbiting could easily be dismissed. Even Barbézieux, though a minister, was not in the King's inner circle or a member of the *conseil d'en haut*. His criticism could be dismissed with the support of powerful allies like Chevreuse and Beauvillier, and friends like Huxelles and Rose. Prominent among Callières's detractors was Vauban himself, the architect of the *pré carré*, the country's defensive perimeter in the north, and his criticism could not be dismissed as carping from the sidelines.

---

[15] *Letters*, 75.
[16] *Letters*, 78, 86, 88. Rose was also suggesting at the time that Callières might be sent to Poland.
[17] *CP Hollande* 164, Callières to Louis XIV, October 18, 1696.

Callières knew that France had no more capable or devoted public servant, for he and Vauban had been had been friends, and socially they ran in many of the same circles. The daughter of the Duke de Chevreuse, whose marriage to Morsztyn's son Callières had arranged, was a close friend of Vauban's daughter, "one of the loveliest widows in France," Vauban wrote in a letter to Callières, in which he also referred to their mutual friends M. and Mme de Valentinay, the parents of his daughter's husband, who were, regulars at the fireside of Mme d'Huxelles. [18] Vauban had been an early contact for Mollo, as we have seen, and recognizing Vauban's influence as the architect of French defences, Callières had gone to great lengths to keep him informed and on his side as the negotiation took shape. In July of 1694, as he was waiting for Mollo to arrive in Paris, he had written to Vauban about Mollo, describing him as a "very good fellow," and on August 12 he had written to Vauban to say that Mollo had just arrived in Paris – "the friend from whom I sent you a letter to which you have responded."[19] Vauban and Callières had much in common. Upwardly mobile men of modest antecedents, provincial gentlemen (at best in the case of Callières) rather than members of the nobility, they saw the world in similar terms from different perspectives, military and diplomatic. Vauban's career had been spent in the service of Louvois and the Le Tellier clan, while Callières had served the rival Colberts, but like many another soldier, having seen the horrors of war first hand Vauban had become convinced of the need for peace and economic reform to relieve the suffering of the population. The two men also saw eye-to-eye on grand strategy. Both believed in a France contained within its "natural" borders: the Rhine, the Pyrenees, and the Alps, and they were opposed to the imperial overstretch of military adventures in Italy and Spain. Most important, perhaps, both men had the moral courage to speak truth to power.

In short, Callières had every reason to hope that Vauban would be his ally, not his opponent, in the search for peace. In a letter to Huxelles on October 4, Callières wrote in a light tone: "I have heard elsewhere of what you write about the scolding[20] of M. de Vauban. It comes from the fact that he isn't in the know, like several others who think they know every-

---

[18] *Papiers de Vauban*, Vauban in Paris to Callières in Holland, March 15, 1697. See also Virol, *Vauban*, 12.

[19] *AN, Fonds Rosanbo, Papiers de Vauban* 261 AP 50, Carton L. dossier 3: *Lettres de Vauban à M. de Calières (sic), secrétaire de cabinet du roi, 1694-1697*, hereafter *papiers de Vauban*. Two of the letters are in fact from Callières, not to him, and he would not become a secretary to Louis XIV until 1698.

[20] *Gronderies.*

thing ...."[21] In fact, as Callières probably knew, Vauban's criticism was a good deal more forceful than a scolding. A violently-worded letter he wrote on September 13, 1696 to the playwright Jean Racine, who had abandoned the theater for the position of court historian has survived, despite Vauban's injunction to burn it after reading. Vauban wrote:

> No sooner had I arrived in Paris than I found foreign envoys spreading rumors of peace on terms extremely dishonorable for us. Among other things, they write that we have offered as a last resort to return Strasbourg and Luxembourg in their current state. If that is true, we are handing our enemies the means to put the spurs to us .... Those who give such advice to the King are doing a good job of serving the enemy cause .... Burn this letter, please.[22]

Callières would have known of Vauban's 1694 *mémoire* to the King entitled 'Forts the King could abandon in exchange for a Treaty of Peace.' In it Vauban had stressed that Luxembourg should be surrendered only on condition of "a total demolition that would not leave one stone standing on another."[23] In July of 1694, Callières had written to him, ostensibly to congratulate him on the victory at Brest, and after a reference to the Mollo channel in which he noted that "the matter you are familiar with appears to me to be on the right track," Callières wrote:

> You have given me real pleasure by sharing your views with me as to the manner in which you believe peace can be made with the Emperor and the Empire, the more so as I share your views on the subject. As the city of Luxembourg is an obstacle to peace I would be grateful for your views. If the King decides to negotiate with the Dutch on the basis of the Treaty of Nijmegen, what fortresses do you believe we could give back to the enemy since Luxembourg was not ceded to us by Nijmegen? I do believe we should never give it up, but are there perhaps some other fortresses nearer to the border we could give back without exposing ourselves too much. If should wish to share your views on this it will remain strictly between us.[24]

Vauban's response has not survived, but he must have declined to rise to this bait, since Callières tried again a month later:

> I am also of your view with regard to keeping Luxembourg ... but the Dutch are committed by treaty not to negotiate with us except on the basis of the Treaty of Nijmegen, and thus it will be a matter for us of deciding what to

---

[21] *Letters*, 78.

[22] Quoted in Mesnard, ed., *Oeuvres de J. Racine*, Tome VII. Vauban wrote '1696'. The correction of the date to 1697 by the editors is mistaken. By September of the following year, the Ryswick treaty was about to be signed without the surrender of Strasbourg, and this was well known in Paris. See also Dangeau, *Journal* entry for September 13, 1697.

[23] Lynn, *The Wars of Louis XIV, 1667-1714*, 170.

[24] AN, *Papiers de Vauban*, Callières in Paris to Vauban, July 10, 1694.

give in exchange if we want to keep it .... That is why I ask you what forts it would be least disadvantageous for the King to give up in exchange, if the King should resolve himself to do this. Everything you write to me is only hypothetical, as you know, and will remain strictly between us. The most likely current proposals involve Ypres, Menin, Tournai, Condé, and Maubeuge. All are very important, but some may be less necessary than others, and no one is I believe a better judge of this than you. If you consider that they are more necessary than Luxembourg, what if we resolved to relinquish it razed?[25]

THE HIGH COST OF DISOBEYING INSTRUCTIONS

Now, to meet this savage criticism and the carping at Versailles, and exploiting the absence of a specific reference in the draft treaty, Callières suddenly decided on his own, without instructions, contrary to his earlier assurances and exploiting a loophole in the draft Treaty, to inform the allies that the fortifications of Luxembourg would be demolished by France prior to the return of the town, rendering the city useless as a military barrier – just as he had earlier suggested to Vauban. It was a major miscalculation, and it caused a crisis in the talks. On October 30, Heinsius reported to the Dutch Ambassador in Stockholm that "the French are playing tricks on us about the fortifications of Luxembourg."[26] Negotiations came to an abrupt halt, with angry charges of bad faith from the allies who were understandably furious over this last-minute French chicanery. The English envoy, Matthew Prior, reported to London on November 2 that "the whole Congress, and particularly the Dutch and Spanish ministers, have charged Dijkveld to tell his incognito friend that if he does not recede from this point all hopes of a treaty are utterly cut off. Cailiers [sic] says that he cannot do it without express order from the court, which accordingly he has writ for, though I look upon this to be an artifice of Cailiers." The Spanish minister, Don Quiros, was furious – "as mad as the Catholic religion and a hot temper can make any man," reported Prior.[27] George Stepney wrote to his patron at the Treasury Sir William Trumbull on October 30 that "I am of your opinion that the French are not in earnest when they talk of a peace. This is plain from Caliers (sic) flying back and saying he had not orders to offer Luxembourg otherwise than demolished, which does not come up to what the allies pretend, nor what this gentleman promised six weeks ago."

---

[25] *AN, Papiers de Vauban,* Callières in Paris to Vauban, August 12, 1694.
[26] *Les français nous font des chicanes ...*, Hein, *Het archief,* 214.
[27] *Calendar of the Marquis of Bath preserved at Longleat, Wiltshire,* London, Manuscript Commission, 1908, vol. III, 95-6.

In response to the allied protest, Callières promised to write for instructions but he suggested that the response would probably not be to the liking of the allies.[28]

It is an understatement to say that this was disingenuous. Callières did not need orders from Versailles to drop the condition on Luxembourg he had suddenly sprung on the allies, for he had done it solely on his own hook, and as soon as the King learned what he had done, he immediately ordered him in sharp tones to withdraw it, writing in a November 12 instruction:

> Your letter of the 8th tells me that you have still not carried out the order I gave to you to remove the difficulty you created with regard to the restitution of Luxembourg in the state in which it is now, and although I do not doubt that by now you will have dropped this claim, if you have not already done so you must do so now, without losing more time.

Making matters worse, in a November 11 dispatch that had crossed with the King's order, the stubborn Callières had dug his heels in even further: "nothing would do more to delay the negotiations than to retreat from just claims made in Your Majesty's name .... Thus I remain firm not to give way with regard to the new fortifications in Luxembourg." He argued that if he stuck to his guns, in return for dropping the condition he could get a reduction in the number of forts to be surrendered in exchange for Luxembourg from four to three. On the 19th, clearly furious by now, the King again ordered Callières to cease and desist: "I told you in my instructions of the 4th to remove the difficulty with regard to the fortifications of Luxembourg. They were so clear that I expected them to be carried out, but your letter of the 11th tells me you still have not done so."

Finally, on the 26th, Louis XIV wrote to his untried envoy for the fourth time, in peremptory tones which conjure up the imperious Sun King of the famous Rigaud portrait. His instructions were normally couched in polite terms, and it was often left to his Foreign Minister to warn that the King was displeased. This time there was no need for that: "Monsieur de Callières, I have ordered you repeatedly to remove this obstacle immediately for the sake of peace in Europe. It suits neither my dignity nor the sincere desire that I have to restore peace to Christendom to negotiate over such an article. You must tell Mr. Boreel that I do not wish to suspend the negotiations over this condition."[29]

Humiliated, charged with bad faith by the allies and with insubordination by the King, Callières had no choice but to back down. He

---

[28] TNA, SP/1/1/129, Stepney to Trumbull, October 30, 1696.
[29] *CP Hollande* 164, Louis XIV to Callières, November 26, 1696.

did succeed in attaching a face-saving provision that Spain should reimburse France for cost of the Luxembourg fortifications, but even this was dropped in the document which was eventually submitted to the Swedish mediator on January 31.[30] Louis XIV was not used to having his envoys repeatedly defy his direct orders, and in the midst of these exchanges, he informed Callières that he was sending two Ambassadors senior to him. (Callières had tried earlier to persuade the allies to keep the negotiation at the level of envoys with plenipotentiary powers, rather than Ambassadors, with some support from the Dutch, but the Austrians and the Spanish would have none of it.[31]) The aging and half-blind Honoré Courtin, a veteran envoy who had represented Louis XIV in England in 1665, would lead the delegation, with Harlay as his second, and Callières would assist them as the third-ranking member.

It was a disaster for Callières. Alone in Holland with no one to consult, and criticized at Versailles by Vauban and others for exposing France to danger when he was only doing the King's bidding, his nerve had failed him at a critical moment. By persisting in the too-clever-by-half Luxembourg gambit in order to deflect the backbiting at Versailles, he had lost credibility with the allies. Worse, far worse, the King's confidence in him had been fatally shaken. Louis XIV was too experienced to disown his own envoy, and he sent Callières money for his expenses, but his decision in the same period to send two more senior Ambassadors to supersede him sent an unmistakable message of no confidence. The Marquise d'Huxelles urged Callières not to resent the new appointments, and he responded unconvincingly that this was the farthest thing from his mind. It was true that he had set the peace process in motion through "pure zeal," quite by himself, but he would be only too happy to see it brought to fruition by someone else. In fact, his only desire was to return to private life: "If I have any other thoughts, I consent that you should withdraw your esteem and friendship ...."[32] It is unlikely that the wise Huxelles was fooled for a moment.

THE LADY WHO MARRIED ANOTHER

To make matters worse, the lonely Callières was also dealing at the same time with a sharp personal disappointment, if not a broken heart. His Dutch colleague Willem Boreel had tried to persuade him that he should marry, on the grounds that his books were no substitute for a wife. Callières told Mme

---

[30] Hein, *Het archief*, 225.
[31] See *Letters*, 200-1, and TNA, SP1/1/136, Stepney to Trumbull.
[32] *Letters*, 121-2.

d'Huxelles that he had turned the well-intentioned suggestion aside with the quip that those who married were certainly right to do so, but those who didn't weren't always in the wrong either. But as Mme d'Huxelles knew very well, the thought had more than crossed his mind. The marriage of his parents had been a happy one, at least judging from his father's writings, and there was no reason why as he rose in the world he should not take a wife.

The match Callières had in mind for himself was a very grand one, with an Ambassador's daughter from one of the first families of France. Anne, Demoiselle de Cominges, was an intimate of Mme d'Huxelles. Her father had been Captain of the Guard of Queen Anne of Austria during the Fronde, and he had taken Monsieur le Prince himself into custody, a demonstration of his unswerving loyalty to the crown. In 1661, the young Louis XIV had sent the blunt spoken soldier as his Ambassador to Charles II of England. Lacking the ability to speak English, and stiff in his manner, he had not been a success.[33] His unmarried daughter Anne, now in her thirties,[34] was a woman of learning, though perhaps not a beauty like her mother, known as the *belle Cominges*. Saint-Simon says that she was a "maiden lady of great wit, virtue, and some fashion."[35] She and Callières had struck up a passionate friendship by the fireside of Mme d'Huxelles.

---

[33] Cominges had been assisted in this embassy by Honoré de Courtin. There is a charming account of it in English by Jean-Jules Jusserand, written when he was the French counselor of Embassy in London, *A French Ambassador at the Court of Charles III*. (Jusserand later served as French Ambassador to the U.S. and became a friend of President Theodore Roosevelt.) Cominges spoke no English, and Charles II found him difficult and unreliable. At a banquet in London hosted by the Lord Mayor, his efforts to be sociable were rebuffed, and he complained bitterly of the offense to the King. Louis XIV had burned cities for less, but, anxious to cultivate the connection with Charles II, the King counseled patience with the uncivilized English. Courtin reported to the Foreign Minister, Lionne, that the difference between France and England could be summarized easily: in France, our master can walk all over his own people, Courtin told Lionne, but in England, the King is obliged to walk alongside his. Anne's mother Sibylle d'Amalbi, joined her husband at the English court, where she made a great splash. From a prominent family of Bordeaux magistrates, she was the *Césonie* of the précieuses, the group satirized by Molière in *Les Précieuses ridicules*. Anne had three brothers, all of whom fought in the wars of Louis XIV. One was killed in Germany, and another was wounded twice as a naval officer. The third, Louis, was so tall and fat that a particularly heavy caliber of cannon shell was named a *"gros Cominges"* – a term that was still in use in the French Army in the nineteenth century.
[34] In the *Histoire genéalogique de la maison de France* of Père Anselme (VII, p. 667), she is listed as the fourth child of Gaston and Sibylle de Cominges. Her sister, Louise-Henriette, presumably younger because she is listed as the last of the five children, had entered a convent in 1684.
[35] *S/S* IV, 499: *"vieille fille de beaucoup d'esprit ... de vertu, et assez du monde."*

They shared an interest in politics, but the social gulf between them was a wide one.

In June of 1696, barely arrived in Holland, Callières asked Huxelles whether Anne was still in Paris, or whether she had gone to the fashionable Abbey of Fontevrault for a rest cure. A few days later, he thanked Huxelles for passing on his compliments. Informed by Huxelles that Anne was back in Paris again, he was overjoyed: "I am delighted to hear she is in good health and that she has come nearer, though I don't know when I will be able take advantage of this. At least now I will be in a position to receive news of her, and as I know of her true worth I take pride in my fondness (*attachement*) for her." [36]

On October 26, 1696, as his growing prominence encouraged him to hope, Callières made the nature of his feelings even clearer to Huxelles:

> I am very happy that Mlle de Cominges has borne witness to you of the state and sentiments of my heart, which must have persuaded you that you are not sowing in a fallow field. What could I not say to you of the beauty of the sentiments of my evangelist, which have attached me to her with a perfect regard for many years! I say nothing to you of the clear lights of her intelligence, for it would be temerity and indiscretion for me to tell you what is as plain as the light of day. She has written a very charming letter to me about all the honors and benefits of my position, which she sees, just as I do, as being principally in that it enables me to contribute to the public good, which for her and for me is the only thing to be desired in this world, or at least the thing to be preferred over all others. [37]

The only way to read this is that Callières had declared his suit to Mlle de Cominges, encouraged by Anne's effusive letter of congratulations on his appointment. Writing to Huxelles a few days later, he returned to the subject. Their relationship was based on a common devotion to public service as the supreme good, he wrote, and "it is this conformity of view that has contributed so much to my fondness for her." But at this point, it seems that something caused Callières to draw back. There are other references to Anne de Cominges in his letters to Huxelles, but no more talk of fondness. The lonely Callières, aided and abetted by the matchmaking Marquise, appears to have taken her letter of congratulations as the opening for a declaration of some sort, and been rebuffed.

Did Anne's family intervene to call a halt? It seems likely. Friendship between a lady and a gentleman who shared a passion for politics was one thing, but marriage between a Callières and a Cominges

---

[36] *Letters*, 86.
[37] *Letters*, 98-9.

was quite another. Such misalliances did take place occasionally, to the scandal of society but also its grudging acceptance. As Mme de Sévigné's daughter had said wickedly of her son's marriage to a girl of lesser parentage who brought a large dowry, "manure is sometimes needed for even the best fields."[38] But there had to be a compelling financial justification, and Callières was far from rich enough to offset the handicap of his dubious genealogy.

The following year, Anne de Cominges married a senior magistrate in Bordeaux, "First President" of the provincial *Parlement*. His name was Jean-Baptiste le Comte, Captal de La Tresne, and the family was a grand one. (Captal, literally Captain, is a Gascon title meaning Lord or Baron.) Saint-Simon who knew the family well says that she decided to make "the end of a coachman" – that is to finish up with a flourish, a pun on the name La Tresne.[39] They had no children, and he died in 1703. Anne outlived her elderly husband by only a few years, dying herself in 1708. When she returned to Paris from Bordeaux, as we know she did from references to her in Huxelles's letters to La Garde, she would have seen Callières again. Perhaps they resumed their talks about public affairs by the fireside of the Marquise.

In June of 1700, returning from a mission to Lorraine, Callières thanked Huxelles for telling him about an increase by the King to the pension of "Madame the First President of Bordeaux." This is followed immediately by a reference to a well-known passage from a play by Guarini, the lament of the *Faithful Shepherd*:[40]

> O Spring, youth of the year
> Beautiful mother of flowers
> Of new plants, and new loves
> Yes you return
> But the bright and happy days of my joys return not with you.
> With you returns only the sad and sorrowful memory
> Of my dear lost treasure.

It was an indirect way of reminding his patron the Marquise – and perhaps also her friend Madame the First President – that he had not forgotten.

---

[38] When this witticism was repeated to the young man's parents they failed to see the humor in it. See Duchêne, *Mme de Sévigné ou la chance d'être femme*.

[39] *S/S* IV, 499, n.8. Saint-Simon spelled the name 'La Traisne'. His father had been a friend of the Captal.

[40] *Letters*, 286-7. *Il pastor fido* by Giovanni Battista Guarini, Act II, scene I, author's translation.

THE RYSWICK CONFERENCE

> It usually takes less time for an envoy to conclude an affair he has been entrusted with than it takes for an Ambassador to pack his bags for the trip.
> – François de Callières, *On Negotiating with Sovereigns*

With negotiations in abeyance pending the arrival of his new colleagues, the disappointed Callières, no longer in charge, still had the thankless task of arranging the logistics for the arrival of his senior colleagues and plenipotentiaries and their considerable entourages. There was also the question of the venue for the peace conference to resolve. Initially the Emperor of Austria had demanded that the conference be on his territory. In January of 1697, given the choice by the allies of the cities of Maastricht, Nijmegen, or Breda, Callières countered with the proposal of the royal palace at Ryswick, halfway between Delft and The Hague, which in apparent collusion with the Dutch he visited privately in November.[1] The Austrian Ambassador, Count Kinski, dragged his feet over the venue, and Callières told Huxelles that the Austrians were like ladies who have to be forced into granting favors they would be better advised to give with a good grace, since the end result would be the same. The other allies eventually agreed to Ryswick, forcing Kinski to go along. The Ryswick palace had two separate but equal wings and a central courtyard, facilitating the elaborate protocol arrangements that were needed for the arrival and departure of the delegations. (See the engraving in Figure 8.) Both sides formally accepted the mediation of Sweden in the person of Count Lilienroot, the Swedish Ambassador. He had a beautiful young wife, and Callières told the King that the gift of a diamond necklace worth 15,000 francs to Mme Lilienroot would improve the mediator's disposition towards France. The King agreed, and Callières presented it to her. Bidding for mediators was a favorite indoor sport, and both sides played the game.

---

[1] *Letters*, 115-16.

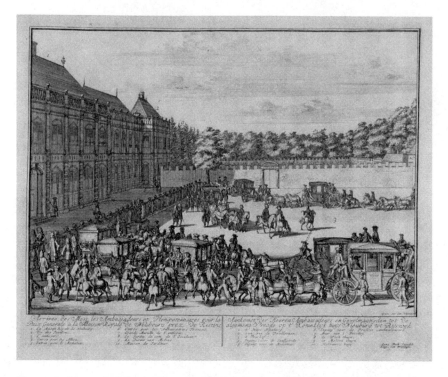

Figure 8. "Arrival of the Ambassadors at Rywsick," showing the arrival of the French delegation. (Museum Rijswijk.)

The aged Honoré Courtin, whose eyesight was so weak that he depended on his daughter to read documents for him, prevailed on the King to relieve him of the appointment. On December 6 he wrote to Callières that "the Marquise d'Huxelles and M. de Harlay will have told you of the pressing reasons that caused me to beg the King very humbly to dispense me from going to the country where you are." His doctors had told him that the humidity of Holland would cause him to go completely blind, he told Callières. He hoped that Callières would bring the business to a successful conclusion and that he would be given "the reward you deserve."[2] In Courtin's place Louis de Verjus, Count de Crécy, was appointed, with Harlay now to head the delegation. Crécy was an experienced negotiator who had headed the French delegation at Ratisbon in 1684, and he was a colleague of Callières's in the Academy, though he would never write a

---

[2] *BnF*, NAF 3298, *papiers de Callières*, Courtin to Callières, December 6, 1696.

Figure 9. Jean-Baptiste Colbert, Marquis de Torcy, French Foreign Minister, 1696-1715.

word for publication. Callières was the lowest ranking of the three men, though all had the grand title of Ambassador Plenipotentiary. Saint-Simon's comment which probably reflect his later conversations with Callières is that "the addition of a man of such low rank still left Callières third, he who had brought the business to this point, and who was fully conversant with all the details of the negotiation."[3]

The two French plenipotentiaries traveled to Holland in some state, and Harlay's wife joined him to preside at his table. She was a great friend of Mme d'Huxelles, as stout as Harlay was thin as a skeleton, says Saint-Simon, who detested Harlay. Crécy proceeded separately, and both envoys made a point of calling on the Marquise d'Huxelles before their departure, testimony to her political influence.[4]

Reduced to administrative tasks, Callières did his best to find his colleagues accommodations commensurate with their status as

---

[3] *S/S* I, 341.
[4] *Letters*, 225.

representatives of the Sun King. With the arrival of some forty plenipotentiaries from all over Europe, rents had skyrocketed, but with the help of his Dutch friends Callières secured two fine houses, both of which still stand in Delft. For Harlay he took the former palace of William the Silent, the *prinsenhof*, where today's visitors can still see the mark left in the wall by the assassin's bullet that killed the founder of the House of Orange in 1584, and for Crécy he rented a nearby house belonging to the Canal Board, the Gemeenlandts-huis. Callières himself remained in more modest quarters in a former convent.[5]

There were a thousand details for Callières to attend to. From Paris, Harlay wrote to say that he had set aside 10,000 francs for rent and carriages, and would do nothing without Calliere's approval. He hated to bother Callières with these trifles. Had Renaudot told him that another passport was needed from the Dutch? It was for a considerable personage. He would explain when he got there. He understood that Renaudot had taken receipt of the money for Callières's expenses from the King.[6]

By the end of March, 1697, Harlay and Crécy had arrived and the three emissaries began their work together. There were rumors in Paris that relations between them were not always harmonious, but there is no evidence of this in their reports, which were drafted almost entirely by Callières in his hand. In contrast to the Harlay-Callières mission of 1694, this time the King and Torcy asked them to write a single dispatch and to share all their information, and with one or two exceptions they seem to have worked together well enough.

Although all three plenipotentiaries were technically of the same status, the difference in their respective rank was apparent. In a letter from Delft dated June 27, 1697, a confidential informant wrote that Harlay had a magnificent train, with "many officers and very fine carriages with black and white spotted horses." He presided over a table with eighteen settings and an elegant service. Crécy, for his part, set twelve places at his table, with an entourage of fewer officers and only four or five servants, including some musicians who had left, and four pages, reported the observant spy. As for Callières, his household was even less impressive than Crécy's, the informant wrote, with only two pages and six or seven servants. With evident disappointment, he reported that none of the three had engaged in any romantic intrigue, although he did claim later that Harlay's advances to

---

[5] *Letters*, 202. This building does not appear to have survived.
[6] *BnF*, NAF 3298, *papiers de Callières*, Harlay to Callières, letters of February 14 and March 3, 1697.

a pretty young girl over dinner had caused her father to send her away to the country to protect her virtue.[7]

Callières knew that a conference with forty or more plenipotentiaries representing the states of Europe would be unwieldy to the point of dysfunction. As he told Huxelles, previous European peace conferences had taken years to reach agreement. With the support of the Dutch with whom he had increasingly friendly relations – "modest and sensible people" he described them to Huxelles – Callières had urged that envoys not be sent at the level of ambassador in part order to keep the protocol complications to a minimum, as well perhaps as to preserve his own role, but once the first ambassador had been sent there was a scramble not to be left out. Callières told Huxelles that cries of "Excellency" echoed in the streets of The Hague as the great men greeted each other: "The common people of the Hague are so used to this word that it is one out of every two they utter, and whenever you ask them for something they say 'yes Excellency', and 'no Excellency', to the point that the title will become so ordinary that nobody will want it any more." The curtain was rising, wrote Callières, and the actors were putting on their costumes.[8]

As the peace conference began with elaborate ceremony, the fate of Carlos II, the sickly and childless Hapsburg monarch of Spain, hung heavy over the proceedings. The general view at the conference was that Carlos wouldn't last out the year, and everyone knew full well that his death could precipitate a violent contest over his inheritance between Austria and France. When Huxelles asked Callières a little naively if it wouldn't be better if Carlos died sooner rather than later so that the conference could sort out his succession while it was still in session, Callières responded gently that it would be better if he stayed alive for a few more years so that Europe could benefit from at least a brief respite from war. An agreement to partition his inheritance between the powers would be difficult to reach. In any case, it was all in the hands of God, and there was no point in building "castles in Spain" over what might happen.[9]

---

[7] *BnF, Fonds Clairambault* 1125, 142-3 and 149. The informant's name is concealed in numerical code, and the letters are to Pierre Daguerre, a French merchant based in Amsterdam who had been used by Croissy an emissary to the Dutch in 1693, *Recueil des instructions*, Tome 21, 414-15.

[8] *Letters*, 268.

[9] *Letters*, 181.

AN IMPRISONED SPY

There was also the imprisonment of a French spy to attend to. Roger de Piles was a member of the household of the veteran French Ambassador Michel Amelot who had served the King in Venice and in Portugal and who would go on to represent him in Spain. In 1692, Piles had been commissioned to travel to Holland, posing as an art dealer, in order to make clandestine contact with the peace party in Holland behind the back of William III, through the bourgmestre of Dort, or Dordrecht, a man named Halwin. Roger de Piles was arrested after his arrival, his belongings which included valuable paintings were confiscated, and he was confined to the fortress of Lowenstein where the Princes of Orange kept their prisoners of state. Huxelles was close to the Amelot family, and particularly to Mme Amelot who was a cousin on her mother's side, and both women wrote to Callières to intercede for Piles. Callières did his best. He told Huxelles that Piles was being well treated in the Lowenstein fortress, he spoke to the Dutch, and he asked Mollo to intervene, all to no avail.[10]

In June of 1697, in a report in Callières's hand, the three negotiators reported to Torcy that "one of us," almost certainly Callières, had been told by Boreel that he hoped to obtain the release of Piles provided expenses for his trial and upkeep in prison were paid.[11] But William III was obdurate, and Piles was not released after the Ryswick Treaty was signed in September on condition that he leave the country immediately. He had put the almost five years of his confinement to good use by writing an important work of art history while in prison, his *Abrégé de la vie des peintres*, published in 1699.[12] As for Halwin, Piles's clandestine contact, Callières reported to Versailles that no stone had been left unturned to obtain his rehabilitation, but that the Dutch response was understandably curt whenever the subject was raised.[13]

A FAMOUS COUNTESS

Callières continued to occupy himself with Poland while in Holland. The death of Sobieski in 1696 opened the field once again to rival French and Austrian claimants, just as in 1674. This time, Louis XIV's candidate was the Prince de Conti – one of the candidates Callières had proposed in 1674 at a time when he had been a child. Frederick Augustus, the Saxon Elector,

---

[10] *Letters*, 151, 177.

[11] *BnF, NAF* 1663, *négociations de Riswick*, 198.

[12] See Puttfarken, *Roger de Piles's Theory of Art.*

[13] *BnF, NAF* 1663, October 16, 1697.

was the Austrian candidate, but the Elector wanted to hedge his bets. In April of 1697 Callières reported a dramatic tale of intrigue to the King:

> Sire, an officer of about 90 years approached me and asked that I repeat what he would say to no one but Your Majesty. (I said I would be the judge of that.) He said he would put the life and fortune of a great prince in my hands, and he showed me a letter with a great seal, which he assured me was that of Frederick Augustus.[14]

The emissary a Baron Rose, told Callières that he had previously approached Forbin-Janson – now Cardinal de Janson, and the King's Ambassador in Rome – with an offer from his master to abandon the Austrians in exchange for French support for his election. But the Cardinal had told him that it was too late, as the decision had already been made to support Conti. In the event of a stalemate, perhaps something could be done. Unsatisfied by this response from Callières's former colleague in Poland, Frederick Augustus had sent his envoy off again in search of a better (or perhaps more credulous) channel to Louis XIV. A friend in Denmark who knew Callières had told him that he could be trusted, or so the Baron told Callières, and traveling only at night to avoid detection, the Baron had come to Delft. He told Callières that if the Austrians found out what he was up to his master the Elector would be lost.

The deal the Baron proposed was that the Elector would agree to withdraw his troops from Hungary where they were confronting the Ottomans. This would create an Army of 90,000 men to be placed in the service of France, and it would of course also increase the Ottoman pressure on Austria. In exchange, Frederick Augustus would need only a modest annual subsidy from France of 800,000 écus, or 2.4 million francs. (Callières himself noted to Torcy that this was a bit high.) Rose said he would return to Hamburg to await the French response.

In a cover note to Torcy, Callières explained that there was a woman behind all this. Frederick Augustus had a passion for a Mlle de Königsmark, "the sister of the man who was killed by order of the Duke of Hanover for having had an affair with his daughter-in-law." As a consequence of her brother's murder, Mlle de Königsmark was passionately pro-French, Callières wrote, and she had a considerable ascendancy over Frederick Augustus, with whom she had a child.[15] A little

---

[14] *BnF*, NAF 1663, 114 and following.

[15] Her brother Philipp Cristoph, Count von Königsmark, had been the lover of Sophia Dorothea, wife of Prince George of Hanover, the future King of England, and he had been killed in 1694 while attempting to escape. For her part in the affair, Sophia Dorothea, the mother of the future George II of England, was confined to the Castle of Ahlden for the remainder of her life. Aurora von Königsmark is described by Voltaire as "the most
(continued)

breathlessly, always alert to the possibility of a Polish intrigue, and perhaps also too anxious to exploit an offer Cardinal de Janson had rejected, Callières told the King that there was no time to lose. Someone should be sent to Dresden immediately with a strong cipher and powers to negotiate with Frederick Augustus. But there was no response from Versailles, and a month later on May 22 Callières told Torcy that Rose had written from Hamburg that in the absence of a reply Saxon troops would remain in Hungary for another year.[16] In the event, the Polish election of 1696 went badly for France. The election was followed closely by Callières in Holland who appears to have been the intermediary for some of the dispatches of his friend the Abbé Melchior de Polignac, the French Ambassador.[17] With Austrian support, Frederick Augustus reversed a first vote by the Polish nobility in favor of Conti, and he was duly elected King. It was not his last dalliance with France through the intermediary of Callières, as we will see.

A FAMILY AFFAIR

There was also an awkward business for Callières to resolve involving Harlay's son, the young Cély, who had come to Holland with his father's considerable entourage. He is described by Saint-Simon as having "great wit and even greater debauchery and wildness."[18] A confidential informant in Delft reported that "the Count de Cély goes from belle to belle without forming an attachment to any of them, and occasionally we see him lavishing caresses in the middle of the street on loose women of low degree." His father tried to keep him from going to the theater for fear that he would fall in love with an actress. Inevitably Cély got into a brawl with another of the other young gentlemen accompanying the delegation. As Callières reported the affair in a collective dispatch to Torcy written in his best hand, Cély and another young gentleman, M. de Sainctot of the clan responsible for the ceremonial introduction and reception of ambassadors at Versailles, had nearly come to blows over a bar girl. A third party, the Abbé de Lannion, went to Cély's father and demanded that Cély be sent home. When Harlay demurred, Sainctot went to the Hague and threatened to

---

celebrated woman of the last two centuries," and her child with Frederick Augustus grew up to be Maurice de Saxe, perhaps the most famous soldier of a later time, *Histoire de Charles XII, Oeuvres completes,* Tome XXII, Paris 1821. 89-90.

[16] *BnF,* NAF 1663, 173.

[17] Callières defended Polignac against the criticism at court of his lavish spending in support of Conti; see *Letters,* 48, 69, etc. Polignac was disgraced as a result, but he rose again to favor, serving (along with the son of Mme d'Huxelles) as a French negotiator at Utrecht.

[18] S/S I, 389.

attack Cély in public.[19] Fearing a public scandal, Harlay asked Callières and Crécy to intervene. They convoked Sainctot and counseled with him "in the King's name." He should have some to them first. Had he done so, Harlay would have reprimanded his son severely. (Dangeau recorded that he had "mistreated French gentlemen in the entourage of the other plenipotentiaries," and that the King was displeased.) In the end, the two young bloods agreed to embrace and set aside the quarrel. Lannion who had a family connection to Harlay passed himself off as a Count in Holland, caused a scandal by trying to meet privately with William III, and the King ordered him home.[20]

IN PRAISE OF THE DUTCH REPUBLIC

Callières admired the Dutch state and its republican institutions, though he was obviously careful not to reveal that in his reports to Versailles, and he made an explicit connection between Dutch prosperity and the climate of freedom of opinion. In his letters to Huxelles he wrote of the cleanliness of the towns and the canals, and the beauty of the tiles decorating the houses – in contrast to Paris, the broad streets had sidewalks. He visited the tomb of William the Silent in Delft with its funeral statue by de Keyser, and at Huxelles's request he sent her an engraving. He particularly respected and admired Johann de Witt, the Dutch leader whose murder by a mob had been provoked by the French invasion of 1672, and he sent Huxelles de Witt's portrait, recalling that he had once glimpsed de Witt in the streets of The Hague attended by a single servant, carrying a small satchel of black velvet in which were kept "the most important affairs of Europe." He was a "truly great man," writes Callières, a leader who combined erudition and political skill. When de Witt was warned of his impending assassination and it was suggested that he strike first, Callières quotes him as saying that he would rather suffer an injustice than commit one.[21] He recounted a story he had from Dijkveld of the chivalrous reception of Cardinal de Retz by de Witt at a time when he was a fugitive from Louis XIV. He described the paintings in the Amsterdam City Hall celebrating republican virtues with scenes from antiquity, placed there so that the magistrates of the city would be constantly reminded that "neither fear nor favor must keep them from doing their duty."[22]

---

[19] *BnF*, NAF 1663, 138.

[20] *Letters*, 260, and Dangeau, *Journal*, May 22, 1697.

[21] *Letters*, 176.

[22] They are still there today in the former City Hall, now the Royal Palace. One painting by Govert Teunisz Flinck shows the Roman Consul Curius Dentatus refusing bribes from foreign ambassadors, content with his meal of roasted turnip. The other by Rembrandt's
(continued)

Influenced by the open-minded and tolerant culture around him, Callières took on some of the local coloring, and his letters to Huxelles reflect this. He visited the laboratory of Van Leeuvanhoek in Delft and peered through a microscope for the first time, drawing the moral that in that invisible world each tiny organism was content to sit on its own little hill without bothering its neighbors. He quoted a Dutch friend as wondering why Louis XIV would want to invade Holland when he had such a pleasant country of his own to rule. For that matter, he asked Huxelles, why would the Prince of Orange want to become King of such a fractious and trouble-making country as England, when he was already the ruler of such a well-ordered state as Holland?[23]

Callières followed English affairs closely and intelligently while in Holland, receiving information from confidential informants across the Channel and passing it on to Versailles. To Huxelles, he wrote that the address of William III on the opening of Parliament in October of 1696 was full of good sense. In his private letters to Huxelles, he never refers to the French Protestants who had fled to Holland after the revocation of the Edict of Nantes as "heretics," or even as adherents of the *religion prétendue réformée* or RPR, the standard shorthand of the time used by French officials, but as "our refugees." To put it mildly, these are not the opinions one would expect from an orthodox envoy of Louis XIV. They reflect instead the moderate views expressed by Callières's father, who had fought with the Dutch against Spain, and who had admired their love of liberty.

As time went by – Callières was in Holland without a break from May of 1696 until December of 1697 – he grew increasingly close to his Dutch counterparts, including the irascible Dijkveld. Although Dijkveld was over 70, he was as vigorous as a young man, Callières wrote to the Marquise:

> When he grows a little heated in our discussions, which happens occasionally, I tell him that of the two of us he is the younger man by virtue of his excitability, and I am the older by virtue of my calm. He doesn't mind, and rather likes the idea that he is youthful since it promises a long life. We get along well together though charged with opposing interests, and when we have disagreements and different interests to uphold I tell him that we must not quarrel. If our masters had nothing to disentangle, we would not have been honored with their full powers to bring their differences to an end.[24]

---

pupil Ferdinand Bol depicts the bravery of the Roman Envoy Caius Fabricius and his refusal to be intimidated by the trumpeting elephants of King Pyrrhus.

[23] *Letters*, 72.

[24] *Letters*, 102.

Callières told Huxelles that the Dutch "are becoming quite used to me, and I am not at all thought of as an enemy. On the contrary, my departure is feared because they hope my stay will contribute to the peace that is so much desired here."[25] Mme d'Huxelles believed that he would be asked to stay on in Holland as Ambassador after the peace, or so it appears from his letters to her, and she was well informed in such matters. Instead it was his rival Usson de Bonrepaux who was named Ambassador. The appointment must have been particularly galling to Callières. Bonrepaux was an enthusiastic persecutor of Huguenots who had made a fortune in the service of Seignelay at the Naval ministry. The usually charitable Callières has nothing good to say about him in his letters to the Marquise.[26]

Allowing for some manipulation by both sides – there was after all a great deal at stake in these personal relationships – it is easy to believe that his Dutch counterparts liked Callières. Mme d'Huxelles wanted engravings of their portraits, and Callières promised to send them if he could find them: "You will see in them two handsome and good heads, and two very agreeable likenesses, not at all serious and off-putting as people wrongly believe statesmen must be." Boreel was as "a man of great worth, very much the honnête homme, pleasant, gay in conversation and extremely good company, very wise and moderate …."

THE CURTAIN FALLS

It was not until early May that the formal proceedings finally got underway at the Ryswick palace with the elaborately choreographed arrival of the plenipotentiaries in their carriages.[27] As Callières had foreseen, the conference soon bogged down in wrangling over protocol and procedure. To the irritation of the representatives of William III, the Austrian Ambassador, Count Kinski, played for time and waited for instructions from Vienna, refusing to say what he would accept as an alternative for the return of Strasbourg. The other principal sticking point was the modalities for the recognition of William III, or as Matthew Prior put it with his usual lapidary wit, how and when Louis XIV would "own the King." The procedural compromise Callièers had agreed to involving a certification by the Swedish mediator that France would extend recognition simultaneously with the signature of the Treaty still left unresolved the issue of the status of James II at Saint-Germain. William wanted the Stuarts expelled from

---

[25] *Letters*, 85.
[26] *Letters*, 121-2
[27] See Figure 10.

Figure 10. "A Bridle for the French King." William III sits secure on the pedestal, while Louis XIV below, recoiling in terror, says "what I stole I will refund," while female figures attempt to slip a bridle over his head. (British Museum.)

Saint-Germain-en-Laye as well as an explicit commitment from Louis XIV not to intervene in English affairs by promoting the Jacobite cause.

Finally, frustrated with the inability of the unwieldy conference to come to terms with these issues, William III proposed and Louis XIV agreed to a secret meeting between their personal representatives – Marshal Boufflers, the French commander in Flanders, and Lord Portland, William's close friend and principal advisor. The two men met over a period of weeks and a deal was finally struck. James II would stay at Saint-

Germain, but Louis would promise not to assist the enemies of William III, be they at home or abroad.

There was some miscommunication as the deal worked out in the Boufllers-Portland channel was committed to paper around the conference table. The Austrians were unhappy that the bilateral negotiation had excluded them, and refused to specify what they would take in exchange for Strasbourg. Alertly, the French negotiators drove a wedge between the allies by setting a deadline, and when the Emperor failed to meet it, the French declared that Strasbourg was no longer on offer, leaving the Austrians to either accept the terms of the Treaty or fight on alone. As Callières confidently predicted to Mme d'Huxelles, outflanked and preoccupied by the Ottoman threat, the isolated Austrians came around in November after all the other allies had signed.

AN UNPOPULAR PEACE

The Treaty (more properly treaties) signed at Ryswick marked the first general peace in Europe in a generation. It was the completion of Callières's 'Great Work', as he had described it to Huxelles in ironic reference to the *magnum operum* of the alchemists.[28] Louis XIV had paid a high price. He had been forced to give up many of his conquests of the 1680s. The Dutch had restored their barrier against French aggression, and Luxembourg had been returned to Spain with its new fortifications intact. Louis XIV, the scourge of heresy in France, had been obliged to recognize the Protestant champion William III as the legitimate King of England. From the allied perspective, the pride of Louis XIV had been humbled, and the threat of universal monarchy had receded.[29] Still it was a better deal than the French could have expected a year earlier, when they had been resigned to giving up Strasbourg as well as Luxembourg if necessary. Thanks in part to the Austrian miscalculation, while Luxembourg was ceded, Strasbourg would remain in French hands until 1870. The defection of the Duke of Savoy from the allied cause had helped, and France had played a relatively weak hand well, exploiting the divisions of the allies. Callières deserves some of the credit for this, but the principal strategist was the King himself.

---

[28] In their introduction to the standard English edition of *On Negotiating with Sovereigns*, which has the title 'The Art of Diplomacy', based on a misreading of the Huxelles letters, Keens-Soper and Schweizer misconstrue Callières's several references to the *grand oeuvre* of the peace negotiations as allusions to the writing of that book. Callières is making a joke.
[29] See the engraving at Figure 10, "A Bridle for the French King".

Saint-Simon later claimed that the loss of Luxembourg was the fault of Harlay, and that Callières had complained to him about this – indeed, that he had been "inconsolable" over it. But this was Saint-Simon's way of making the hated Harlay the scapegoat for an unpopular agreement and absolving his friend Callières. It does seem likely that Callières allowed Saint-Simon to think this – the Duke wrote that "I have heard him say this many times"[30] It is also possible, indeed probable, that there were tensions between Harlay and Callières. But it was the King, not Harlay, who had disavowed Callières's ill-advised attempt to devalue the citadel as a bargaining chip by threatening the destruction of its fortifications.

In the early morning hours of September 20, it was finally done, and Callières drafted the triumphant report from the three plenipotentiaries to the King on the signing of the Ryswick Treaties: "This peace, Sire, is the more glorious in that it is Your Majesty who has shaped it and prescribed all the conditions, and that it is to Your Majesty alone that Christendom owes its tranquility."[31]

In historical terms Ryswick marked only a brief respite before the death of Carlos II plunged France once more into war with its former adversaries, but history is lived forward, not backwards, and at the time, the Ryswick Treaty was celebrated as the dawning of a new era of European peace. There was a service of thanksgiving in St. Paul's Cathedral, and William III commissioned a commemorative silver table and mirror for Kensington.

In France, however, reaction to the Ryswick Treaties was far less favorable, both in court circles and in the court of public opinion. The customary *Te Deums* of thanksgiving were held in the churches and cathedrals across France, but the rejoicing was far from heartfelt, and according to one source local officials in Paris had to coerce the population into setting off the traditional fireworks in celebration on threat of fines.[32] Renaudot wrote sarcastically to Torcy on October 5 that "with regard to the peace, it seems to hear most people talk that they are upset about it. That seems quite bizarre to me ... they talk as if the forts that have been surrendered were their own personal property that has been stolen from them. The thing is that people are still angry with our dear brother, the former Prince of Orange. So Virtue is persecuted."[33] The pious Mme de Maintenon voiced the general ambivalence. She thanked God for the

---

[30] *S/S* I, 415: *j'ai ouï assurer ce fait souvent à Callières, qui ne s'en pouvait consoler.*

[31] *BnF,* NAF 1663, *négociations de Riswick,* Harlay, Crécy, and Callières to the King, September 22, 1697.

[32] Courtily, *Annales de la cour et de Paris,* 122.

[33] *BnF, Clairambault* 1057, *lettres autographes de Renaudot,* 24.

sentiments of peace He had inspired in the heart of the King, but surely "it was a kind of disgrace to give back what had cost so much effort and bloodshed."[34]

The scapegoats were the three negotiators. A bitter broadsheet was hawked in the streets of Paris:

> De Harlay, Crécy, and Callières
> Have made peace.
> Ah, what plenipotentiaries they are!
> Have such clever fellows ever been seen?
> It was these able ministers,
> Who in just one day,
> Gave back thirty-two cities,
> Not to mention Luxembourg.
> Why they barely saved Paris![35]

Harlay's scapegrace son Cély was commissioned to carry news of the signing back to Versailles. His doting father wrote privately to Torcy that he had not been able to bring himself to deny his son the honor of bearing the news of peace, but he was worried that he would misbehave and that this would turn out to be his ruin. Would Torcy try to see that he behaved himself for once?[36] On behalf of the three plenipotentiaries, Callières wrote that Cély had promised to "make good speed to report to Your Majesty," but the young scoundrel lingered in taverns along the way, arriving well after the news had already reached Versailles from other sources. The King gave him 12,000 francs as a present anyway and told him to be wiser in the future. Cély decided to take it in diamonds instead, like a proper young nobleman.[37]

FROM PRINCE OF ORANGE TO KING OF ENGLAND

Now that France had recognized William and peace had been made, the three plenipotentiaries could call formally on the English King on behalf of Louis XIV. Callières had several private audiences with him, obviously wanting to take the measure of the Sun King's principal adversary. He was favorably impressed. William III spoke French fluently – "with a slight lisp," Callières told Huxelles – and one evening they had talked about a variety of things for over an hour. The King was a good conversationalist,

---

[34] *Correspondance générale de Mme de Maintenon*, Tome IV, 184 and ff.
[35] Quoted in the Boislisle edition of Saint-Simon, *Mémoires de Saint-Simon*, IV, 235 n.2.
[36] BnF, *Clairambault* 1125, f. 148, Harlay to Torcy, September 23, 1697.
[37] Dangeau, *Journal*, October 6, 1697, and Sourches, *Mémoires*, IV, October 7, 1697.

Figure 11. William III of England. (British Museum.)

with a good sense of humor, said Callières. He watched his words carefully, but he was not as circumspect and close-mouthed as his reputation had it. On the contrary, he was simple and modest, easy to talk to, relaxed in manner – in short, the very model of an *honnête homme*. Before returning to England, William III told Callières that he would not take a naval escort across the Channel. He had no need of one, he said, as he trusted to the good faith of Louis XIV. Callières was struck by this grand and suitably royal gesture.[38]

Only one thing bothered him, William told Callières, and that was Louis XIV's choice of Ambassador, Count Tallard. William was particularly sensitive to slights from Louis. He noted that for his part he was sending Lord Portland, the first gentleman of his household, to Versailles. While Tallard was certainly acceptable to him, he thought that the King might send someone of higher rank, a Duke or a Marshal of France, as a personal emissary. He had looked into the precedents, he told Callières, and his predecessors had been granted this courtesy.[39] William sent the same message through the Count d'Auvergne, who had come to Holland to recover his property at Berg-op-Zoom as part of the Ryswick settlement, but Louis XIV was unmoved, and Tallard alone went off to London.

PRESENTS ALL AROUND, AND A REWARD FROM THE KING

As the conference came to a close, in accordance with the prevailing custom in such matters, both the Swedish mediator Count Lilienroot and the indefatigable Mollo received the considerable sum of 36,000 francs as a gesture of thanks for their efforts from Louis XIV. (They presumably received presents from the allies as well.) In support of the gift to Mollo, Callières argued to the court that he had worked hard to keep the city of Amsterdam on the right side. He noted that Mollo had taken risks in establishing a private channel to Amsterdam – after all, Roger de Piles and his Dutch confederate had been arrested for doing the same thing, he reminded Versailles – and Mollo had sacrificed his business interests to the French cause, faithfully discharging all the tasks he had been given. In the future, he would continue to be a useful channel to Amsterdam, Callières predicted, accurately as it turned out, since Mollo would continue to be a French go-between for another decade and more. As for Lilienroot, the Swedish mediator, while he had been difficult over Strasbourg, the Count deserved a reward as well, though "we have only discussed this in general terms through the intermediary of his wife, who has always appeared to us to be eager to promote the interests of Your Majesty."[40] In addition to negotiating her husband's gift, the beautiful Mme Lilienroot had obviously played more than a decorative role in the talks themselves.

---

[38] *Letters*, 271, 274, 279-80.

[39] *Letters*, 274-5, and *BnF*, NAF 1663, Crécy and Callières to Louis XIV, November 29, 1697.

[40] *BnF*, NAF 1663, Harlay, Crécy and Callières to Louis XIV, September 22, 1697.

As the Ryswick curtain lowered, far from feeling triumphant at the completion of the 'Great Work', Callières was in an understandably dyspeptic frame of mind. He was well aware of the domestic sniping over the Treaty and its cost in territory, and his financial affairs were in bad shape. Despite the money the King had sent to him, he told Huxelles that he would be in straitened circumstances after he paid all his debts. Exchange costs had eaten up a quarter of the money he had brought from France, and he would have to cut expenses to the bone. Once he was back in Paris, he would come to her suppers to save money, and his only desire was to return to her fireside as soon as possible.[41]

Adding salt to the wounds was the King's choice of Callières's rival, Usson de Bonrepaux, as the new Ambassador to Holland. Callières hoped he would not be left hanging on uselessly while waiting for the dilatory Bonrepaux ("*bon repos*," he wrote to Huxelles), who was being transferred from Denmark and apparently in no hurry to get to Holland. It was kind of Huxelles to say that he should have had the job himself, he wrote bitterly, but Bonrepaux was a better choice since Bonrepaux was rich, having taken the precaution of first making his fortune at the Naval Ministry. Positions as envoys were "ruinous and painful for a man who has only great zeal and industry," wrote Callières.[42]

As soon as the ink was dry on the first set of agreements Harlay left Holland, leaving Crécy and Callières to oversee the conclusion of the bilateral treaty with the Austrians.[43] Finally, at the end of November, the King finally granted Callières permission to leave Holland without waiting for Bonrepaux's arrival. His last letter to Huxelles was sent on November 28 as he was on the point of leaving Delft. He must have made a slow progress in the winter with the muddy roads, as his presence at Versailles is not noted until almost two months later, on January 26 of 1698.[44]

Eventually the King decided on a suitable reward for his three plenipotentiaries.[45] They were unpopular – according to one report they were afraid to show their faces in the streets of Paris – but Louis XIV was far too experienced in statecraft to turn his back on men whose only crime was to have carried out his orders. In a complex financial transaction, the King installed Callières one of his four private secretaries, replacing

---

[41] *Letters*, 273-4.

[42] *Letters*, 274.

[43] The King was displeased by Harlay's departure, and he is said to have reminded his father-in-law Chancellor Boucherat, that Harlay had agreed not to come back until everything was settled, Sourches, *Mémoires*, IV, October 29, 1697.

[44] Sourches, *Mémoires*, V, January 26, 1698.

[45] Dangeau, *Journal*, February 23, 1698.

Bergeret who had been Croissy's deputy at the foreign ministry. Each private secretary served for three months, and the post carried with it a *brevet de retenue* of 20,000 *écus*, or 60,000 francs – essentially a promissory note to be paid by the estate of the previous holder of the office. The post had been vacant for some time – Bergeret had died in October of 1694[46] – and the financial aspects are confusing. A sum of 50,000 francs went to Crécy from the *brevet de retenue* as part of the deal, and his son was made a gentleman in waiting. Harlay, who was already wealthy, received an additional 5,000 a year. The King asked Crécy to go to Aix in connection with an affair involving the Palatinate, but there is no indication that the King considered Callières for another foreign mission. Louis XIV had decided to keep him close to his own person.

---

[46]Sourches, *Mémoires*, IV, 393, n.4.

BETWEEN TWO WARS

Our hope is in the moderation, the piety, and the devotion of the King.
– The Marquise d'Huxelles to the Marquis de La Garde

The four years between Ryswick and the outbreak in 1702 of the decade-long war of the Spanish Succession saw frantic negotiations between England and France to avoid the threatening conflict. Carlos II of Spain lingered near death without an heir. If William III and Louis XIV could reach a bilateral agreement over his succession, they would be in a position to dictate terms to the rest of Europe, avoiding a conflict neither monarch wanted. Callières had anticipated the need for such an agreement, and during the Ryswick talks he had been careful to tell Louis XIV that both Boreel and Dijkveld thought Holland would be favorably disposed to a deal over Spain. Anthonie Heinsius, the Grand Pensionary who dominated Dutch politics, was more skeptical, but he agreed to let William III try to negotiate a bilateral deal with France for a buffer zone on Holland's borders. While French troops massed near the Spanish border, and a French fleet maneuvered off the Spanish coast, all sides understood well that a winner-take-all approach to the Spanish succession by France would recreate the coalition of the League of Augsburg, but there was a spirit of compromise in the air after Ryswick, and a strong desire – at least in London and Paris – to preserve the peace.[1]

The hard bargaining that ensued between France and England over Spain and its possessions, which included much of Flanders, Italy, South America, and the West Indies as well as Spain itself, produced two partition treaties. The first agreement was signed between France and England on October 11, 1698. It placed Joseph Ferdinand, the seven-year old Elector of Bavaria, son of Maximilian Emmanuel, on the throne of Spain as the successor to Carlos II. He was to inherit the Spanish Netherlands, the West Indies, and Sardinia as well. The Spanish had not been consulted, and they took understandable offence at the deal reached over their heads. As for the Austrians, kept in the dark as well by their erstwhile allies, they were furious too, and promised to sabotage it. The Treaty might still have had a

---

[1] See Grimblot ed., *The Letters of William III and Louis XIV and of Their Ministers*, vol. I.

chance of implementation had not Joseph Ferdinand quite unexpectedly died in February of 1699, sending the negotiators back to the drawing board. The second Partition Treaty concluded in March of 1700 resembled the first except that the Archduke Charles, son of the Austrian Emperor, was to have Joseph Ferdinand's share. Again the Austrians declined to join, and the Emperor Leopold and his council prepared for another conflict with France.

There are glimpses of Callières operating at court during this period as a source for English envoys, but his role was clearly secondary as one of four private secretaries at Versailles, his credit damaged by the adverse public reaction to Ryswick. Matthew Prior who was a member of Lord Portland's embassy to France reported in May of 1698 that he was "pumping Callières to get a sight of the original Treaty of Breda that ended the Anglo-Dutch war of 1665-1667. (It contained a precedent the English wanted to cite.) A year later in May of 1699, with his characteristic breezy wit, Prior wrote that "I am closeted and catechized about my Lord Portland's retreat by all the world from Monsieur le Prince down to Callières" – an indication of Callières's modest place in the pecking order at Versailles.[2]

A MARTIAL REVIEW, AND "PURE LOVE"

In September of 1698 at Compiègne, where Louis XIV held a grand exercise designed to overawe Europe with the spectacle of French military might, we catch another sight of Callières at court. Commanders of units had bankrupted themselves to outfit their troops in the finest uniforms and plumes, and a mock siege and assault was carried out under the watchful eye of the King, with Mme de Maintenon looking on discreetly from her the interior of her carriage, using a mirror. The foreign envoys at Versailles spoiled things by declining to attend because of a protocol fuss over the marking of their tents, much to the frustration of Louis XIV.

Callières dictated an account of this military extravaganza to a secretary and sent it to Mme d'Huxelles, but he was clearly more interested in the book he was reading at the time by Fénelon, now Bishop of Cambrai, the author of the biting 1694 letter of reproach to the King. Entitled 'Maxims of the Saints on the Contemplative Life',[3] it defended the

---

[2] Jealous of the favor his rival the Earl of Albemarle enjoyed from William III, Portland had withdrawn from public life.

[3] *Explication des Maximes des Saints sur la vie intérieure*, 1697. Fénelon's defence of Mme Guyon angered the King and Mme de Maintenon, and a prolonged polemic ensued between Fénelon and his rival Jacques-Bénigne Bossuet, Bishop of Meaux. After a two-year *(continued)*

doctrine of "pure love" espoused by the Bishop's friend Mme Guyon, who was close to the wives of both Chevreuse and Beauvillier. Mme Guyon had been disgraced and imprisoned for her heretical views, and the tolerant Callières suggested to Huxelles that she would have been better advised to emigrate to Holland where she would have the freedom to preach as she wanted.[4]. He was less concerned by Fénelon's allegedly heretical opinions than by his lack of common sense. He thought that Fénelon's mystical notion of perfect love was at odds with the reality of human nature. "Why propose ideas of perfection and disinterested love we can never attain, and which only serve to delude us?," he wrote sensibly to Huxelles.[5]

A MISSION TO LORRAINE

Among the provisions of the second Partition Treaty negotiated between France and England after the death of the little Archduke was the relocation of the Duke of Lorraine to Milan. He had not been consulted about this deal reached by England and France over his head, and it was considered necessary to gain his consent after the fact. Ryswick had restored Duke Leopold to his little principality surrounded by French territory, and he was married to Louis XIV's niece. They were an attractive and happy young couple, beloved by their people who had suffered under the earlier French military occupation. For reasons of family honor, it was important to Louis XIV that Duke Leopold appeared to agree with a good grace to go along with the deal even though he had no choice whatsoever in the matter, and for the delicate errand of obtaining his unforced consent Louis XIV selected Callières. The mission was supposed to be confidential, but Matthew Prior thought that it would not be a secret for long, and he was as usual right. On June 8, Callières wrote to Huxelles that "I found myself in the Gazettes today."[6]

The Duke and Duchess charmed Callières. Their seven month-old son had just died, but the Duchess was already pregnant again, "some small consolation" Callières wrote to Huxelles. On his initial arrival at Nancy he had put up at an inn, but the Duke moved him to a splendid private apartment in the palace. There were diversions every day, music and plays and balls, and the little court was a pleasant one. The Duke's younger

---

investigation by the Vatican, parts of the work were condemned and Fénelon was confined by the King to his diocese, where he remained for the rest of his life.
[4] *Letters*, 79.
[5] *Letters*, 281.
[6] *Letters*, 288.

brother François, age eleven, showed off his dancing skill for Callières, and Callières observed the pilgrimage and feast of "summer Saint Nicholas" which is still celebrated today in Nancy.[7]

It was not a taxing negotiation. Without irony, Callières observed to Huxelles that whenever the Duke appeared in public his subjects implored him on bended knee not to leave them, but Leopold had no real choice except to comply with the King's wishes, even though the ink on the Ryswick Treaty Callières had helped to negotiate was barely dry. To the Duke, Callières stressed the advantages of Milan and its surrounds. It was a much more desirable and economically viable possession than Lorraine, he argued, and the young Leopold was wise enough, or well enough advised, to place himself in the hands of Louis XIV. As a traditional farewell present to a departing envoy, the Duke gave Callières a large diamond, the one he left to Renaudot in his will, and by early July he was back at Versailles, his short and rather *pro forma* mission accomplished to the satisfaction of all.

ONE LAST POLISH GAMBIT

On November 1, 1700, Europe's long death watch came to an end and the unfortunate Carlos II breathed his last. As Harcourt, the French envoy to Spain, made his way back with the contents of the will, the Marquise d'Huxelles left no doubt about her fears and hopes for peace: "our hope is in the moderation, the piety, and the devotion of the King," she wrote to the Marquis de La Garde, "that he will choose to take a course that is already glorious enough rather than creating the risk of a new war."[8] When the Marquise d'Huxelles learned that Carlos II had left his Kingdom and all his possessions to the grandson of Louis XIV, the Duke d'Anjou, she knew that a decision by Louis XIV to accept the will would probably mean war, and she followed the deliberations at Versailles hour by hour from her salon on the rue Sainte-Anne. She wrote that "the King held two councils yesterday, and only a half hour ago the ministers were with him in Madame de Maintenon's apartment." When after much debate in the *conseil d'en haut* the King decided to accept the will and install a Bourbon on the Spanish throne, she conveyed the drama of the moment to La Garde:

---

[7] *Letters*, 286.
[8] Rylands, MS French 93, letter of November 4, 1700.

Figure 12. Louis XIV receiving James II of England at Saint-Germain-en-Laye.
(British Museum.)

All the courtiers embraced the King about the knees, tears in their eyes, when he declared the King of Spain and showed him to them, calling on him to be a good King, and to always conform himself to the manners of a nation that had called him to rule with such expressions of love, to govern it with a just goodness – but always to remember that he was a Prince of France.[9]

In the midst of these fateful developments, a Polish emissary appeared in Paris, and Callières could not resist rising again to the bait. He was Major General Jordan of the Saxon Army, sent by the Frederick Augustus to test the waters as part of the habitual game of playing France off against Austria.[10] The French Ambassador in Warsaw, the Marquis du Héron, was overly familiar with the tricks of the Polish King, and perhaps Frederick Augustus calculated that he might find a better reception in Paris through Callières, who had shown himself an eager partner in his clandestine discussions with Baron Rose in Holland. Torcy gave him the task of negotiating with Jordan, and he undertook it with his customary zeal. He

---

[9] Rylands, MS French 93, letter of November 18, 1700. Saint-Simon's account based on Dangeau's *Journal* is very similar.
[10] Cf. *Recueil des instructions des ambassadeurs.*

met with Jordan privately at his own house, and he told Torcy that he had drawn up an agreement between France and Poland that reflected the new European situation in the aftermath of the the acceptance of the will of Carlos II.[11] As usual, the problem was money. Augustus did not have the cash to pay his troops. In exchange for a French subsidy of 80,000 *écus* a month, or 240,000 francs, he offered to keep a full 33,000 men under arms, who would be in a position to attack Austria in the spring in the event that the Emperor chose to declare war, as seemed likely. (Frederick Augustus's price had gone up since the mission of Baron Rose, and the number of troops on offer had gone down, but this time he was offering to attack the Austrians directly.) Callières told Torcy that he thought he could bargain Jordan down to 200,000 a month – the same subsidy France was paying to Sweden, he noted – and he thought that Jordan would settle for three months up front. He argued that it would be a worth the expense to put pressure on the Austrian Emperor who was bound in the *Milanese* where the Duke of Lorraine was supposed to relocate. Intelligence reports from Vienna suggested that the Austrians were already raising and equipping an additional twenty regiments.

To ensure the Treaty's implementation, Callières suggested to Torcy that "presents" – less politely known as bribes – should be given to Jordan as well as to the Grand Marshal of the Polish Crown, Casimir Bielinksi. (Bielinski had married one of Morsztyn's daughters, though Callières did not mention this to Torcy.) Would Callières have taken a cut of these presents himself if they had been paid, in exchange for his role as the French negotiator? The possibility cannot be excluded. In any case, displaying his expertise in these matters, Callières told Torcy that bribing ministers was standard practice in the countries of the North: "I know from various accounts I heard while I was in these countries that ministers have to be personally interested in the implementation of Treaties made in the name of their masters if they are to take effect."

Callières argued that if Polish troops were sent into Silesia to stir up a revolt against the Emperor, this might make it unnecessary to send French troops to Italy to forstall an Austrian move against Milan. (The Italians, "suspicious by nature," would not look favorably on French troops crossing the Alps, Callières noted – as if Italian suspicions of French troops on their territory were not well founded.) The Emperor would probably send troops through Venice rather than the Alps, a good route "as I know from having travelled it in a carriage from Innsbruck to Venice."[12]

---

[11] *BnF, Fonds Renaudot* 7492, C. to Torcy, December 5, 1700 "in the evening, Paris."
[12] *BnF, Fonds Renaudot*, 7494, 48 and following.

(Callières had seen it in 1674, on the way back from Poland to Milan to report to the Duke of Savoy.)

Torcy eventually initialled the treaty with Poland but it was never ratified, and it seems doubtful that any money actually changed hands. In Warsaw, du Héron reported that Augustus II had no intention of implementing it, and the following year the Polish King signed a deal with the Emperor instead. Over Grand Marshal Bielinski's protests – perhaps French presents had some effect after all – Augustus arrested du Héron, in violation of the immunity of envoys, on the pretext that he was refusing to leave the country. In retaliation, Louis XIV detained all Polish nationals in France, releasing them only after the safe return of his Ambassador. Once again, Callières had argued for a negotiation with Poland with far too little scepticism about the real intentions of Augustus II.

BY THE KING'S SIDE

It is a mistake to despise the post of secretary to a great man. None has ever failed to rise in fortune.
– Jacques de Callières, *On the Fortune of Gentlemen of Birth*

On January 6, 1701, at the ripe age of 89, Toussaint Rose died, and on January 14 it was announced that Callières would have his post of principal secretary. It was an important position. Rose, a familiar presence in the salon of the Marquise d'Huxelles, was a formidable character, known as President Rose, after his office as head of the Paris Chamber of Commerce, and Louis XIV had inherited him from none other than Cardinal Mazarin. Callières thus became the second, and the last, principal secretary at Versailles, through the long reign of Louis XIV.

There would have been no lack of contenders for the lucrative and influential position. Having observed Callières closely, and perhaps also on the recommendations of Torcy, Chevreuse, and Beauvillier, the King must have concluded that his energy and zeal could be useful, provided he were kept close to home. From now on he would remain with the King at all times. In addition to the influence that came with proximity to Louis XIV, the post brought Callières an additional 10,000 francs a year.[1]

It was not a clerical position. Too much attention has been paid to Saint-Simon's characterization of the incumbent as the "pen," the person responsible for imitating the handwriting of Louis XIV. Saint-Simon was a reactionary, attached to the increasingly antiquated feudal trappings of a modernizing French state, and there is no evidence that Callières could counterfeit his master's handwriting. His responsibility was rather to draft, or supervise the drafting of, the King's voluminous correspondence. That would be an influential position in any government, but especially so in an absolute monarchy.[2] The "Bureaucrat-King," as he has been called, kept his hand firmly on the machinery of state, considering that diplomacy and war were the principal duties of a monarch.[3] It would have been up to Callières

---

[1] Dangeau, *Journal*, January 14, 1701.
[2] This could be a highly technical and complex business involving the subtle gradations of openings and closings. See Sternberg, 'Epistolary Ceremonial'.
[3] See Rule's 'Louis XIV, Roi-Bureaucrat', and 'The King in His Council'.

to see that the King's decisions and those of the *conseil d'en haut* were translated into writing. The office should not be confused with the later purely honorific *charge* of secretary to the King which could be purchased, and which brought with it noble status. Callières was not a clerk but the head of the King's private office, more influential than many men with grander titles, and he was at the center of the apparatus that had evolved to manage the needs of the most powerful state in Europe and its overseas dependencies. During Torcy's term in office as Foreign Minister, which coincided roughly with Callières's term as principal secretary, the budget of the Secretary of State for Foreign Affairs more than tripled and the size of the bureaucracy nearly doubled, with a growing institutionalization of the conduct of foreign affairs in all their ramifications, from propaganda to a "black chamber" with the task of breaking foreign codes.[4]

Callières's portrait was painted in this period by Hyacinthe Rigaud, but no image of him has survived, a considerable disservice to the biographer and the reader alike.[5] We have to make do intead with Saint-Simon's portrait in words of Callières at Versailles:

> He was a tall, thin man, with a large nose, the head thrown back, distracted, civil, respectful, who from years of residence abroad had acquired foreign manners and a disagreeable exterior appearance that ladies and fashionable young men found it hard to countenance. But this impression disappeared as soon one spoke with him of serious matters.[6]

Callières worked in close collaboration with Torcy. Judging from the occasionally sharp "I told you so" tone of his notes to the minister, their relationship was almost that of equals. (This is in sharp contrast to Renaudot's dealings with Torcy, much more that of master and servant.[7]) Callières was closely connected to the increasingly influential Chevreuse, who had no formal government portfolio but who is described by Saint-Simon as operating as a virtual prime minister, as well as with Beauvillier, who was a member of the *conseil d'en haut*. This appears to have give him a power base of sorts of his own. Thirty years after his first clandestine trip to Poland, he was finally in a position to advance the public good as well as his own ambitions, and he made the most of it.

---

[4] See the classic Picavet, *La diplomatie française au temps de Louis XIV*, 325, as well as Bély, *Espions et ambassadeurs au temps de Louis XIV*.

[5] We know this from the painter's workbooks: Roman, *Le Livre de Raison du Peintre*, which refer to a *portrait en buste*.

[6] *S/S* I, 346.

[7] See Duffo, *Lettres inédites de l'abbé E. Renaudot*, in which Croissy and Torcy scold Renaudot for failing to carry out various errands, including personal ones.

As Callières assumed the office of principal secretary, war appeared to be on the horizon. The King having decided for the Spanish succession, the Duke d'Anjou, now Philip V of Spain, set out on the long road to Madrid. He was accompanied by Beauvillier and Callières wrote Beauvillier a long letter expressing the hope that he would return to Paris as soon as possible: "I hope you will come straight back from Irun, leaving the princes to make their grand tour without you."[8] Reviewing the dire international situation for Beauvillier, Callières wrote that the Austrian Emperor was bent on war. We continue to press the King of Poland to make peace with Sweden," he noted, but it was probable that the Poles would take sides with Austria, and that even Sweden would be forced to support the Emperor's claim to Milan, as would the German states and the "League of Grisons," the Swiss cantons. It might be possible to co-opt a few of the German princes, but they would want subsidies and guarantees. There was no time to lose or the Emperor would get to them first. There was one bright spot, and this was in Canada, where peace had broken out: "I am enclosing two letters I have received for you Monseigneur. One is from my brother, who has concluded a peace with the Iroquois and the other savages of America who have long tormented our colonies in New France."[9]

The other letter was from Mollo – "the Resident of Poland in Amsterdam who as you know served us well in the negotiation of the general peace" – and he had a favor to ask. With France and Spain now united under Bourbon rule, Mollo wanted the position of Spanish Resident in Amsterdam. The present incumbent was a Jew named Belmont who was no friend of France, Callières wrote. Mollo had written to Torcy and according to Torcy the King was favorably disposed, but the King thought Mollo should write to his grandson the King of Spain directly. Mollo was zealous and loyal, Callières reminded Beauvillier, and he could be a useful advisor in the present situation. The Spanish ambassador to Holland, still the same Don Quiros who had been there during the Ryswick talks, was favorably inclined to his candidacy. Would Beauvillier speak on Mollo's behalf to the new King of Spain? Callières concluded on a somber note: "I have just received a coded letter from Mollo in which he reports that he believes that war has been decided on in Holland."

---

[8] *Fonds Renaudot*, NAF 7487, 407-413. Irun was the crossing point on the Spanish border.
[9] Louis-Hector's 'Great Peace' with the Iroquois and other native peoples was not formally signed until August of 1701 – but Callières's letter is dated January 1 of that year, when Beauvillier was on the road with the princes.

A PLEA FOR PEACE

Notwthstanding Mollo's pessimism, it appeared in the early months of 1701 that peace with England and Holland might be possible even with a Bourbon on the throne of Spain. William III was kept on a short financial leash by a war-weary Parliament, and while England hesitated Louis XIV connived with Maximilian Emmanuel, the Viceroy of the Spanish Netherlands, to take over his forts and evict their largely Dutch garrisons without firing a shot, placing the Dutch in a precarious position. The Dutch received a French emissary, d'Avaux with open scorn and disproportionate demands for concessions while they played for time and prepared for war.

Sensing an opening, Callières drafted a radical proposal for a political offensive to halt the slide towards war. It may have been intended as a brief to be presented at the *conseil d'en haut*, perhaps by Beauvillier.[10] It is in any case a remarkable document. (An English translation is at Annex B, for the interested reader.) In essence, Callières argues for an appeal by absolutist France to the English Parliament and to Dutch opinion, over the head of both William III and Anthonie Heinsius. Distinguishing between what he called the personal interests of William III and those of the "English nation" as represented by Parliament, he argues that William was bent on launching a war before France could recover from the last conflict. But the English Parliament though jealous of France by its "very nature" was exhausted and burdened by debt, and reluctant to place arms in William's hands again lest he make use of them against its liberties. Callières predicts, rightly, that William did not have long to live – he would die within a few months – and he argues that William was desperately trying before he died to convince the Dutch that the only way to ensure their security was to attack France. On the other hand, the Dutch wanted peace; anyone who doubted this failed to understand them, Callières argued.

William was hoping that France in its typically impatient way would take the initiative by declaring a pre-emptive war on Holland, Callières maintained. But to do so would be to play into William's hands and enable the Dutch to present themselves to the rest of Europe as the victims of unprovoked French aggression, just as they had done in 1672. Instead, France should avoid at all costs being the first to break the peace, and offer the Dutch "reasonable guarantees" for their security. As at Ryswick, the winning strategy would be to raise doubts in Dutch minds

---

[10] *Mémoire sur les moyens de conserver la paix, Fonds Renaudot*, NAF 7487, folios 430-41. The paper is undated, but based on the context it must have been written about October of 1701, after the French occupation of the Spanish Netherlands.

about the alliance with England, and drive a wedge between the Dutch and Austria. He proposes that France take the first step by sending envoys to Holland as well as to England.

To the objection that it was beneath the King's dignity to send embassies to those who were preparing for war against him, Callières contended that on the contrary this is the only sensible thing to do: "if we only maintained embassies to honor those we send them to this would be justified, but as we generally send them to countries we are suspicious of, as authorized spies, in order to be well informed as to the situation there, and in order to establish and maintain networks with the people of the country and to encourage movements against the government .... It would be an offence against sound policy not to send them."[11] If the offer of security guarantees were rejected by the Dutch, the King would gain the high moral ground and be better-placed to gain international support if it came to war.

Callières urged that when William III crossed the Channel back to England, which he expected would be in November of 1701, envoys should be sent to both England and Holland bearing draft treaties that would be made public so that they could be debated in Parliament as well as in the assemblies of the seven Dutch provinces. To Louis XIV, the quintessential authoritarian ruler and the Most Christian King, he argued that "the free peoples of England and Holland have not yet lost the power to change the plans of those who govern them," and "this is the only way to elicit the free opinion of the English and Dutch nations." A manifesto inviting the other states and princedoms of Europe to act as guarantors should also be made public as a gesture European opinion.

Callières attached two draft treaties spelling out the security guarantees he proposed to offer the Dutch, one with France, and the other with Spain. France would offer to withdraw from the Spanish Netherlands and create a demilitarized buffer zone, restoring the barrier the Dutch had lost, and both France and the Spain of Philip V would grant the Dutch the equivalent of most favored nation trading status.[12] He suggested this initiative would be greeted with "joy" in Holland, but even if it were rejected, Louis XIV would have "persuaded all Europe of his moderation."

It was an extraordinary proposal. In effect, Callières was recommending to the absolute ruler of Versailles that he appeal to the representative institutions of Protestant England and Holland over the head

---

[11] In Chapter IX of *On Negotiating with Sovereigns*, by contrast, Callières argues that it is an offense against God and Justice for an Ambassador to incite rebellion against the prince to whom he has been accredited.

[12] *Fonds Renaudot*, NAF 7487, 413-420.

of his fellow monarch William III. As for the choice of Ambassador to Holland, Callières himself would be the obvious candidate to repeat his success at Ryswick, though this was left unstated.

The fate of this brief, preserved by Callières in draft among his papers which are interspersed in the *Fonds Renaudot*, is not known. If Beauvillier or Torcy ever raised it in the *conseil d'en haut*,the discussion would probably not have been prolonged. The King was sensitive to these arguments to some extent. In order to avoid the appearance of being the aggressor, Louis XIV did delay an invasion of Dutch territory. (Saint-Simon was highly critical of this "false and pernicious policy" on the grounds that it had ceded the initiative to the adversaries of France.[13]) But Louis had no intention of converting the Spanish Netherlands into a neutral buffer zone. On the contrary, even as Callières was citing what he believed to be the King's reluctance to dismember his grandson's possessions as a possible objection to the demilitarization of the Spanish Netherlands, Louis XIV was having Torcy sound out the French Ambassador in Madrid with regard to an outright annexation of that territory by France. The Ambassador advised against it – Philip V was still in the process of consolidating his power, and it would make him look like a French pawn – and so Louis contented himself with having his grandson declare him Regent of the provinces, annexation in all but name.[14] At this stage, he had no intention at all of ceding control of the Spanish Netherlands, and Callières's arguments would have fallen on deaf ears.

In September of 1701, James II died at Saint Germain, and Louis XIV immediately recognized his twelve year-old son as the legitimate King of England. Not to have done so would have meant turning the Stuarts out of Saint-Germain, awkward in the extreme for Louis XIV, but his hasty action reinforced the assertions of William III to reluctant Tories that there was no alternative to war, leading Parliament to vote the necessary credits. William died in March of the following year, but on May 15, 1702, the Grand Alliance of Austria, England, and Holland formally declared war on France and Spain.

It would be fully as long and ruinous a conflict as Callières had predicted, and a catastrophe for France.

---

[13] *S/S* II, 50.

[14] Clark, 'From Nine Years War to Spanish Succession', as well as Veenendaal, 'The War of the Spanish Succession in Europe'.

LAST MISSION TO LORRAINE – LAUGHTER AND TEARS

In November of 1701, Louis XIV sent a force under Tallard, his former Ambassador in London, to occupy neutral Lorraine, acting to preempt the Austrians who had designs on the strategic little state surrounded by French territory. (Since the second Partition agreement had remained a dead letter, the Duke was still in Nancy.) The Duke was being courted and pressured by the Austrian Emperor who had granted him the title of "Royal Highness" and the Palatinate town of Landau had already been taken over by imperial troops. With good reason, Louis XIV feared that Nancy might be next. As is often the case when a great power confronts a smaller state, the pre-emptive French invasion was justified as a measure to ensure the Duchy's own security. It was a brutal business, a violation of Lorraine's neutrality justified by military necessity, and to preserve appearances Louis sent Callières back to Nancy to secure Duke Leopold's consent to his own occupation, just ahead of Tallard's forces.

Huxelles followed the developments closely. A correspondent reported to her on December 1 from the front that Callières had spent the night in Toul, and that he would present himself the next morning at the Duke's levée to convey the French ultimatum. In the meantime Tallard's force proceeded up the Moselle River, with 13 battalions and 30 pieces of artillery towards Nancy. Huxelles's source wrote sympathetically that at the little court in Nancy "where last night there was only dancing … tomorrow morning there will be tears."[15]

Arriving at Nancy with Tallard's guns already in position, Callières informed the Duke that the King found it necessary to occupy his capital, and he hoped that the Duke would consent. According to an eighteenth century historian of Lorraine who contended that Callières "wanted to serve his master and establish his own glory by a duplicitous démarche," Callières suggested to the Duke that his few troops put up a token show of resistance. Leopold responded that "the world knows that Nancy cannot be defended, and I have no troops with the exception of my guards. I would be taken for a rash fool relying on the justice of my cause alone if I were to attempt to resist your master."[16] Declaring that there was nothing to negotiate, he and his pregnant wife, who was after all the niece of Louis XIV, abandoned their capital for Lunéville, leaving Tallard's troops to beat down the city gates without any pretence of resistance.

---

[15] Rylands, MS French 94.
[16] Chevrier, *Mémoires pour servir à l'histoire des hommes illustres de Lorraine*, Tome II, 13-15.

Putting the best face on the occupation of Lorraine, Renaudot's *Gazette* explained that it was all for the young Duke's own good:

His Majesty sent his cabinet secretary the Sieur de Callières ... to the Duke to tell him that it was absolutely necessary that the King should provide for the security of the city, which had for some time been threatened by the generals of the Emperor.... Having set forth his reasons for wanting to preserve a strict neutrality, the Duke retired to Lunéville with the Duchess. But there is no doubt at all that they will both soon return to Nancy....

But the Duke and Duchess stayed in Lunéville, refusing to return to their own palace while it was under French military occupation, and the *Gazette* dropped the claim that their return was imminent.

It was Callières's last mission abroad, an inglorious one at best. He had been cast more in the role of *consigliere* to a Mafia don than that of negotiator, a *herault d'armes* conveying an ultimatum in advance of the guns. This time there was no diamond from the fairy-tale Duke and Duchess as a parting gift.

INSIDER AT VERSAILLES

There is some evidence in this period of Callières's growing influence at Versailles. Following the arrival of Philip V in Spain, a remarkable alliance developed between Marie-Anne de la Trémoille, Princess des Ursins, who was the head of the Spanish Queen's household, and Mme de Maintenon in Versailles, the morganatic wife of Louis XIV. These powerful women soon dominated the relationship between the two Bourbon monarchies, and according to Saint-Simon, the principal ministers at Versailles, including Torcy, Beauvillier, and Pontchartrain, the Naval Minister, were so troubled by the situation that they all asked the King to relieve them of all responsibility for Spanish affairs. Pontchartrain maintained an agent in Madrid to look after his interests and those of the navy ministry, in the person of François Amboise Daubenton de Villebois, the brother of Philip V's confessor, and two letters from Daubenton de Villebois to Callières have survived.[17]

With the first, in December of 1702, Daubenton de Villebois cautiously sent Callières a memorandum on the budget of the Spanish

---

[17] *BnF*, NAF 7487, 339 and 441. The *Fonds Renaudot* catalogue identifies the writer as Fr. Gillaume Daubenton, Philip V's confessor, but this is an error as the signature makes clear. Daubenton de Villebois had served earlier as the official in charge of the fur trade in Canada, and this may account for his connection to François. He later became the senior clerk in the Navy ministry under Pontchartrain.

navy[18] – "in conformity with your orders, which have been found to be in conformity with those of the Princess des Ursins and M. le Comte de Pontchartrain," he wrote, but he asked Callières not to tell Pontchartrain that he had done so. By the time of the second letter, written almost a year later in October of 1703, the situation at the Spanish court had deteriorated to the point that Daubenton was openly critical of Mme des Ursins, and he he offered to send Callières copies of his entire correspondence with Pontchartrain if Callières would send him the money to hire someone to transcribe them. It was a risky business for Callières to be plotting secretly with Pontchartrain's agent behind that powerful minister's back, and Mme de Maintenon might not have been pleased either if she had known of the clandestine exchanges.

A CONFRONTATION WITH DANGEAU

For all of his proximity to the King and his growing prominence, Callières was still vulnerable to the slights of those with better-attested quarters of nobility. There was no love lost between him and the Marquis de Dangeau, the pompous court chronicler who was his fellow member of the *Académie française*. Callières made fun of Dangeau in his letters to Huxelles, and it is clear that Dangeau was not a member of her set of the great and good. Madame, the earthy German Princess from the Palatinate, widow of the King's brother, recounted a story in her letters to her Aunt Sophie in Hanover which was making the rounds at Versailles involving confrontation between Callières and Dangeau which illustrates both Callières's courage and his ready wit.

In Madame's telling, seeing Callières in the corridors at Versailles, Dangeau had called out to "Monsieur Callières," without using the *particule de noblesse* that signified noble birth, a deliberate insult. Callières ignored him. Dangeau called again, and there was still no response. After a third attempt, the Marquis demanded to know why Callières refused to answer. "What is it, Monsieur Angeau?," Callières finally replied. "Why don't you call me by my right name?," demanded the furious Dangeau. "You took one *de* from me, so I'm taking two away from you," responded Callières.[19] A violent slanging match between the two men ensued over who would be better remembered by posterity, and Callières was probably fortunate that Louis XIV had imposed a strict ban on duels. It clear that Madame's sympathies were with Callières.

---

[18] *L'argent de la flotte.*

[19] Quoted in Amiel ed., *Lettres de Madame, duchesse d'Orléans,* 216-17. The letter is dated July 10, 1702.

THE RUINOUS WAR

There are few persons who will disagree that as the interests of France must be more dear than those of Spain, peace is preferable to the continuation of a ruinous war to uphold the grandeur of the Spanish monarchy.
– François de Callières, *mémoire* to the King

To English contemporaries, the War of the Spanish Succession that raged in Europe and in the Americas from 1702 until 1712, was 'the Great War.' It was fought on both land and sea, pitting a French Army estimated at 250,000 in 1705 against the combined forces of Austria, Holland, and England. France had the advantage of interior supply lines and unified command under Louis XIV, but the allies had better generals, and at sea England and Holland soon gained the upper hand. Succeeding to the English throne on the death of William III, Queen Anne appointed as her commander on the continent John Churchill, Duke of Marlborough, while the principal general for the Empire was Prince Eugene of Savoy – the quiet younger brother of Thomas, Callières's candidate in 1674 for the Polish throne, once destined by his mother for an ecclesiastical career.

Notwithstanding inevitable differences over strategy, Eugene and Marlborough made a formidable team, and Marlborough and the Dutch leader Anthonie Heinsius developed a solid working relationship. Dutch forces were placed under Marlborough's overall command, and even the commercially minded 'good republicans' of Amsterdam saw French control of the Spanish Netherlands as an intolerable threat to the survival of the Dutch Republic. Amsterdam particularly resented the grant to a French company by Philip V of the *asiento*, the lucrative slave trade with South America and the West Indies. The strategic objective of the two Protestant powers was the same: to humiliate Louis XIV and prevent him from ever threatening them again.

For a time the French held their own. They blocked the advance of Eugene around Milan, where Callières had warned Beauvillier the Austrains would send reinforcements, but in 1703 the defection of Victor Amadeus of Savoy, master of the double-cross, undermined the French position in Italy. Portugal abandoned France and made its ports available to the English fleet. In August of 1704 at the village of Blenheim on the

Danube, the combined forces of Marlborough and Eugene destroyed a superior French force under Tallard, capturing him and either capturing or killing over half of his troops. In the same month, a combined English and Dutch fleet forced the withdrawal of a French fleet under the Count de Toulouse off Malaga, establishing a naval superiority in the western Mediterranean the allies were never to lose.

SPEAKING FOR THE PEACE PARTY

By May of 1705, with the noose tightening around France, Louis XIV and his ministers, especially Beauvillier and Chevreuse, were again in a mood to entertain the possibility of a negotiation, and Callières drafted a paper with the title 'How to bring about peace.'[1] (An English translation is at Annex C.) Its principal points were that a negotiator – and he obviously had himself in mind – should be sent to Holland to negotiate a separate peace with the Dutch, using the same tactics as at Ryswick, and that Spain should be used as a bargaining chip while there was still time.

Callières began with an overall analysis of the general situation. He was certain from his regular letters from Mollo that the 'good republicans' of Amsterdam could be tempted into a separate negotiation, but first they would have to be assured that the talks would take place on the basis of three principles: restoration of their barrier in the Spanish Netherlands, the prospect of commercial advantages, and a partition of the Spanish dominions. Just as at Ryswick, he argued, the Dutch would begin by refusing to negotiate without their allies, and just as at Ryswick the French negotiator would respond that he had the power to discuss the demands of the other allies with them *ad referendum*. In the end the Dutch would agree to separate talks, subject to a ratification of the final deal by their partners.

With brutal realism, Callières outlined the dire military and economic situation facing France. Given the state of the French economy there was no possibility of a military victory: "Our enemies are much better placed than we are to raise and counter-raise great armies, whether by land or by sea, as they have more men and ships as well as the ability to obtain money at lower interest rates."[2] The allies were determined to wage war ruthlessly until they got what they wanted, and they would grind France down until that point came. Spain, and its Italian possessions, was the only high card left in the French hand, and it should be played now, before it too was lost to the fortunes of war.

---

[1] *Moyens de parvenir à la paix, BnF, Fonds Renaudot*, NAF 7487, folios. 423-30.
[2] In the margin Callières wrote (accurately enough): "The Dutch obtain loans at 4%."

To the objection that this would be to negotiate away the patrimony of Philip V of Spain, Callières argued that French interests and not those of Spain should be the only consideration. Spain could again develop as a potential threat to France, he argued, and its dismemberment would be desirable:

> As the interests of France must be more dear than those of Spain, peace is preferable to the continuation of a ruinous war to uphold the grandeur of the Spanish monarch .... A longer war could destroy France without any certainty that it would preserve the Spanish monarchy in its entirety .... We must not put off a negotiation of peace terms any longer, ceding some part of (Spanish possessions) in order to preserve the greater part while we are still masters of the whole .... It remains only to make the correct choice of the peace terms and the means of gaining their acceptance by the Dutch, without exposing the King of Spain to an uprising from his subjects when they learn that this dismemberment is being negotiated.

To prevent this, it would be critical to keep the negotiation over his territories secret from Philip V and his council until it was a *fait accompli*: "when we have agreed with the Dutch to negotiate an agreement, only then and not before, will it be the moment to inform the King of Spain ...."

As for the shape of a deal, Callières outlined several complex combinations of territorial exchanges involving Spanish property. One possibility would be to cede the Spanish Netherlands outright to Maximilian Emmanuel, the Elector of Bavaria, while France recovered Luxembourg. The Austrian Archduke could be bought off with the Kingdom of Naples – preferably without Sicily, but if necessary with it. A second combination would be to give Naples and Sicily to Maximilian Emmanuel. In exchange, the Elector would cede upper and lower Bavaria as well as the upper Palatinate to the Austrian Archduke, for whom a kingdom could be created composed of these territories "just as was done with Ducal Prussia, which is of lesser importance than these lands of the Elector of Bavaria." The Spanish Netherlands would then go to the Elector of the Palatinate.

Callières was confident that an early peace could be achieved on this basis with the Dutch. They were traders at heart, he wrote, and a proposal along these lines would drive a wedge between Holland and England: "There is little doubt," he wrote, "that one or another of these options will be accepted by the Dutch if we begin by satisfying them with regard to their trade, which is the basis of their government. As soon as they are satisfied they will oblige their allies to content themselves with what has been agreed with His Majesty, and there will then be a nearly certain means of obtaining the consent of the English court." If the King would agree to send an emissary to meet the Dutch on the border who was empowered to negotiate on this basis, "an early success may be hoped for" – just as at Ryswick.

Callières spoke for the peace party associated with Chevreuse and Beauvillier, and he managed to co-opt their friend and ally the young Saint-Simon into the effort as well, as the Duke recounts rather naïvely in his memoirs:

> I often saw Callières, who had conceived a friendship for me, and I learned a great deal from him .... Having concluded that it was time to bring an end to the war lest we sink further .... I sketched out a plan in my head without writing it down, more for my own instruction than because I thought I had come up with anything very good or practical. I was surprised when he took a great fancy to it. He urged me to put it down in writing and to present it as a proposal to the three ministers with whom I was in intimate contact. I held out for a few days. Finally, pressed by Callières, I promised that I would speak to them, but I couldn't bring myself to put anything in writing. M. de Beauvillier to whom I spoke first found it a very good and reasonable proposal, as did M. de Chevreuse, and they wanted me to speak to the two others. Their response was in such sharp contrast that modesty might keep me from describing it, but it paints them as they were. Having listened very attentively, the Chancellor[3] responded that he would kiss my ass if it were carried out. Chamillart[4] said gravely that the King would not give up a single windmill of the whole Spanish Succession. At that moment I realized that we were paralyzed, and how much the consequences were to be feared.[5]

By the end of 1705, notwithstanding Pontchartrain's dismissal of any bargaining over Spanish possessions, Louis XIV and his ministers were ready for a negotiation more or less along the lines of the proposal Callières had outlined some months earlier, and the capture of a senior French officer, the Marquis d'Alègre, provided a channel. Released on a sixty day parole with a promise not to return to the fight, d'Alègre went back to Holland armed with a French offer that he presented to the Pensionary of Amsterdam, William Buys. The peace party in Amsterdam was tempted by the deal, or so Mollo reported, but on January 9, 1706, Callières forwarded to Torcy a deciphered report from Mollo to the effect that Marlborough had taken d'Alègre with him back to England to prevent him from continuing the promising dialogue.

Seeing Marlborough as the principal obstacle to a negotiation with

---

[3] Pontchartrain: *"Le chancelier me répondit, après m'avoir écouté fort attentivement, qu'il voudrait me baiser au cul que cela fût executé...."*

[4] Chamillart was the Secretary of state for war and a close friend of Saint-Simon. (This makes four ministers consulted rather than three – unless Saint-Simon isn't counting Chevreuse as a minister – which technically he wasn't.)

[5] *S/S* II, 645-646.

the Dutch, Callières had a recommendation for Torcy: "Given as you know the influence his own interest has over his mind," he said, d'Alègre should be instructed to test the waters by offering the Duke a very large bribe. D'Alègre should flatter him by telling him that only he could make peace, playing on the hatred of the Tories for the Duke, and promise him a "great sum of money" on the conclusion of the peace. No matter how high the sum it would be money well spent in order to prevent more shedding of blood – and besides, it might make Marlborough more amenable to a Stuart restoration after the death of Queen Anne.[6] As Winston Churchill notes in his biography of his ancestor, the Duke received this offer of a bribe with polite interest and possibly a bit more – certainly without the slightest trace of indignation.[7] Torcy wrote later in his memoirs that he had "listened without emotion to various propositions intended to flatter his desire to amass endless riches."[8] But nothing came of it, even though Marlborough would later ask his nephew, Marshal Berwick, whether it was still on the table.

On January 15 Callières wrote again to Torcy enclosing a deciphered letter from Mollo, who reported that the Dutch would prefer to take over the Spanish Netherlands themselves rather than having a foreign prince installed there.[9] Callières thought it had been unwise for d'Alègre to raise the issue of a possible exchange of Milan for Lorraine, since if France were to obtain formal title to Lorraine – expanding French borders to the Rhine – it would raise Dutch fears of French encirclement. It was unwise to suggest anything that as part of a peace France sought to gain territory. Instead, the Amsterdam peace party should be offered commercial concessions and a reduction of French duties on Dutch goods.

With an optimism that had little but Mollo's encouragement to justify it, Callières told Torcy that: "If M. d'Alègre has the time to discuss these matters, I am convinced that a way will be found to reach agreement with the Dutch" – implying that it would be better to send a full time negotiator. Callières appears to have had some impact, as on January 21 1707, the King sent a new instruction to d'Alègre offering the commercial concessions Callières had recommended, "though this is prejudicial to the welfare of my subjects."

---

[6] *CP Hollande* 207, January 9, 1706.
[7] Churchill, *Marlborough*, 69.
[8] Colbert, *Mémoires*, I, 113.
[9] *CP Hollande* 207, January 15, 1706.

"NO PEACE WITHOUT SPAIN"

In England, meanwhile, opinion was hardening against a peace. The ruling Whigs had adopted the slogan "No peace without Spain," and while by this time Louis XIV was more than willing to trade off his grandson's possessions in return for a general peace, he was still unwilling to see a Hapsburg replace Philip V on the Spanish throne. Throughout the fighting season of 1706 the war continued on its various fronts with no end in sight. On May 23 at Ramillies north of Namur, Marlborough again routed a French army, forcing a headlong French retreat from much of the Spanish Netherlands. Just as Callières had feared, this removed a trump card from a now greatly weakened French hand, making a deal in exchange for the Spanish Netherlands moot.

Mollo and Callières continued to correspond, and on June 29, 1707, Callières forwarded a lengthy set of recommendations to Torcy along with Mollo's report of his meeting with the head of the Utrecht city council, Veillandt, as well as several other "well-disposed" Dutch officials. The meeting had taken place at Mollo's country house between Amsterdam and Utrecht, "where," said Callières, "I began the negotiation of the last peace with the late M. Boreel."[10] The Dutch officials were ready to talk, but only after Louis XIV had agreed to make the Partition Treaty the basis for the negotiation, and again Callières argued strongly to Torcy that dismemberment of Spanish possessions would be in France's national interest, as a Bourbon dynasty in Madrid would eventually represent a threat to France. "You are aware, Monseigneur," he wrote to Torcy,

> that many able envoys (*ministres*) are persuaded that the Partition Treaty would have been much more advantageous to France than the creation of a Bourbon dynasty in Spain that would eventually become a dangerous rival to France .... The same envoys say that they would have preferred to see some province united to the French monarchy, or the division of the Spanish monarchy among several princes, rather than the passing grandeur of a cadet branch that will not fail to exhaust France if we support it against the will of all Europe, alarmed at the present union of the two principal crowns of Christendom.

It was an extraordinary case for the private secretary of Louis XIV to make to the King's Foreign Minister.

Callières drew up a draft response to be sent to Veillandt through Mollo, noting as he did that Veillandt was known to be "an enemy of the English." Its thrust was that the King could accept the Partition Treaty as the basis for a negotiation, provided that Veillandt could deliver the Dutch

---

[10] *CP Hollande* 207, Callières to Torcy, "à Paris ce 29 juin 1706," 205-15.

to the negotiating table and agree to keep the offer secret. As a way of camouflaging this major concession, Callières proposed an elaborate and duplicitous contrivance that would probably have been unworkable in practice. Veillandt would be shown an unsigned letter, and that letter would be deciphered in Holland on the basis of another letter from France, which Veillandt would then be asked to send back. If he failed to respond favorably, Callières argued, there would be no great risk, since an unsigned letter could always be disavowed as a forgery. There were risks in such a course, Callières allowed, but the risks of continuing a ruinous war were greater.

Torcy must have declined this elaborate and impractical artifice, since writing from Paris on July 23, 1706, Callières continued to press the minister for an offer to Amsterdam of a negotiation on the basis of the Partition Treaty. Forwarding the usual deciphered letter from Mollo, this time he attached a draft reply, telling Torcy that "I will await your reply with your orders for the post that will go on Monday at noon, should you decide that I should write in this sense or in such other manner as you may be pleased to convey in accordance with His Majesty's intentions." The response three days later from Torcy at Marly was a dose of cold water:

"I read to the King the letter you received from Mollo on the 15th," Torcy wrote. "His Majesty wishes that you should respond simply that you have nothing to add to that which you have already written to him, and that it is inappropriate for him to insist on the need for new concessions [*de nouvelles grâces*] before he has given a response to the offer you have already conveyed with regard to His Majesty's intentions. Moreover, prudence requires that he moderate his zeal, lest in seeking to advance the prospects for peace he give those who seek to delay it new ways of undercutting the success of his good intentions."[11]

While this was politely put, it was an unmistakable rebuke, and the minister spelled out the message so that it could not be missed: "I stress this last point because information from Holland suggests that [Mollo's] enthusiasm is committing the King and significantly harming the progress of peace."

BYPASSED

Concerned that the Dutch might be tempted by a separate negotiation, Marlborough and his agents kept a close watch on the border, and at one point the Duke thought that Callières was already in Holland. On September 15, 1706 he wrote to Heinsius that "I am assured that M. de

---

[11] *CP Hollande* 207, Torcy to Callières, July 26, 1706, 222 and following.

Callières is in Holland; I beg you will let me know the truth." Heinsius responded in a teasing mode: "I can't be certain that M. de Callières may not be in the country. It does seem to me that I would know something of it, but it is true that there are many false rumors in the country, stemming I think from the proposals the French have made, which do not appear to me to be completely known ...."[12]

Meanwhile, French channels to the Dutch proliferated. A Dutch magistrate from Rotterdam named Hennequin had established a connection to Chamillart, the Secretary of State for War through Pierre Rouillé de Marbeuf, France's envoy to the Bavarian Elector. (Saint-Simon says that Rouillé was close to both Beauvillier and Chevreuse.[13]) Rouillé gave Hennequin a proposal with instructions to take it straight to Heinsius, offering a negotiation on the basis of the Partition Treaty, just as Callières had recommended, but bypassing Mollo and Amsterdam.[14]

On September 11, having been told of the Rouillé proposals by Mollo though he could not learn the precise details of what they contained, Callières wrote to Torcy in alarm, forwarding two letters from Mollo. If the propositions reported to have been made by Rouillé were unauthorized, they should immediately be disavowed or there would be trouble in Spain – an interesting argument given that Callières had himself been proposing to trade away Spanish possessions behind the back of Philip V. If on the other hand they were genuine, they should be followed up with the magistrates of Amsterdam, "the only persons capable of restraining Heinsius." The Dutch leader would be extremely hard to deal with: "I know this from experience, since as long as I negotiated with Dickveldt who was the Prince of Orange's man and that of Heinsius they played for time, whereas with Boreel who represented Amsterdam we settled most of the principal articles of the Treaty of Ryswick." Perhaps a formal peace conference should be proposed – and why not at Ryswick? It would be critical to keep

---

[12] Hoff ed., *The Correspondence of Marlborough and Heinsius*, 267.

[13] *S/S* II, 532.

[14] Colbert, *Mémoires*, I, 110-11. The tangled skein of French diplomacy during this period is not always easy to unravel, and it sometimes appears to have confused the participants themselves. Following Arsène Legrelle, Lucien Bély has identified four distinct and interwoven channels, but this may be clearer in retrospect than it was at the time. Among those involved in addition to Mollo and Hennequin was an agent for the Duke of Holstein-Gottorp, Hermann Petkum, who worked with equal zeal for England and for France, as well as Count Bergeyck, who represented the Elector of Bavaria, Maximilian Emmanuel, in the Spanish Netherlands. The use of these multiple and contradictory channels to the Dutch run by different ministers in Versailles gave Heinsius and Marlborough the sense that the French were both overly eager and deliberately duplicitous – not without justification.

Amsterdam in the picture, and to move quickly to agree on the outline of peace before the fortunes of war turned again against France: "I will come to you tomorrow evening so that in the event you have the King's instructions for a response I can deliver it by the mail the day after tomorrow, Monday, before noon, in order to save time."

Having conferred with the King, Torcy's response to Callières was sharp and negative, and he prepared a draft for Callières to send to Mollo himself "by order of the King," not trusting Callières to convey the message in his own words. Callières was instructed on the King's authority to tell Mollo very directly to stay out of the way:

> I have received your letters of the 16th, 20th, and 23rd of this month. Do not be trouble yourself over the truth of the propositions put forward by Sr. Hennequin, and if doubts are raised, say he is authorized to advance them. Do not undercut this negotiation, and restrict yourself to reporting on developments without showing the slightest eagerness to involve yourself, just as I do not want to be involved myself as I do not have any authorization to do so and do not wish to incur a direct ban on writing to you.[15]

Torcy's threat was clear: if Callières and Mollo continued to interfere, they would be ordered to cease their correspondence.

Chamillart, meanwhile, who was running the Hennequin channel, was furious at Callières and Mollo, and he wrote angrily to Hennequin that he was throwing up his hands:

> It is up to God to give peace to men. It is from Him that I will expect it. In the meantime, I will do the best I can to promote the war. As He is just, I hope He will save us from the oppression in which we find ourselves. Your friend Count d'Avaux must be furious at this turn of events. I have written to him that I want to have nothing further to do with negotiations from now on. Messieurs Callières and Mollo will benefit greatly – if I am to believe this last person, he has long predicted what I see happening, and that the Pensionary of the city of Amsterdam has insufficient credit to conclude anything with us.[16]

Hennequin to Chamillart responded by complaining of the damage done by Mollo and Callières and "their intrigues," and he urged that Mollo not be told of the details of the French proposal.[17]

Bloodied but unbowed, Callières would not let the matter rest, and on October 16 he wrote to Torcy urging again that Mollo and the

---

[15] *CP Hollande* 207, September 30, 1706. The letter is in Torcy's own hand rather than that of a secretary.
[16] Bély, *Espions et ambassadeurs au temps de Louis XIV*, 109-10.
[17] *CP Hollande* 207, October 3, 1706.

Amsterdam magistrates be brought into the picture. Mollo had been meeting with Veillandt, the Utrecht magistrate, and he had forwarded two letters to Callières, one from Veillandt, which Callières sent along to Torcy. What would be the harm of sharing with Veillandt and Amsterdam the proposals that Hennequin had given to Heinsius and that Marlborough had by now taken to England, Callières asked? Heinsius and his cabal were in the pay of the English, and there would probably be a popular uprising against them. It was a great mistake to be dealing with Heinsius at all. Nothing good would come of it, and if the peace party in Amsterdam were left out it would be more difficult for them to oppose new military expenditures.

Callières even hinted that if Torcy could keep him in the dark, there might be matters he had kept from Torcy too – matters that Callières had apparently taken up directly with the King. They involved a potential mission by a French envoy, obviously Callières, to Holland:

> I recall that three years ago, Veillandt asked me to send a letter from the King with assurances as to the barrier, sufficient guarantees for their trade, and a reasonable satisfaction for their allies, asking that His Majesty send someone to Holland to negotiate on this basis, and he would agree to convene a conference of the States General. I will show you this letter, but as His Majesty did not want to give umbrage to the Spanish he decided not to go forward.[18]

Now that these very proposals had finally been made, Callières argued, to refuse to communicate them to Amsterdam would be to alienate the party on which peace depended, with the risk that when war resumed in the spring the terms would stiffen. "Remember, monseigneur, what I have told you so many times, that peace will never be achieved through the channel of the Pensionary Heinsius, who was elected as a result of the hatred he has for the French. Just as was the case of his master the Prince of Orange, he knows very well that peace will cost him the advantages he has gained through war."

The best way to proceed, urged Callières, would be for the States General to send a secret envoy to Paris, and Heinsius could never do this, not having the power. Thus he thought that the best course would be for him to respond to Veillandt along the following lines:

> Monsieur, having informed King of your good intentions, he has authorized me to convey the attached proposals which have been conveyed at The Hague so that you can cooperate with others. His Majesty has indicated that he is prepared to send one or more ministers to Holland authorized to

---

[18] *CP Hollande* 207, 242 and following.

conclude a sound and lasting peace with your authorized representatives on the basis of these proposals.

It is not difficult to guess the identity of at least one of the envoys Callières had in mind for the mission, but again his draft response was not approved.

Mollo complained to Callières that his credibility with the Amsterdam burghers was being sacrificed to no end. Either use me as an intermediary, he wrote, or tell me you don't want me, so that I can be available another time. Whenever he was given proposals, the Dutch responded that they had already received better terms through Hennequin.

On October 25, an agitated Mollo wrote directly to Torcy. Marlborough was coming from England to confer with Henisius carrying a response to the Hennequin proposals, and Mollo thought it would contain exorbitant demands. Callières had told him in a letter of the 15th that the proposals had been sent, and his Amsterdam friends had asked Mollo to ask Callières to send them a copy. He thought they would try to moderate the English response if they could only be put in the picture.[19] But Torcy politely turned aside Mollo's request for the Hennequin proposals, telling him that his only task was to determine whether the King's offer to meet had been accepted.[20] Eventually, as Callières had recommended earlier to Torcy, the King decided to offer a public peace conference to take place "on a place situated between the two armies, or between Mons and Brussels."[21] Hennequin protested, knowing that the Dutch and the English would never agree to what they would regard as a trick of the tyrant of Versailles, and nothing came of it.

ONE LAST TRY

As the fighting season of 1707 approached, Callières drafted an extended analysis of the situation in Holland entitled "How to Achieve Peace." It amounted to a critique of past French dipomacy and the neglect of the Mollo channel.[22] Callières argued that if the King's proposals had been transmitted by Mollo through Veillandt to Amsterdam in the first place, instead of by Hennequin to Heinsius, they would have been sufficient to establish at least a basis for negotiation. Callières lamented to Torcy that but by the time he had replied to the Dutch overtures through "M. de Leven in Leiden" – Pieter van Leeuven, identified by Torcy in his memoirs as a pro-peace voice – under pressure from Marlborough, the Amsterdam city

---

[19] *CP Hollande* 207, October 25, 1706.
[20] *CP Hollande* 207, November 10, 1706.
[21] *CP Hollande* 207, d'Avaux to Hennequin, October 18, 1706.
[22] *CP Hollande* 208, *Mémoire touchant les moyens de faire la paix*, February 1707.

council had voted to oppose the Hennequin proposals as well as the idea of a public peace conference. Callières proposed an elaborate and probably unworkable gambit to forestall a new military campaign in the spring. A letter should be sent to Veillandt, in code, which he could read but not keep, offering talks and an immediate ceasefire while negotiations proceeded. Philip V would be asked to abandon Spain to the Archduke in exchange for Milan – by this time already in allied hands anyway – and the fortress towns of Ypres and Menin could be given to the Dutch for their barrier. To the objection that this could provoke an uprising in Spain, Callières noted that "given the large number of troops His Majesty will soon have in that country" the safety of the King and Queen should not be a problem. Callières followed this with another set of recommendations only a month later along similar lines. This time he suggested that Philip V be given a rump Italian Kingdom in Sicily, Naples, and Sardinia. The allies would have six months to accept or reject the deal, with a cessation of hostilities in the interim to enable him to withdraw his troops in Spain: "it will be agreed by the Treaty that the Archduke, as King of Spain, will not be able to trouble the subjects of the monarchy whether in Europe or outside Europe as a result of their loyalty to Philip V."[23]

In the meantime, an increasingly desperate Torcy, pressed no doubt by the King, decided to reactivate the Mollo channel. Writing to Mollo directly, he asked him to meet with Hennequin to find out why there had been no response to the French proposals conveyed through Rouillé – and in a postscript added from Marly, he hinted that the French might be able to improve on them. Back now in the loop, Callières wrote to Mollo alerting him to Torcy's letter, and on April 14, Mollo responded to Torcy in high excitement. (Mollo's letter was addressed to "Monsieur Salomon, merchant banker, rue Quinquempoix.") As he had already written to Callières on the 11th, he wrote, he had received Torcy's letter of the first "containing eight numbered pages, with two new ciphers," and he had deciphered it personally, "working day and night." He would go to see the first regent of Amsterdam on the next day, and as instructed he would tell the Dutch that they would be pleased with the barrier they would get – though he wished that Torcy would arm him with the details that were not hard to guess at. In a cover note to Torcy, Callières argued again that Mollo could not be effective unless he was given the text of the proposals already conveyed through Hennequin.[24]

The Dutch response to these signs of increasing French desperation

---

[23] *BnF, Fonds Renaudot*, 7488, 210-21, *projet de paix générale*, March 1707.
[24] *CP Hollande* 208.

and internal incoherence was predictably negative, and on the 18th, Mollo wrote sadly to Torcy that there had been a hardening of opinion even within the Amsterdam peace party. Now he was afraid that the Dutch would not be willing to talk at all without the agreement of their allies – perhaps a secret emisssary could be sent?

From Amsterdam, where he had gone because he had "no confidence in the post from The Hague to Paris," Mollo reported to Callières on the 20th that he had heard from Hennequin that "people at Versailles" were saying that if Hennequin had been the channel instead of Mollo instead the Dutch response would have been positive. This was not true, said Mollo, and rewriting history he told Callières that "On the contrary, I urged his use and hoped for his success. Please stop people from writing such fantasies [songes], which could render me useless." This was of course exactly what Callières had been writing and saying, as Mollo was well aware.

Torcy responded on April 28th, again directly to Mollo, very much along the lines of Callières's February and March mémoires: "I have your letters of the 14th, the 15th, the 18th, and M. de Callières has shown me the one you wrote to him on the 20th." The minister told Mollo that he had reason to believe – "and I don't write this lightly" – that Philip V would agree to a rump Kingdom in Savoy and Nice without Milan, and both Ypres and Menin could be given to the Dutch for their barrier "though this would be a great loss for the King." He trusted that that this would not come back to haunt him, and that he would not be told later that he had already agreed to this "simply because I raise the idea with you." He hoped that all Mollo's hard work would not be in vain.

On April 21, however, in a letter that crossed with Torcy's, Mollo reported that Marlborough had left Holland and was travelling to Berlin and Hanover to shore up the allied coalition. The implication was that nothing could be expected by way of a reply in his absence. On the 24th, Mollo wrote to Callières that he was urging people to take Hennequin's proposals seriously and not to see them as an attempt to drive a wedge between allies – which was of course exactly what they were.

By May 1, 1707, with troops again on the move and no response from the Dutch, Torcy had soured on Mollo again. He wrote to Mollo to tell him that he had been indiscreet, and that he had spoken publicly about the French proposals. What did he have to say for himself?

This appears to have ended the involvement of Callières in these chaotic back channel non- negotiations with the Dutch, which appear to have confused the French themselves at times, and which certainly conveyed a growing sense of French desperation to the Dutch. It was left to Torcy himself to go finally to Holland after a series of further French defeats, only to be humiliated at Gertruydemberg.[25] The allies demanded not only that Louis XIV agree to the removal of his grandson from the Spanish throne, which he was prepared to do, but that in addition he commit to the removal of Philip V by force. This was too much, and French opinion rallied to the side of the aging monarch. What had started as a dynastic conflict in pursuit of Bourbon ambitions was transformed into a war of national survival, the nobility melted its silver plate, and France fought grimly on.

When a Treaty was finally signed at Utrecht in 1713, its terms were far more favorable to France than those Torcy had offered the Dutch four years earlier. Philip V kept Spain, though he lost his Italian possessions. France lost the Hudson's Bay – Callières had managed to preserve at Ryswick, as well as Acadia, present-day Nova Scotia. England acquired a share of the American trade from Spain, including the lucrative *asiento*, the right to trade slaves. Mollo continued to act as an intermediary at Utrecht for Torcy, but Callières appears to have played little or no role.

CALLIÈRES AND THE NEGOTIATIONS: A VERDICT

From a strategic perspective, Louis XIV would have done well to heed Callières's warnings of impending disaster. His analysis of the weakness of the French position and the need for concessions to prevent a war France could not win was accurate and prescient, but he was always one concession ahead of the King – a reminder that sometimes in government the only thing worse than being wrong is being right too soon. After Marlborough's victories at Blenheim and Ramillies, Louis XIV advanced proposals that were increasingly attractive to the allies, but they were always too little, too late. By 1704, when Callières proposed the demilitarization of French-occupied Flanders as a buffer for the Dutch, the King was still hoping to turn the Spanish Netherlands into a French dependency, and he refused to loosen his grasp. When Callières first proposed the Partition Treaty as a basis for negotiation, the King was still hoping to keep his grandson on the throne of Spain, and he abandoned that objective only after it was too late to obtain reasonable terms from the allies, just as Callières had feared. When Spain's Italian possessions were lost, and there was nothing left to abandon but Spain itself, Louis was forced to accept even that humiliation. France was fortunate in the end that

---

[25] For an interesting take on the historiography of all this, see Bély, *Les larmes de Monsieur de Torcy*.

the Dutch overplayed their hand and that the Tories came to power in England.

But while Callières was right on grand strategy, his tactics were another matter. It seems unlikely that there was ever a deal to be made through a peace party in Amsterdam. In the very early days of the war, when the Dutch were bearing the largest share of the allied burden alone, Amsterdam might have seized on his proposal for a demilitarized zone in the Spanish Netherlands as a barrier, though it is hard to see how such an agreement could have been enforced given the well-founded allied distrust of Louis XIV. The powerful Amsterdam merchants were clearly tempted by the trade concessions, but there was never any serious possibility of a popular uprising in Holland against Heinsius as Callières suggested with more hope than realism. The Grand Pensionary dominated the Dutch political landscape, and Dutch opinion broadly agreed with him that France would remain an intolerable threat to the security of Europe until Louis's pride was humbled.

In short, the divide-and-conquer tactics that had worked to some extent at Ryswick – though not nearly as well as Callières later claimed – would not work again, and his repeated assertions that the road to peace necessarily went through Amsterdam and Mollo were became increasingly incredible. In the end, after Torcy's humiliation at Gertruydemberg it was a back channel negotiation with London, not Amsterdam, that worked out the outlines of the deal at Utrecht. England rather than Holland, proved to be the key to peace.

It is not clear why Callières was not used again as a negotiator. That he wanted to be sent to Holland, convinced that he could bring the Dutch around, is plain from the briefs for the King in which over and over he rehearses the tactics he used at Ryswick and promises a quick success if his recommendations are followed. Instead, he and Mollo were told by Torcy and the King to stay out of the way. When in early 1707 the Hennequin channel proved to be a dry hole, Torcy unleashed Mollo again with hints of an even better deal, but Callières stayed at Versailles.

There is some evidence of Callières's influence over the evolution of French policy, and Marlborough who had a well developed agent network, thought he was a key policymaker at Versailles. Among the sources of Marlborough's intelligence was a "black chamber" in Celle, or Zell, where mail passed through territory controlled by the Duke of Brunswick, and correspondence to and from French envoys could be intercepted and deciphered. The volume of the mail requiring considerable triage, the code-breakers were instructed to concentrate on any communications from Callières as potentially the most important source of intelligence with regard to French plans and intentions.[26] As we have seen, at one point Marlborough was sufficiently worried that Callières was already in Holland trying to establish a separate channel to the Dutch to cause the Duke to write to Heinsius.

It may be that the King considered that it would be too compromising of his person to send his own private secretary with peace proposals he might later have to repudiate. Against this, he finally sent Torcy himself to be humiliated by the Dutch. It is more likely that the problem was Callières himself. He was too closely connected to the peace-at-any-price faction of Chevreuse and Beauvillier. The King had experienced his stubborn independence before at Ryswick. Once unleashed, he might well be hard to rein in again. Frustrated in his ambition to repeat his Ryswick exploit, Callières had concluded that a fundamental change in the strategic situation was necessary in order to establish the conditions for a negotiation with the Dutch. His search for an exit strategy had by this time led him away from Flanders and Holland to a very different place: the highlands and lowlands of Scotland.

---

[26] Bély, *Espions et ambassadeurs au temps de Louis XIV*, 142.

THE SCOTTISH DIVERSION I:
LORD LOVAT'S LAMENT

Monsieur de Callières, the Hero of our Cause.
– Simon Fraser ('Lord Lovat')

In the early months of 1703, an exotic visitor was received by Louis XIV in the throne room at Versailles. His name was Simon Fraser, and he called himself Lord Lovat. He was the chief of the Clan Fraser, and he had come to propose that he lead an invasion of Scotland to restore the Stuarts. The meeting went well by one account, Fraser was initially tongue-tied in the Sun King's presence, but later Louis told Queen Mary that he hoped that Fraser had been as pleased with him as he had been pleased by Fraser.

Emerging from the meeting, Fraser compared notes in the antechamber with Torcy and a second official he describes lyrically in his memoirs:

> He was a man of a clear and solid understanding, of a superior genius, and consummate in everything that constitutes the character of an able minister. He was better acquainted with the affairs of foreign countries than the natives themselves. But what was most admirable in his character was his rare integrity and inviolable probity, and that he was the best friend that ever existed. He was so invincibly attached to his word and his friendship, that no power and no misfortune on earth could ever lead him to depart from them, or prevent him from supporting oppressed innocence, and asserting the truth with which he was acquainted.[1]

The reader will have recognized in this description the Secretary of Cabinet to the Most Christian King, known to Fraser and the Jacobites as the "Marquis de Callières."

---

[1] Fraser letter to Colonel Nathaniel Hooke, March 30, 1704, Hooke papers, Bodleian Library, Mss. Add. 25, 88.

Figure 13. Simon Fraser, Lord Lovat, in his prime.

Then in his thirties, Fraser was tall and well made, not at all the jowly caricature sketched by his friend William Hogarth before his execution for treason in 1747 at the age of 80.[2] A man of charm and presence, he was the very model of a Scottish *montagnard*, as the French called the Highlanders. Fraser considered that he had been cheated of his title and the Fraser estates that went with it by a conspiracy led by the Marquess of Athol. The Clan Fraser still recognized him as its feudal chief,

---

[2] See Figure 13. There is a thorough and well-documented biography of Fraser by Mackenzie: *Simon Fraser, Lord Lovat, His Life and Times*. MacKenzie, who had served in India, memorably compares the relations between England and Scotland to those of the Raj in Delhi and the tribes of the Northwest Frontier in what is now Pakistan.

but he had fallen afoul of Scottish law when in an effort to assert his claim to the title he had bedded the dowager Lady Lovat by force, while bagpipes skirled in the background to muffle the lady's piteous cries. Restored to her kinsmen, the lady would only prosecute Fraser for the lesser offense of "rapt," or abduction, rather than outright rape, but this was enough. Branded an outlaw in Scotland, Fraser fled to England and took an army commission under William III. Tiring of the life of an impecunious officer, and determined to reclaim his birthright, he made his way to the exiled Stuart Court at Saint-Germain, having first taken the precaution of converting to Catholicism and impressing the pious Queen Mary with his fervor for the true faith. It was thanks to the Papal Nuncio to France, Monsignor Filippo Gualtieri, the Queen's advisor, as well as the good offices of the Queen's friend Mme de Maintenon, that he had succeeded in gaining access to the Sun King.

THE JACOBITE DOSSIER

Callières's interest in Scottish affairs was far from altruistic. It reflected his conviction that Scottish disaffection with England could be used to open up a second front, forcing Queen Anne and the Duke of Marlborough to withdraw forces from the continent and creating new possibilities for a negotiated settlement of the war of the Spanish Succession on terms more favorable to France. He had inherited the Jacobite account at Versailles from his old friend Renaudot, who since 1688 had managed English affairs for Seignelay, Croissy, and Pontchartrain. The Anglophone Renaudot had fallen afoul of the internecine warfare at the exiled Stuart court at Saint-Germain, whenat one point, as a tactic to gain support in England for a negotiated Stuart restoration, the French court had pressured Saint-Germain to transmit a document to Protestant sympathizers by which James II promised to "protect and defend the Church of England." As the document's unlikely drafter, Renaudot was accused of free-lancing, and in his papers there is an exculpatory account of his dealings with English and Scottish affairs, written about 1693, in which he protests that he acted throughout in strict accordance with instructions from Torcy and other ministers. [3]

---

[3] *BnF, Fonds Renaudot*, NAR 7487, 260-1, undated and unsigned but in Renaudot's hand. He was accused of rash conduct involving an agent named Montgomery and another named Jones. Renaudot protested that he had always acted under the direct orders of Seignelay and Pontchartrain, and that he had employed the *mot de Fabius* – advised delay. While Renaudot's role as spymaster and liaison to Saint-Germain in the 1690s has long been recognized, the far more prominent part played by Callières from 1702 until 1708 is reviewed here for the first time.

The little Jacobite court at Saint-Germain-en-Laye was a viper's nest of intrigue, and after the death of James II in 1701 the pious Mary of Modena was never sure whom to trust apart from her confessor. There were two principal factions: on one side was Lord Perth, tutor and governor to the young heir to the throne, and his younger brother Lord Melfort, both fervent Jacobites. They were Scots, convinced that they would eventually have to fight their way back to Scotland, and that they could do so only with French support. The cautious Earl of Middleton, an Englishman who was Queen Mary's Secretary of State, led the opposing faction. His preference was for a negotiation to restore Stuart rule on the death of Queen Anne in England, and to this end he maintained clandestine contacts with Marlborough and others in England who were worried by the prospect of Hanoverian succession. Sensibly, Middleton sought to preserve a margin of maneuver in order to avoid becoming a French pawn, fearing that in the end (as eventually happened at Utrecht in 1713) the Jacobite cause would be sacrificed as part of a French deal with England.

In Scotland, public opinion was equally divided but increasingly anti-English. The failure in 1699-1700 of an ambitious scheme launched by Scottish investors for a colony and trading post on the Isthmus of Panama at Darien to be known as New Caledonia, torpedoed in the Scottish view by perfidious English investors, had embittered the Scots. The ambitious Duke of Hamilton, principal leader of the Scottish parliament, was known to have Jacobite sympathies, and Hamilton exploited the rise in anti-English feeling after the Darien disaster to increase his popularity.

The roots of Scottish disaffection with England ran deep. Many if not most Scots viewed 1688 as an invasion by "Dutch William" rather than as a glorious revolution. In 1689, while the Scottish parliament deliberated over whether to offer the Scottish throne to William III, John Graham of Clavershouse, Viscount of Dundee, had ridden out from Edinburgh under the guns of the castle to lead a rebellion from the Highlands. A charismatic general, at Killiekrankie 'Bonnie Dundee' commanded a Highland force against a largely Lowland army, and the charge of the Highlanders had carried the day. But Dundee himself was fatally wounded, and his rebellion was defeated at Dunkeld only a few months later. The martial ardor of the clans at Killiekrankie left a lasting impression on both English and French minds.

By the beginning of the new century, winds of change were blowing in Scotland, and it seemed that all the country lacked for a successful rebellion was another charismatic leader. The Duke of Hamilton trimmed and tacked, with one eye on his wife's financial interests in England and the other on his own ambitions for the Scottish throne. In May of 1703, the Scottish Parliament defied Westminster by voting to allow

French goods free access to Scotland, and in the following year Edinburgh adopted the Act of Security rejecting Hanoverian succession in Scotland, leading Westminster to retaliate with a threat to ban all Scottish exports to England.

It was Torcy who had referred Fraser to Callières as his principal contact with the French court, and when it was decided to send Fraser back to Scotland as an emissary to the Scottish lords, it was Callières who drafted the formal commission for Fraser from the King.[4] Invoking the memory of Dundee, it asserted that he would doubtless have conquered Scotland if he had not been killed, and that the "experience and the knowledge His Majesty has of the bravery and zeal of the Highland lords of Scotland for his service allow of no doubt that they will employ all their forces to maintain the right of His Britannic Majesty against the new usurpation planned in England in favor of a foreigner." After all, the commission suggested slyly, "The royal family is Scottish in origin, and it is up to Scots to defend and uphold the honor and rights of their ancient monarchy against the schemes of the English, who have long sought to oppress them, and to treat them as they are treating the Irish."

In order to assist the Highland lords in taking up arms in order to "oblige the South" to declare for the Stuarts, Fraser and a travelling companion, John Murray, were given the sum of 40,000 francs to arm the clans,[5] and they were authorized to promise that France would send officers to help with military training. If they were not prepared for an immediate uprising, Fraser and Murray were to use the money to prevail on the Duke of Hamilton to seize control of Edinburgh for the Stuarts. If Hamilton declined, they were to return to France with the funds unspent.

There was a "special note" attached. "Well-informed sources at Saint-Germain" – read Fraser – were sure that he could command no fewer than ten thousand clansmen, and that many other Highlanders would join with him. A descent by the Highlanders on Edinburgh would present no great risk since they could retreat easily to their "inaccessible mountains," where they would make short work of any number of pursuing English troops. Having risked everything to come to France, Fraser was owed a "decent reward"[6] for his expenses. Modestly, he would also like to be made a Chevalier de Saint Louis, the highest chivalric order in France. As for

---

[4]*BnF* 7487, *Fonds Renaudot*, 370-379, *Mémoire pour servir d'instruction a Milord Lovat chef des Frazers et député des autres chefs des clans ou tribus des montagnards d'Écosse, et à M. Morray, gentilhomme écossais, allant en Écosse pour le service du roi de la Grande Bretagne*. Large portions of the draft instruction are in Callières's hand.
[5] *Leurs vassaux.*
[6] *Gratification honnête.*

Murray, as a French officer he could be offered the inducement of a promotion on his return.

The commission demonstrated Callières's ignorance at this point in his involvement of the complexities of Scottish politics, as well as his credulity with regard to Fraser's extravagant claims. Fraser commanded perhaps 100 men of his clan – nothing like the 10,000 he claimed – and the Scots lords would need a lot more than 40,000 francs if they were to descend on Edinburgh, as events were to show.

THE SCOTS' PLOT

Fraser's party set out in May of 1703, and by August he was in Edinburgh. Before proceeding to the Highlands, motivated by a burning desire to settle accounts with his rival the Marquess of Athol whom he believed had cheated him of his birthright, as well perhaps as a desire to play both ends against the middle, Fraser took the precaution of meeting in Edinburgh with the Duke of Queensbury, Queen Anne's High Commissioner. Queensbury offered him money and a passport for safe conduct in exchange for political intelligence about Saint-Germain, but the High Commissioner's report to Queen Anne noted that he suspected Fraser's motives. [7]

In the Highlands, a council of Jacobite leaders assembled under Perth's son at Drummond Castle to hear Fraser out, but they failed to agree on a leader for the uprising. Unimpressed by the paltry offer of 40,000 francs and French military training, clearly a half measure, they commissioned Fraser to return to the French court to obtain more concrete proof of French support. After one more secret meeting with Queensbury in Edinburgh, Fraser made his way back to France, arriving in Paris in January of 1704 after various adventures in Flanders. His initial welcome from Queen Mary was a warm one, and even the cautious Middleton initially expressed pleasure at his safe return.

Before long, however, reports reached France that the news of Fraser's clandestine trip had stirred up a public hornet's nest in England. Gualtieri, the Papal Nuncio, passed on a published report from a London gazette to the effect that a "most infamous person lacking good name and reputation" by the name of Captain Fraser, a convicted rapist, had been in clandestine contact with the Queen's High Commissioner in Scotland. [8] Other reports were equally incriminating, and at Saint-Germain and Versailles the battle over Fraser raged back and forth, while what came to be called the "Scots' Plot" caused an outcry in London. Fraser responded

---

[7] MacKenzie, *Simon Fraser*, 121.
[8] Gibson, *Playing the Scottish Card*, 28-9.

with righteous indignation. It was perfectly true that he had met with Queensbury, he wrote to Mary of Modena, but only in an attempt to "turn his heart."

The appearances were damning, but Callières took Fraser's side, convinced of his innocence and good faith despite mounting evidence to the contrary. At one point, Fraser writes in his memoirs, having passed a bad night in Paris, he went in the early morning to Versailles, arriving "at seven am to the Marquis de Callières, who always protected him, being better acquainted than any other person with his loyalty and zeal." In Fraser's telling, Callières promised to speak to Torcy about "that scoundrel Middleton," and having done so Callières returned to tell Fraser that he had nothing to fear.

In February of 1704, Callières drafted a "*Memoire* on the Scottish Enterprise" that proclaimed Fraser's innocence.[9] He declared that "we have carefully examined all the charges made against Milord Lovat, the chief of one of the Highland clans recently returned from Scotland with original letters that are not suspect, and we have found these accusations to be baseless." The paper was more sophisticated in its analysis of Scottish politics than the instruction for Fraser he had prepared the year before, and Callières claimed a new expertise in Scottish affairs, declaring that "for over two years we have worked with all the necessary zeal to examine all the reports from Scotland, whether oral or in writing, in order to determine the true state of this Kingdom." The conclusion was inescapable: Scotland was ripe for rebellion.

It was true, Callières allowed, that there were divisions in Scotland between Presbyterians and the Church of England (*les épiscopaux*), but that there was a general agreement to separate from England was evident from the laws newly adopted by the Edinburgh Parliament refusing to pay the expenses of the English troops garrisoned in Scotland. Moreover, the Scottish lords had bought weapons in Holland with which to arm their "vassals," and a bill presented in Parliament in favor of Hanoverian succession in September had not only failed, its sponsor had narrowly escaped arrest. The Scots knew that England would never grant the Scots freedom of trade, for that would ruin England's own commerce. There was no need to trust to clandestine reports from agents: "it is easy to judge from all these public actions that the aim of the entire Scottish nation is to shake off the yoke of England ...."

---

[9] This *mémoire* exists both in the *AAE, CP Angleterre* 217, in a clerk's hand, presumably the one prepared for the *conseil d'en haut*, and in the *BnF, Fonds Renaudot*, NAF 7487, 195ff, in Callières's hand.

It only remained to set a rebellion in motion, and that would not be difficult, given the martial virtues of the Highland tribes. Callières provided a helpful primer for the King and his council as to the manners and customs of the primitive Scots:

> The Highlanders of Scotland who make up about half of this Kingdom are without question the most courageous and zealous in the service of their King and the royal House of Stuart. They live on little, inured to work and fatigue, and devoted to their chieftains whom they follow blindly when ordered to take up arms because that is the condition on which they hold their lands. They view them as their princes, with the power of life and death over them. Several of these Highland chiefs can field a good number of their clansmen armed with muskets, swords, and great bayonets and bucklers that they protect themselves with while fighting. Some have two thousand, and some have three thousand, and they can easily field ten thousand under arms with under than fifteen days notice ... which is enough to begin and induce the rest of the kingdom to follow ....

Attacking Middleton, though not by name, Callières suggested to the King that despite everything he had done for the exiled Stuarts, some there took the extraordinary position that there was a distinction to be made between Scottish interests and those of Louis XIV:

> They have said more than once to persons worthy of trust that this enterprise would be good for France, but not for them. One would like to believe that they have other plans they think are better, but it is easy to show that they are wrong when they distinguish between the interests of their King and those of Your Majesty, who has protected him with such generosity.

This faction at Saint-Germain had the nerve to complain of the Ryswick Treaty, Callières wrote – by which Louis XIV had disavowed the Stuarts, it will be recalled, in favor of William III. They even claimed that an uprising in Scotland would spoil the chances for a negotiated return to power in London. In short, it was painfully clear that "they prefer a residence in Saint-Germain to one in Edinburgh."

Attacking Middleton's position that an uprising in Scotland was a "mirage,"[10] Callières argued that the policy of negotiation with Queen Anne's ministers was the real mirage, and Middleton's clandestine contacts with the Tories were foolish distractions.[11] Anne had shown herself a determined enemy of France, exhausting England in men and money to dethrone the King of Spain. In emotional and personal terms calculated to appeal to Louis XIV, Callières charged that she had plotted with Victor

---

[10] Middleton's term was *visions*.

[11] *De vains amusements.*

Amadeus of Savoy to bring violence to the heart of France by supporting the revolt of the Camisards in the mountainous Cévennes region, and that she had sent money and military advisers to "these monstrous fanatics in Languedoc." Surely this breach in the rules that ought to govern relations between sovereigns, even when they were at war, justified assistance to the righteous cause of the Highlanders in Scotland.[12]

With a cold realism of precisely the sort Middleton feared, Callières suggested that even if an uprising only led to a civil war in Scotland, that would be fine from the French perspective. After all, the English were the principal enemy of France, and "there is nothing more just and natural that to carry the war to their island. Your Majesty has no need of the advice of the ministers of the Court of Saint-Germain, and no need be guided by their policy, which is more English than French."

Besides, Callières argued, the Scottish cause was just. Scotland was an ancient ally of France seeking only to restore its independence under its rightful King. What more reason was needed to provide the Scots with the French protection they sought? It would force an English withdrawal of forces from the continent to deal with the rebellion, and the Dutch would have to sue for a separate peace.

To this end, Callières urged that the King should assert firm control over Saint-Germain by convincing Mary of Modena to allow Louis XIV to assume personal control of her affairs, bypassing her own advisors. The Papal Nuncio, Gualtieri, could be relied upon to generate a letter from the Pope to the pious Queen, instructing her that her religious duty was to commend herself entirely to "the profound wisdom and well-tried generosity of Your Majesty."

Aside from its cynical readiness to fight to the last Scot, the weak point of Callières's proposition was the absence of a suitable leader for the Scottish rebellion. It had become clear even to Callières that Fraser was not suitable for the role, and Middleton had seized on reports of his meetings

---

[12] The revolt of the Camisards was entirely home-grown in its causes, generated by the repression of an indigenous religious movement by French dragoons, and while Protestant opinion in England and Holland was sympathetic to the Camisards, little if anything seems to have been done to help them. A few thousand Camisard rebels sheltered by a sympathetic population managed to tie down large numbers of troops France could not easily spare, including the Irish Brigade, which was particularly zealous in its attempts to exterminate the "monstrous fanatics." A few months after Callières's mémoire, Marshal Villars succeeded in negotiating a deal with the principal Camisard leader, a former baker's boy named Jean Cavelier, in exchange for an offer to make him a General in the French Army. The conflict sputtered on at a reduced level until 1715 after Cavelier escaped to England, ending his remarkable career as the Governor of the Isle of Jersey.

with Queensbury to discredit both Fraser and the notion that that Scotland was on the verge of an insurrection.

For months, the battle at Versailles and Saint-Germain over Fraser continued to rage. Preserved among Callières's papers is a *mémoire* in which he rebuts Middleton's charges against Fraser.[13] It was true that the High Commissioner had offered Fraser rewards if he would come over to the government side, Callières admitted, but Fraser had rejected them. Queensbury was after all a friend of Fraser's from his earliest youth. Without the slightest pretence of objectivity, Callières adopted the indignant voice of Fraser himself: "He declares that it is remarkable to see himself accused instead of the praises he deserves, having sacrificed all in the service of his King. Before he came to France two years ago as an emissary of the Highlands chieftains to offer their services, he had been in the peaceful possession of his seat, one of the most pleasant in the country, with a thousand men bearing arms, ready to follow him anywhere .... If he had wanted to abandon the King's cause, he could have recovered these possessions." In fact, of course, Fraser had been a wanted man without prospects when he turned up at Saint-German.

Callières concluded with a final attack on Middleton and a call for action: "Lord Lovat declares further that it is easy to see that those who govern the court of Saint-Germain, being English by birth and inclination, cannot bear to see Scots, whom they hate, have the glory of restoring their King." The risks were low, and the potential gains high: A "Scottish diversion," he wrote, could enable "the restoration of the peace of all Europe."

Under increasing fire at Saint-Germain, Fraser continued to rely on Callières for advice and counsel. He wrote to Colonel Nathaniel Hooke, the Irish commander of a French regiment, that "I will always be guided by Callières and let him do whatever he sees fit, for I will always be pleased with whatever he does for me, and think myself happy at any time to be guided by him."[14] But the tide turned gradually and inexorably against him, as more evidence surfaced of his double-dealing. It did not help his cause when Fraser wrote a typically intemperate letter to Queen Mary in which he proclaimed that "Jesus Christ would come in his clouds" before she would restore Scotland to its rightful King.

In desperation, Fraser wrote to Hooke that the only hope was for Gualtieri and Callières to lobby Mme de Maintenon, who was increasingly

---

[13] There are two versions of this document in the *BnF, Fonds Renaudot*. The one at NAF 7487, *Mémoire sur les affairs d'Écosse, février 1704*, f. 380-386, is in a court hand. The original in Callières's hand is at NAF 7492, f. 173-8.

[14] Hooke, 113.

hostile to him: "Our Queen's tears are ready and powerful with the other lady." He pleaded with Hooke to intervene with the two men: "I know that the Nuncio and Monsieur de Calliers have such a good opinion of your judgment and are so much my friends that they will do anything for me that you will propose to them."[15] For his part, the Nuncio warned Fraser that Queen Mary was now determined to ruin him.

At Saint-Germain, the battle lines were drawn ever more clearly, and Callières was in the midst of the fray. Colonel Hooke was at the front, and he told Fraser to write to him in care of Callières, while to Torcy Hooke wrote that Queen Mary had complained to him that he was failing to keep her informed of his dealings with Callières and Torcy.[16] Hooke added that Middleton had summoned him, offering a cipher so that he could inform on Versailles, but that he had declined to accept.

In March of 1704, a letter arrived from Scotland from the Duke of Perth's son, Lord Drummond, who had hosted Fraser's meeting with the Highland chiefs, and Fraser sent it by express courier to both Hooke and Callières, proclaiming that it cleared him of all charges. His situation appeared to improve further with the belated arrival of John Murray, his traveling companion, who defended him. Gualtieri, the Nuncio, advised Hooke that it would be better for Callières than for Hooke to bring all this to the attention of Versailles – otherwise it would be just one foreigner defending another. On May 20 Callières wrote to Hooke triumphantly but prematurely that Murray's arrival had "dissipated all doubts" about Fraser.[17]

From the front lines with his regiment, an increasingly worried Hooke continued to bombard both Callières and the Nuncio with letters. Having had no response to three letters to Callières, he wrote to the Nuncio on July 13 from the "Camp of Offenburg," a town on the Rhine opposite Strasbourg, that this was so unlike Callières that he was afraid that his letters with their criticism of the Queen might have fallen into the hands of Saint-Germain, in which case "all is lost." Would the Nuncio ask Callières if he had received them? Callières responded on July 26 confirming receipt of the three letters, but he reported that nothing was being done to advance things: "At Saint-Germain they are only working to prove on the basis of documents from England that Lovat is guilty, and the rest is neglected." An anxious Hooke told Callières that a friend had written to him that there was conclusive evidence of Fraser's guilt, and "I beg of you Sir, to tell me if it

---

[15] Hooke, 101.
[16] Hooke, 129.
[17] Hooke, 150.

is true."[18] After some delay, Callières replied cautiously, and the tenor of his response suggested that even he had growing doubts about Fraser. Noting that he was writing without a cipher which limited his ability to be frank, he told Hooke that "I don't believe that the man you speak of to me is as guilty as you have been told, and the evidence, which they say is clear as day, doesn't seem so to me. It does seems to me that he wanted to use the trust placed in him to destroy his principal enemy, the one you know,[19] and in that regard I will not attempt to defend him. But for the main part of the business, I can't see that he has ruined anything, or that he acted with an ill intention. He simply lacked judgment and proper conduct on certain occasions. It would take too long to explain the whole affair to you, and I will put that off until your return.[20]

In the end, just as Hooke had feared, the tears of Mary of Modena swayed Mme de Maintenon. The King sided with Middleton, ruling that Fraser was guilty as charged of conspiring with English agents in Scotland. Fraser was consigned without trial to prison in the town of Angoulême, some 280 miles away. He would remain there in detention for over a decade under more or less comfortable circumstances, while a pension continued to be paid to him by Louis XIV.

LORD LOVAT'S END

Fraser was deserted in captivity by many friends at Versailles, but the loyal Callières was not one of them. In 1713, after the expulsion from Saint-Germain of the Stuart court, when Fraser petitioned for a pardon and a position in French service, Callières "indisputably the best friend in the world" he wrote, intervened in his favor with Gualtieri, back in France for a visit to his old friend Louis XIV, now wearing a Cardinal's hat. Fraser in his detention had made a friend of the Countess de La Roche, an influential woman with whom he claimed a kinship. In a hand by now shaky with age, Callières wrote: "Here is a letter for Your Eminence from the Countess de La Roche on behalf of Lord Lovat, together with a *mémoire* by way of an apologia for his past conduct, as well as another letter from this Lord to me, in which he begs me to commend his interests to you .... I told Lord Lovat that in light of your past kindnesses to him I had no doubt that you would intervene with His Britannic Majesty on his behalf, and that I would

---

[18] Hooke, 155.
[19] The reference is to the Marquis of Atholl.
[20] Hooke, 156. Callières's response is dated August 26, 1704.

Figure 14. "Jacobite Hopes Dashed." The Stuart Pretender, "Perkin" is shown being drawn by monsters named "popery," "tyranny," and "slavery," over the prostrate bodies of "toleration," "liberty," "moderation," and "property." Perkin Warbeck was a pretender to the English throne. His dubious claims had been espoused by King James IV of Scotland with an invasion in 1496 of England. (British Museum.)

second this, but that he should be patient, and wait for a favorable occasion."[21]

Fraser eventually escaped (or was allowed to escape) from France, returning to Scotland in time to participate in the Jacobite uprising of 1715 – but on the government side. Turning his coat once again, not for the last time, he led the Clan Fraser against the Jacobites, helping government forces suppress the uprising and gain control of Inverness. In exchange, he received the return of his Highland estates, and the title of Lord Lovat. His final adventure came in 1745, when switching sides for the last time he supported the uprising led by Charles Edward Stuart. This miscalculation resulted in his death on the executioner's block at the age of 80. Before his execution, the old rogue cited the tag from Horace: *dulce et decor est pro*

---

[21] British Library, additional manuscripts 20368, Callières to Gualtieri, letter 29.

165

patria mori, it is sweet and fitting to die for one's country. Verses attributed to Samuel Johnson were more apt:

> No Tory pities thinking what he was
> No Whig compassions, for he left the cause;
> The brave regret not, for he was not brave;
> The honest mourn not, knowing him a knave.[22]

Callières had backed the wrong horse.

---

[22] Quoted in 'The Newgate Calendar', a popular nineteenth century work, available online at http://www.exclassics.com/newgate/ngintro.htm. It contains a lingering account of the execution of Lovat under the heading 'Traitors, Rebels, and Assassins.' A celebrated engraving by Lovat's friend William Hogarth depicts him on the eve of his execution.

THE SCOTTISH DIVERSION II: INVASION

In other times, we would have spent millions, and thought them well spent, simply to bring the Scottish nation to the state it is in today. Since Providence has brought it to this state without any effort or expense on our part, how can we refuse to take advantage of this?
– François de Callières, *mémoire* to the King

With Fraser confined at Angoulême, in Scotland relations with England continued to deteriorate. For a time, war seemed inevitable, but cooler heads and shared economic interests prevailed, and Commissioners were appointed with the mandate to negotiate the union of the two countries. There were riots in Scotland in protest, but in October of 1707, against the background of what might be politely termed English transfer payments, some of which went to indemnify investors in the Darien venture, the first Parliament of Great Britain convened, and Scotland lost its status as an independent state.

Daniel Defoe, spying in Scotland for Robert Harley, the Speaker of the House of Commons, painted the increasingly sour mood in a series of letters to London. From Edinburgh on October 24, 1707, Defoe reported that Highlanders in clan dress were roaming the streets, and that the temper of the population was incendiary: "I had not been long here but I heard a great noise, and looking out saw a terrible multitude come up the High Street with a Drum at the Head of them shouting and swearing and cryeing out 'All Scotland would stand together, No Union, No Union, English dogs', and the like." Fearing for his life, Defoe thought of Jan de Witt, the Dutch statesman admired by Callières who had been torn apart by a mob in 1672, and quickly made himself scarce.[1]

These circumstances again seemed to favor the Scottish Diversion – or the Scottish Enterprise as it was more politely termed in deference to the sensibilities of Saint-Germain – and Callières's friend Colonel Nathaniel Hooke replaced Simon Fraser as the French court's chosen instrument. Hooke was a far better choice. Born in 1664, and educated at Trinity College in Dublin, he had led an adventurous life in pursuit of lost

---

[1] Richetti, *Life of Daniel Defoe*, 118.

causes. In his youth he had been associated with the ill-fated rebellion of the Duke of Monmouth, the illegitimate son of Charles II, serving as chaplain to Monmouth. Escaping to Holland after Monmouth's defeat at the Battle of Sedgemoor, he had returned to England to be pardoned by James II, and after the Williamite revolution of 1688 he became a fervent supporter of the Jacobite cause, having converted to Catholicism. Arrested and confined to the Tower of London, he was released in time to fight at the Battle of the Boyne and to be evacuated with French forces, eventually placing his sword at the service of Louis XIV.

Despite this chequered past of shifting loyalties, unlike Simon Fraser, Hooke was a man of honor who believed in serving one master at a time. After receiving his discharge from James II he acquired French nationality, and to the end of his life he was the faithful servant of Louis XIV and France. He was decorated with the Order of Saint-Louis, and he served as the French envoy to Poland and Saxony in 1711 – an appointment in which it seems likely that his friend and ally Callières had a hand.

In early 1702, Torcy had sent Hooke undercover to Holland, and there he had succeeded in penetrating the inner circles of the English and Dutch leadership, sending back a stream of intelligence on the basis of contacts with both Marlborough and the English Ambassador to Holland, Lord Stanhope. On his arrival in Holland in May, the first letter he received was from Callières, anxious to know whether he had arrived safely, and it was none other than Francisco Mollo who handled Hooke's clandestine correspondence with Torcy after war broke out later that month. In his reports to Torcy, the tough-minded Hooke cast cold water on the prospect of splitting the Dutch from the English to which Callières and Mollo were much given, and it is clear that Torcy attached great value to the intelligence Hooke obtained. The Minister asked Hooke to stay in Holland and take a position under Marlborough from which he could continue to spy for France, but Hooke refused on the grounds that this would be dishonorable.[2] Torcy blew his cover to Middleton at Saint-Germain, to Hooke's horror, and Marlborough – who had Saint-Germain penetrated – almost certainly suspected that Hooke was a French agent, but careful as always to keep his options open, the Duke gave him safe conduct through English and Dutch lines. On his return to France, Hooke was rewarded with a commission as a Colonel in the French Army.

Hooke proved to be as steady and discreet as Fraser had been unreliable and self-serving, and he and Callières established a strong

---

[2] See Byrne, 'From Irish Whig Rebel to Bourbon Diplomat'. Chapter V describes Hooke's mission to Holland based on his correspondence with Torcy (and Callières) in the *AAE, CP Angleterre supplément*, 3.

relationship of mutual confidence. (Although the evidence is not conclusive, Callières appears to have sent him a manuscript copy of *On Negotiating with Sovereigns*, to which Hooke responded warmly.[3]) Hooke had wondered to Callières whether he would ever be fully trusted by Torcy and the King,[4] but his mission to Holland in 1702 removed any remaining doubts about his loyalty. As an emissary to Scotland, Hooke was preferable to Fraser in other respects as well. He carried a French commission, and as a senior French officer he could speak for France. Irish by origin, he had no Scottish connections or interests to distract him from his duty as the envoy of Louis XIV.

COLONEL HOOKE GOES TO EDINBURGH

In March of 1705 Callières rehearsed the arguments for the Scottish enterprise in yet another passionately worded "*Mémoire* on Scottish Affairs" (an English translation is at Appendix D). It began with a history lesson for Louis XIV and the *conseil d'en haut*. There was an innate antagonism between England and Scotland, Callières argued, based on history and the English domination of Scottish trade. The English were determined to subject Scotland just as they had subjected poor Ireland, but the difference was that the Scots were a warlike race, and they could base themselves in the Highlands "where the English have never managed to subdue them, despite their more numerous armies, which the Scots always find the strength to defeat, subsisting on oatmeal, milk, and the turnips that are found everywhere," an interesting take on Highland ecology. Even Cromwell had never able to conquer the Scots, and he had been forced in the end to buy them off. The Scottish lords could command their "vassals" absolutely, and the Highlanders spoke the same language as the Irish, Callières explained helpfully. The distance between Scotland and Ireland could easily be crossed in small boats at Kintire. Now was the time to exploit this state of affairs, with England and Scotland on the brink of open warfare after the adoption by the Scottish Parliament of the Act of Security. Even the "English of the court of Saint-Germain" – Middleton and his

---

[3] On February 6, 1704, Hooke wrote to Callières: "I will have the honor of thanking you tomorrow morning for the book you had the kindness to send to me. I will read it with a great deal of eagerness and careful study." In a side note to his copy of the letter, Hooke adds that the book in question was the manuscript of *De la manière de négocier*, which would not be published for another twelve years. (Hooke papers, Bodleian Library, Add. Mss. 25, 55.)

[4] Hooke asked Callières to intervene on his behalf with Torcy to persuade him 'that I have no other interest at heart than that of France, which I regard henceforth as my country', Byrne, 'From Irish Whig Rebel to Bourbon Diplomat', 119.

faction – had now been obliged to accept this: "The alarm taken by the English Parliament and the laws it has passed to oppose the laws adopted by the Scottish parliament ... are the irrefutable proof... that the time has come to take advantage of this favorable inclination of a nation as warlike as the Scottish nation to force the King's enemies to purchase peace on terms that are glorious for His Majesty ...." The Scots were so aroused against England that "they are talking now of demanding from the English the return of the three counties of Northumberland, Cumberland, and Westmoreland, which formerly belonged to Scotland, which the English only hold by virtue of a lease that has expired." The English had banned the sale of Irish woollens in Scotland, and all these measures had only stiffened the Scots in their determination to resist. The Scottish lords had bought arms and munitions in Holland and they were preparing the clans for battle in monthly reviews. Presbyterians and Episcopalians alike were united as never before in their resolve to oppose the English. "Two well-informed Scottish officers recently arrived from Scotland report that military reviews take place every month, and that they amount to more than 80,000 men. In the Province of Ayre alone they have seen 17,000 armed Scots." English press gangs were kidnapping Scots for service on English ships, and eleven Scots had been taken, leading the Scottish High Sheriff to march into England and kidnap eleven English heads of family in retaliation. Queen Anne had failed to find a single Scot who would accept the post of High Commissioner. She had been warned that if she persisted in demanding the revocation of the Act of Security and acceptance of Protestant succession by the next Scottish Parliament, there would be an uprising of the "entire Scottish nation."

Callières disposed of the objection that with armies in the field in Italy, Spain, Flanders and Germany Louis XIV lacked the necessary resources. The reverse was true, he argued: by obliging England to withdraw from the continent troops that were "the most redoubtable we face," the Scottish Diversion would "end the need for His Majesty to maintain such large armies in so many different countries." "In other times," Callières argued, "we would have spent millions, and thought them well spent, simply to bring the Scottish nation to the state it is in today. Since Providence has brought it to this state without any effort or expense on our part, how can we refuse to take advantage of this by considering proposals to easily and cheaply bring it to fruition?"

In such circumstances, urged Callières, an emissary should be sent to the Scottish lords immediately. His description of the ideal envoy sounded a lot like Colonel Hooke. He should be "a man of ability who knows the language and the laws of the country and who is not attached to or in the service of the court of Saint-Germain." Empowered to speak for

Louis XIV, he would tell the Scots that "His Majesty asks only of them that they take the measures they believe best suited to establish their independence from the English, who are the enemies of His Majesty as well as theirs." The envoy would carry a letter from the King, which Callières outlined in detail:

> Its substance would be that His Majesty having learned with displeasure that the Scottish nation finds itself in peril of being placed under the yoke of the English, who by the laws adopted in their last Parliament have shown themselves determined to overturn the basic laws of the ancient Kingdom of Scotland and to reduce the Scots to the same slavery as the Irish, and knowing of the ancient attachment of the Scots for his forebears, who gave them protection and the right of residence in the Kingdom of France, cannot see them in this peril without offering them his royal protection from the usurpations of the English.

The emissary would not propose to the Scottish lords – at least at this stage, as Callières put it carefully – the restoration of the Stuart Pretender, since the Scots were not united on this point, though they were all equally determined to throw off the English yoke. Better to leave that to a later time. The emissary would carry a letter from Louis XIV to the Duke of Hamilton pledging to take into account his personal interests – euphemism for the offer of a bribe.

Above all, it was essential that this be done behind the back of Saint-Germain:

> It is essential to negotiate initially with the Scots only on behalf of the King, and to conceal the knowledge of all the details of this negotiation from the Court of Saint-Germain. This is because we know from long and unhappy experience that no secret is safe there, and that within this Court are concealed emissaries who would inform the ministers of Queen Anne of every development ....

There was little doubt that Saint-Germain has been thoroughly penetrated by English spies, Callières asserted. In fact, he had a source who could confirm this to the King personally:

> A foreigner of the first rank who was in the service of our enemies during the last war and who now serves the King of Spain has told well-informed persons (*gens dignes de foi*) that when he was in the enemy camp the best and soundest intelligence he received came from the agents King William maintained at the Court of Saint-Germain. They informed him not only of the plans of Saint-Germain against him, but also of our plans against other enemies and of our order of battle on both land and sea. This foreigner is now totally committed to the King's interests, and he will be willing to give the

same testimony directly to His Majesty if he should wish to ask him for it. In that event we offer to reveal his name.[5]

Yes, Callières acknowledged, it was true that the Scots had sent word through the Duke of Perth that they needed 5,000 men from France before they could consider an uprising, and the King did not have five thousand men to spare or the ships to transport them to Scotland, but there was a way around this. The men could be found in Scotland, and the officers sent from France: "we propose to send sixty Irish, Scottish, and French officers, taking them from those discharged from the Irish and other regiments in His Majesty's service." As for ships, "in order to transport these sixty officers with arms for five thousand men we will need only one frigate of thirty or forty guns, which can be done in secret provided the Court of Saint-Germain isn't informed." Finding funds for the expedition would not be a problem, Callières contended. A little creative financing would do the trick. Bonds could be issued on the Hôtel de Ville generating a total of 400,000 francs, and an additional 300,000 would come in the form of matching funds from a "foreign power" that Callières did not name – almost certainly Pope Clement XI, a strong supporter of the Jacobite cause who had already advanced money through Gualtieri to Mary of Modena.

The strategic benefits to France would be incalculable, Callières contended. With all their troops on the continent, the English would be in no position to oppose the expedition, and they would have to abort their plans for an attack on Cadiz and the invasion of Spain through Andalusia. Until the Scots had agreed to mobilize no money would change hands, and there was little or no risk for France and everything to gain: "this enterprise … will in all likelihood be followed by a quick and glorious peace, since the Dutch seeing the English occupied at home and unable to come to their assistance will be obliged to negotiate with His Majesty and to accept the terms he is graciously pleased to offer for the security of their state and their trade."

Callières's position that Hooke's mission should be undertaken behind the back of Saint-Germain proved to be unrealistic. In order to overcome the last objections to his trip, Hooke was forced to meet alone with Queen Mary on June 5, and she promised to approach the King. Hooke wrote to Callières that "I studied the Queen's demeanor while she was speaking, and as I know the sentiments of her heart well, I am convinced that she is entirely in support of the plan."

On June 8, Lord Perth wrote to Hooke to tell him that the Queen had indeed spoken to Louis XIV, and that it had been agreed to send him:

---

[5] This may well be the Elector of Bavaria, Maximilian Emmanuel.

My dear Colonel, you know how I am situate at the King's table, the King being betwixt the Queen and me. She was so impatient to tell me news that she whispered to him to tell me that she has spoke and what she asked would be done. Give my service to the two Dukes (i.e. Chevreuse and Beauvillier) and Mr. de Callières.

She asked that he pass on her gratitude to Chevreuse as well, who had obviously been an influential voice in support of the Hooke mission. Perth quoted her as having said: "I am sensible of all that I owe to (Chevreuse)." Through Perth, the Queen conveyed her thanks to Callières for his "goodness and interest in her affairs."

Interestingly, however, on June 10, writing to Torcy, Hooke asked that Callières not be told immediately of the Queen's approach to Louis XIV: "I beg of you that M. de Callières should know nothing of this démarche of the Queen, at least for the moment." It seems likely that given Callières's strong opposition to any discussion of the mission with Saint-Germain, Hooke was worried that he would tell the King that the trip had been compromised. The Queen had indeed told Middleton of the Hooke mission, and Hooke wrote to Torcy: "You see, Monseigneur, how right I was to be concerned about talking to the Queen. But I hope we can manage the affair .... I will be obliged to receive her orders, but I will only follow yours, and I hope I can keep you from being tormented by the factions and divisions at Saint-Germain ....[6]

Hooke's instructions from Louis XIV are dated June 17, 1705, and they follow the line set out in Callières's March *mémoire* very closely. (Callières probably had the principal hand in drawing them up, although there is no copy in his papers.[7]) Hooke was to sound out Scottish opinion with regard to an uprising in the Highlands, and assure the Scottish lords that the King would take Scotland under his protection if they were prepared to act, but without necessarily espousing the Stuart cause. As Callières had recommended, he was armed with a letter from the King to the Duke of Hamilton hinting that the King would be generous with regard to his private interests, as well with more generic letters for the Marquis of Montrose, the Duke of Gordon, and other Scottish grandees. Hooke was given a travelling fund of 6,000 francs for expenses and a frigate to carry him to Scotland, *L'Audacieuse*, captained by James Carron who knew the Scottish waters well.

Hooke set off for Dunkirk where he was to take ship for Scotland, but there were delays. Adverse winds kept *L'Audacieuse* in port, and on

---

[6] *CP Angleterre* 218, Hooke to Torcy, June 10, 1705.
[7] *CP Angleterre* 219, June 17, 1705, from Louis XIV to Colonel Hooke, with a *pouvoir du roi*.

July 31 he wrote to Callières that "the wind still persecutes me." He was worried that the mission had been betrayed, as two English sloops off the coast were said to be looking for the ship by name. After one false start when the frigate had to return to port, the wind finally shifted, and within four days she was standing off Slains Castle, the seat of the Earls of Errol, today an evocative ruin overlooking the North Sea at Cruden Bay. Lord Perth's sister the Countess of Errol was a fervent Jacobite, and she welcomed Hooke with open arms. There was a brief scare when one of the three frigates that composed the tiny Scottish navy, the *Royal Mary*, Captain Gordon commanding, appeared from the south, but Gordon was a friend, and he and Carron agreed to stay out of each other's way. Hooke sent *L'Audacieuse* off to Norway with orders to return in three weeks to stand off Slains and await further instructions.[8]

In Scotland Hooke moved about freely. Among friends, immersed in a Jacobite sea, he was not betrayed. He reported back that some two-thirds of the Scottish lords were reliably Jacobite in their sympathies, but that since the scandal over Fraser's "Scot's Plot" there had some backsliding, in the absence of a charismatic and determined leader who could bring the quarrelsome Scots lords together under a single banner.

The obvious candidate for the role was the Duke of Hamilton, whose Jacobite sympathies were as well known as his ambition and his need for money. Hooke met with Hamilton in the dead of night at Holyrood Palace in Edinburgh, where the principal officers of state had their apartments. The two men knew each other well, having been fellow prisoners in the Tower of London after Monmouth's defeat. The devious Hamilton received Hooke in his bedroom in total darkness, explaining that he wanted to be in a position to swear on oath if necessary that he had not "seen" him. Hooke handed over the letter from Louis XIV as well as "a document showing that I am authorized to do all that is necessary for the good of Scotland, and for your Grace's own interests in particular." The devious Hamilton withdrew to an adjoining room to peruse them by candlelight.

The conversation between the two men lasted well into the night, and the sparring between the French agent and the Duke ended in stalemate. Hamilton wanted French money up front – to buy votes in Parliament, he said – and the prudent Hooke wanted to see some action first. Hamilton charged that France wanted only was a diversion in Scotland that would force the English to draw off troops from the continent

---

[8] The Hooke mission to Scotland of 1705 is described in Gibson, *Playing the Scottish Card*, 41-65.

– precisely the French aim, as Callières's *mémoires* make clear. Hooke responded that this was a calumny spread by Westminster. If he were exposed and ruined, Hamilton wondered, would Louis XIV make over to him the Duchy of Châtellerault, gift of an earlier French monarch to an ancestor as a reward him for his role in arranging the marriage of Mary Queen of Scots to the French Dauphin? After much debate, and several more clandestine meetings, Hooke concluded that Hamilton was hopeless: "During the three nights I spent in his company it was all endless argument. He asked for one hundred thousand pounds of sterling to bring matters to a break, but he would not bind himself in any way, which brought me to conclude that there was nothing to be done with him."[9]

Hooke was right to suspect that Hamilton was toying with him. His wife's considerable estates were over the border in Lancashire, and they would be forfeit if he sided openly with the Jacobite cause. On September 1, the day after his last meeting with Hooke, the Duke suddenly proposed in Parliament that Queen Anne should be allowed to choose the Scottish commissioners who would go to London to negotiate the terms of a union with Scotland, thus ensuring that the English would in effect be negotiating with themselves. There was an uproar from the Jacobite members when they learned of Hamilton's betrayal, but the measure passed by a slim majority of four votes.

Hooke suffered badly from seasickness, and he returned to France after a harrowing and dangerous voyage somewhat the worse for wear. On September 29, he wrote to Callières en route to Fontainebleau that he would be at court in a few days, and he asked that Callières inform Chevreuse of his arrival and "give an order to one of your people to find me a room, and leave a note at the poste when I get in to tell me where I should go." Callières appears to have invited Hooke to stay with him, since when Lord Perth wrote to Hooke on October 16 he asked that Hooke "give my humble service to Monsieur de Callières and to the Nuncio." (On October 23, Perth asked Hooke to "give my service with all my heart and soul to M. de Callières."[10])

HOOKE'S SECOND MISSION

Despite the inconclusive discussions with Hamilton, the disaffection of the Scots with England continued to grow. In June of 1706 Charles Fleming, a first cousin of Lord Perth, arrived in Paris as an emissary from two of the the principal Scottish leaders, Gordon and Errol. (Maximilian Emmanuel's

---

[9] Gibson, *Playing the Scottish Card*, 59.
[10] Hooke, 371, 436.

officials in the Spanish Netherlands had detained Fleming as a possible spy, and at Hooke's request, Callières intervened with Torcy to secure his release.[11]) On his arrival, Fleming told Callières, accurately as it turned out, that the Scottish Parliament was about to convene to adopt the Treaty of Union. French defeats (*mauvais succès*) in Flanders and in Spain had discouraged the Scots, Fleming said, and he offered to return immediately to Scotland to raise an army of 20,000 men. Callières supported his case, arguing again that once the Scots had taken up arms, the "persecuted Catholics in Ireland" would follow suit, forcing the English to withdraw all their troops from Flanders and Spain.[12]

Finally, in March of 1707, Colonel Hooke returned to Scotland. He had been at the front throughout 1706 at the head of his *Régiment de Sparre*. (After his capture following the negotiated surrender of Menin in July, Marlborough had met with him to try to elicit French terms for a negotiated peace, but the prudent Hooke refused to be drawn.) This second mission must have been preceded by another *mémoire* from Callières but the only trace of it is a revealing cover note to Torcy: "Monseigneur, here is the *mémoire* you wanted from me. I have tried not to leave anything out that may demonstrate the importance of this affair, and I have only set down well-established facts. I hope you can make use of it in the King's service, by adding to it your wise observations in order to dispel the unfortunate hesitation that has resulted in the blocking of the great benefits we could gain from this diversion. But I am afraid that we are like Cassandra in the Iliad, who announced truths no one would believe."[13]

Both Perth and Middleton, for once on the same page, wanted Fleming to go with Hooke, and Perth wrote Hooke on March 3 that his connection to Perth's sister the Countess of Errol could be useful. Middleton argued that since Fleming had not been seen at Saint-Germain he had not been compromised. But Callières, fearful of leaks whenever Scots were involved, responded that "ministers were opposed to his going from the first," and Torcy declined to intervene. Fleming stayed in France.[14]

Hooke arrived at Dunkirk on March 22, 1707, and again there were delays and an indication that Pontchartrain, the Navy Minister, was not

---

[11] Hooke II, 5.

[12] *CP Angleterre 1706, supplément, mémoire* from Callières to Torcy, Versailles, June 8, 1706.

[13] Callières's note to Torcy is juxtaposed with a copy in a secretary's hand of Callières's March 1705 *mémoire sur les affaires d'écosse*, cited above, of which the original is in the *BnF, Fonds Renaudot*, NAF 7487, 360-371. The date of the note is clearly March 1707.

[14] Hooke II, Perth to Hooke, March 3, 1707.

entirely on board with the scheme. He was supposed to have had two ships waiting for him in port, one a decoy, but there was only one, he reported to Callières and Chevreuse, and even it wasn't ready, a little sloop of only 16 guns. Those who sent him obviously cared little for his security: "since an affectionate and courageous zeal is scorned," he wrote bitterly, "I will try to moderate it in the future, as so many others have done." After three days the winds turned adverse. Hooke had to confine himself to his room in an inn for fear of exposure by English agents in the port who might recognize him. "How I wish you ill, for having persuaded me to undertake this trip," he wrote ruefully to Callières.[15] He commended to Callières's care his "second self"—his wife, a former lady-in-waiting to Mary of Modena, who had given birth to a child a few months earlier. On the 24th, still in Dunkirk, poor Hooke wrote again to Callières. The ship was still not ready and he had been sick, with cold sweats and bouts of fainting, but Callières was to say nothing of this to her. In a postscript, he added that the ship was to be ready "by Sunday," but on the 28th he reported to Callières that the winds were still adverse. On April 17, after almost a month during which he was "a prisoner in my room" for fear he would be recognized in the streets of the port, Hooke was still in Dunkirk. Finally after a difficult crossing, the seasick Hooke arrived again off the castle at Slains, reaching Edinburgh just in time to hear the ringing of bells ring on May 1 in celebration of the Act of Union.

The adoption of the Act of Union which carried with it the demise of an independent Scotland solidified Scottish opinion in favor of an open appeal for French assistance, and Hooke easily collected the signatures of the principal lords, excepting only Hamilton, to a "Memorial" to Louis XIV. It promised an uprising as soon as James Francis Edward Stuart, known to history as the Old Pretender, just come of age at 18, could set foot on Scottish soil. The Scots asked for arms and munitions for an Army of 25,000 infantry and 5,000 cavalry. They would themselves supply the senior officers for this force but "we want majors, lieutenants, and sergeants to discipline them" they wrote.[16] Money would be needed too, 100,000 pistoles or 600,000 francs as an initial amount – the same figure Callières had mentioned. Prominent Presbyterians and Episcopalians, Cameronians and cavaliers alike, all joined in the appeal, united for once by the loss of Scotland's independence. Even the conniving Hamilton sent a letter of his own in cipher to Queen Mary at Saint-Germain, using the

---

[15] Hooke II, Hooke to Callières, March 22, 1707.
[16] Gibson, *Playing the Scottish Card*, 93-4.

peculiar alias of Sara Brown, to say that "if help doesn't come soon, all will be at risk."[17]

By June 23, Hooke was back in Paris. The Memorial from the Scots had breathed new life into the Scottish enterprise, and Hooke was anxious to keep its contents secret from Saint-Germain. He wrote to Callières to say that he had called at his house several times but failed to find him at home. He warned that Lord Perth's sister Lady Anne Crosly was indiscreet and not to be trusted. John Murray wrote to Hooke to say that he had run into Lady Anne at Callières's house on the 28th, and she had told everyone present that he had been in Scotland. Referring to Middleton and his faction, Murray wrote that "the blackguard boys know our story exactly in the letter."

With the support of Chevreuse and Beauvillier, Hooke and Callières pressed hard for a response, but there was continued opposition from the rival ministers for the Army and Navy, Chamillart and Pontchartrain. They would have to find the ships and men for the enterprise, inevitably at the expense of another theater of war at a time when France was hard pressed on all fronts, and they dragged their feet.

CALLIÈRES MAKES A PLAN

Finally, on August 1, 1707, a detailed "Proposal by the Duke de Chevreuse, Monsieur de Callières, and Mr. Hooke, for the Scottish Enterprise" was drawn up in great secrecy, eleven pages in manuscript.[18] Thanks to Hooke's notation in English at the top of the first page, we know precisely where and when it was composed. Hooke wrote that "This project was composed by the Duke of Chevreuse, M. de Callières, and me, at the Hotel de Luynes, rue St. Domingue (*sic*), Faubourg Saint-Germain, in Paris, on August 1, 1707. It was sent by the said Duke to M. Chamillart the next day; it is an original in M. de Callières's hand, with some corrections in the Duke's hand."

Callières's proposal was both a detailed planning document and an argument for the enterprise. It declared that the Scots had promised to field a force of 30,000 men and it provided a detailed list of the equipment they needed. Not content with an uprising in Scotland, they proposed to carry the fight into England itself. They would seize Newcastle and its coal,

---

[17] *CP Angleterre* 222, *supplément*, 'Sara Brown' to Queen Mary, May 19, 1707.
[18] *CP Angleterre* 222, *supplément*, 455-461, *Projet par le duc de Chevreuse, M. de Callières, et Mr. Hooke, sur l'enterprise d'Écosse*. The Hôtel de Luynes, demolished in 1900, was built by the famous Mme de Chevreuse (1600-79), subsequently Duchess de Luynes. It was across from the rue du Bac on the corner of the rue Saint-Dominique.

without which London would freeze in the coming winter, and they believed they could take London itself before Queen Anne could call her troops back from Flanders. The force would gain converts on the way: "English history shows that there has scarcely ever been a King who has not been recognized when he has crossed over with troops. Among the many examples are Henry VI and Edward III, who were crowned within three months." (The more recent example of William III was perhaps considered impolitic to cite.)

Before finally committing themselves, Callières wrote, the Scots wanted to be sure that the Stuart Pretender would be himself at the head of his troops. This was the only way to avoid a prolonged civil war. The enterprise would be not a conquest or an act of aggression, but an "act of justice that will restore public tranquillity." Even if Queen Anne did manage to find enough loyal troops to oppose her brother the King, which was by no means apparent, and even if she managed to push the Scottish troops back across the border, she would still be deprived of forces for use against France in Flanders.

The Scots were united "at the moment," the drafters asserted, and strong enough to take over Scotland. They needed only enough troops from France to secure the initial landing, after which those troops could be returned. They had asked for 8,000 troops, and their preference was for the Irish brigades now in France. While they would leave the choice to the King, as leader of the expedition the Scots recommended Marshal Berwick, who had just won a victory for France at Almanza. (As the son of James II and Arabella Churchill, Berwick was both the half-brother of the Pretender and Marlborough's nephew.)

The proposal detailed the considerable logistical requirements of the Scots. French troops would be needed, and enough powder for 30,000 men, six pieces of field artillery, mortars, bombs, bullets, and grenades. Twenty frigates of 20-40 guns each would be required to transport the force. Operational secrecy would be an absolute requirement given the effective English control of the Channel, and the proposal included an elaborate deception plan. Frigates would be pre-positioned at Brest, Rochefort, Port Louis, Le Havre, and Dunkirk. While they were being made ready, orders would be sent to nearby garrisons to prepare for a deployment on the pretext of a relief in place of the garrisons of the Channel ports. Three battalions and a regiment of dragoons would be redirected to rendezvous with the frigates at Dunkirk, and their real orders would be revealed to them only after they had set out.

"As we are prepared to show," the drafters wrote, aware that the proposal would be closely scrutinized by Pontchartrain and Chamillart, each frigate could embark 250 men within two days. Since this piecemeal

method of embarking troops was an innovation, the English would not
detect it. To prevent leaks, Saint-Germain would be kept in the dark as long
as possible, and secrecy maintained at all costs. At the last minute the
Pretender would be bundled out of Saint-Germain in the dead of night,
arriving in Dunkirk with only "a modest suite," If the expedition sailed in
September there would be little risk, as the English rarely sent a squadron
off Dunkirk to patrol the sea-lanes to Scotland so late in the season.
Provided the winds were favourable, the entire invasion fleet could be off
the "River of Edinburgh" – the Firth of Forth translates with difficulty into
French – within two days. The fleet could land in complete safety at Leith,
the Pretender would be proclaimed in the city, and the population would
rally to him.

The drafters dealt with the objection that it would be enough to
simply send arms and powder to the "Presbyterians" of Scotland –
Middleton's counter-proposal perhaps – by saying that this would be a half-
measure. In classic Callières fashion, they argued that "this diversion alone
will ... destroy the Bank of England and the City of London where the
principal financial force of His Majesty's enemies lies," forcing the Dutch
to sue for a separate peace. In a final argument designed to sway Louis
XIV, they maintained that this was the only way to keep Philip V on his
throne of Spain.

For purposes of coordination, the Scots sent an emissary to France.
He was James Ogilvie, the son of the Earl of Boyne, a fervent Jacobite who
would go on to fight in the 1715 rising. (Ogilvie is referred to in the Hooke
papers as the "Younger of Boyne".) Ogilvie had written to Callières on
May 27 to give notice of his intention to come over, and on arrival in
Dunkirk, traveling under the name of Elphinstone, he cited Callières as a
reference to the port administrator. By October he was in Paris. [19] He wrote
to Hooke on the 29th that "Callières did me the honor to call here yesterday,
but I was with the E.M. [Earl Middleton] He has promised to use his
endeavors that my business may be expeded [sic] before the court goes to
Marly."[20] On November 13, Ogilvie wrote to Hooke that "it seems that my
friends at the French court have entirely forgott me, which seems a little
strange to me, and in a disparaging reference to Callières," he complained
to Hooke that "the person I trusted has not credit to raise money." Three
days later, Hooke responded from Versailles that "you will soon have an
ordonnance for 1000 crowns. M. de Callières has followed it with more
earnestness than he would have done for himself."[21] Eventually, Callières

[19] Hooke II, 279.
[20] Hooke II, 502.
[21] Hooke II, 513.

found Ogilvie what in the world of espionage is called a safe house, where he and other Jacobites could be kept in isolation. Ogilvie wrote to Hooke that "I have got a very pretty house at Montrouge by Mr. de Callières's recommendation where you and your lady will be extremely welcome, but no money as yet, which is hard." It was a village Callières knew well, having negotiated its purchase from the Vitry family for Morsztyn as part of the Châteauvillain estate. There Oglivie drafted a paper to be sent back to Scotland, and Hooke offered to put it into French so that it could be shown to Callières. (Despite all his dealings with the Jacobites, unlike Renaudot who was by now out of the picture, Callières still had no English.)

A FAILURE OF NERVE

Preparations for the invasion continued throughout the fall of 1707, very much along the lines of the plan drawn up by Callières, Chevreuse, and Hooke, but far more slowly than they had wanted. As they had recommended, the troop movements to Dunkirk were disguised as routine rotations, and the size of the force at 5000-6000 thousand men was about what they had recommended, but as a timetable September proved to have been hopelessly optimistic. Marrying up so many troops with ships and loading them in preparation for a complex amphibious operation was easier to describe in theory than to manage in practice, even if the relevant ministers had been fully in support of the Scottish enterprise, which was far from being the case.

As the commander at sea, the King chose the Count de Forbin, a sea dog with a well-deserved reputation for dash and bravado. In a distinguished naval career, Forbin had accompanied a French embassy to Thailand, remaining behind to train the Thai navy, and in the current conflict he had commanded Dunkirk privateers with great success, carrying out damaging raids on allied shipping in the North Sea. Forbin was a nephew of the Forbin-Janson who had been Callières's colleague (and critic) in Poland in 1674, now Cardinal de Janson and an influential voice at court after a series of Ambassadorships, including the one in Rome where he had rebuffed Baron Rose.

From the beginning, Forbin was adamantly opposed to the expedition — or so he maintained after the fact in his memoirs.[22] He told Pontchartrain would sooner take the same number of ships and men and attack Amsterdam directly. It was an exaggeration to say that Scotland was on the brink of revolt, he told the minister, and the expedition would be a

---

[22] Forbin left an account in his *Mémoires*, 240-62.

waste of six thousand good men. He doubted that they could even be landed. Informed by the minister of the plan drawn up by Callières, Hooke, and Chevreuse, Forbin was aghast, exclaiming "Who is the fool who drew this up!"[23] Someone who knew nothing of naval affairs appeared to have "counted on his fingers" that twenty ships could embark the six thousand men at 300 per ship, but that asumed they would be slow transports rather than the fast frigates needed to evade the blockading English fleet in the Channel.

Pontchartrain told Forbin to "stop philosophizing" and get on with it, but he did agree to adjust the composition of the fleet to meet Forbin's objections. A powerful naval squadron was assembled that included some twenty fast Dunkirk privateers, each of twenty to thirty guns, escorted by five ships of the line, a total of thirty-three ships. Still convinced that the expedition was doomed, Forbin appealed to his uncle the Cardinal, who was not in on the closely guarded secret, but he declined to intervene, suggesting that instead Forbin speak directly to the King about his misgivings. Forbin did so in taking his final leave of Louis XIV at Versailles, but the King refused to hear him out, forewarned perhaps by Pontchartrain. Forbin's doubts were to have fatal consequences for the expedition.

As for a land commander, the able and charismatic Berwick was the obvious choice, as recommended by Callières, Chevreuse and Hooke. Instead, on Chamillart's recommendation Louis XIV chose the undistinguished Count de Gacé, a Matignon in the market for a Marshal's baton. Saint-Simon describes him as a "good fellow, and an *honnnête homme*, but without wit, capacity, or any reputation for military skill," and implies that he got the position only because of his business connections with Chamillart.[24]

It was impossible to camouflage the movement of 6,000 men to Dunkirk from the English and Dutch agents in the port, but elaborate precautions were taken to disguise their ultimate objective. In early December of 1707, an English agent in Paris reported that Forbin had been given command of a squadron at Dunkirk, though for what purpose he could not say. Even Dangeau was kept in the dark. On February 29, 1708 he wrote that "thirty ships are being prepared at Dunkirk and in the

---

[23] Forbin atttributes the plan to "the bureaus," and it presumably reflected the detailed preparations of the naval and army ministries, but its main outlines were clearly set out in the August 1 plan drawn up at the Hôtel de Luynes.

[24] S/S III, 87-100, contains the Duke's account of the Scottish Enterprise. In his narrative, Hooke goes to Callières after the Act of Union, and Callières enlists Chevreuse and Beauvillier. This conveys the essentials without the messy complications of the facts.

neighboring ports. The ground troops in the coast are deploying, and several other battalions are being sent to the area. This is giving rise to much speculation in Paris and here, and it is even, it seems from the reports, creating concern in Holland and in England."

The first indication that Scotland was the fleet's destination reached Whitehall only in mid-February, and it was not until early March that Queen Anne's ministers learned from their agents in France that the Stuart Pretender had been hustled out of Saint-Germain and taken to Dunkirk, which made the fleet's objective clear. Feuding Whigs and Tories closed ranks in light of the threat, recognizing that a revolt in Scotland could easily spread to Ireland, and even to Flanders where the population was restive under English and Dutch occupation. A squadron under Sir George Byng was quickly assembled to keep watch off the coast. Byng could clearly see the large fleet assembled in the roads, but a shift in the wind on March 1 forced him to pull back to the English coast, leaving behind only a token force to keep watch.

Byng's appearance had convinced Forbin that the enterprise had been fatally compromised, and he ordered the disembarkation of the invasion force, infuriating the nineteen-year Pretender who was recovering from an ill-timed bout of the measles. He wrote to Louis XIV to complain, and by the time the King's reply ordering Forbin to proceed arrived, Byng's fleet had disappeared, and the landing force was re-embarked. To his mother the Queen, James wrote hopefully that "My body is weak but my spirits are high. I hope my next letter will be from the Palace at Edinburgh."[25] The invasion fleet sailed for Scotland on March 6 with the ebb tide.

Reports that their rightful King was on his way with a French fleet soon reached Scotland. One observer wrote that with the exception of those in the pay of the government "in every face was to be observed an air of jollity and satisfaction."[26] One of the French frigates, *Le Protée*, separated by a storm from the main body of the fleet, had arrived early off Leith on the 12th. Emissaries told its captain from the town that the population was ready to take up arms in support of the Pretender, and the Governor of Edinburgh Castle, the Earl of Leven, whose 2,000 troops of doubtful loyalty would be outnumbered three to one by the invaders, considered whether to flee the city.

It was critical that the invasion force be landed before Byng could come up from the Channel. But somehow the highly experienced Forbin

---

[25] Gibson, *Playing the Scottish Card*, 119.
[26] Gibson, *Playing the Scottish Card*, 121.

unaccountably lost his way, making landfall off the coast of Aberdeen, some one hundred nautical miles from his intended destination. Hooke argued for an immediate landing at Montrose, where he was sure the invasion would find support, but Middleton who had also accompanied the expedition argued for returning to Edinburgh. Finally the French fleet arrived off the Firth of Forth, but with a favorable wind Byng caught Forbin at first light on the morning of the 13th preparing to disembark the by now seasick troops.

Had Berwick had been in command, rather than the lackluster Gacé, it is possible that even with the English fleet in proximity the invasion would have proceeded, but Forbin had other ideas. He resolved to save his ships instead, and after a feint he managed to escape with most of the fleet intact. There was a further discussion of landing the Pretender up the coast on the Angus shore, as Hooke had first proposed. Encouraged no doubt by Hooke, the young James believed that Scotland would rise for him even if he landed with only a few troops – but after much heated discussion Forbin's fleet straggled back to Dunkirk, leaving the Scots to reflect bitterly on what might have been.

Poor James, who had conducted himself bravely for a boy of nineteen, wanted to remain in Dunkirk and go from there to fight in Flanders as the "Chevalier de Saint-Georges," the *nom de guerre* he had chosen for himself, but Louis XIV asked him return to Saint-Germain. Saint-Simon describes the scene when James and the Queen and the rest of Saint-Germain presented themselves at Marly on April 20. It was a beautiful spring day as the Saint-Germain party advanced slowly towards the King who waited for them on the steps of the Château. "Sorrow was evident on the faces of these unfortunates," recalled Saint-Simon. To the young James, Louis XIV said gently "I am delighted to see you in good health, but I admit that it displeases me to see you here." Middleton and Perth made their bows. Middleton's was particularly obsequious, says Saint-Simon, and he thought he detected a certain coldness to him in the King's manner. Mary of Modena retired with Mme de Maintenon, while Lord Perth went off with Beauvillier and Torcy. Despite the failure, Forbin was rewarded with a pension, and Pontchartrain received a reward too, leaving Saint-Simon to muse darkly about treachery in high places and to suggest that that, after all, Forbin had served Pontchartrain well "in his way." Forbin himself says that Chamillart and Pontchartrain were mainly interested in pinning the blame for the failure on each other.

The failed French expedition of 1708 has not been of much interest to historians over the years, French or British. Failures rarely are, but it might easily have been a turning point. The tinder in Scotland was dry, and the flames would probably have spread quickly from Edinburgh, as they did a few years later in 1715. It is unlikely that the Old Pretender could have been sustained by the French on the throne of his ancestors for long, but Queen Anne and Marlborough would certainly have been forced to contend with the insurrection, withdrawing troops from the continent and creating new negotiating opportunities. Perhaps as he hoped, Callières would have been sent himself to Holland to exploit them. For over five years, he had pleaded passionately for the Scottish enterprise. At the critical point of execution, through no fault of his own, it had failed, undone by indecisive leadership and a failure of nerve.

CHAPTER FIFTEEN

ELDER STATESMAN

One can find nothing solid to rely on with regard to the actions of the English in light of their lack of logic and their bizarre nature.
– François de Callières to Cardinal Gualtieri

The failure of the Scottish diversion did no good for Callières's credentials as a foreign policy strategist, though he was not to blame for its failure. It was a dismal time at Versailles, as the War of the Spanish Succession dragged on interminably with no prospect of a settlement on terms acceptable to France. Torcy was famously on the verge of tears as he told the King of the concessions he would be forced to offer, and Louis XIV himself wept in a discussion with Beauvillier at the prospect of having to abandon the grandson he had placed on the throne of Spain. Callières had been a prophet of sorts. His warning that Bourbon glory would eventually have to be sacrificed to French interests had been prescient, but by the time Louis XIV and his ministers came around to this view, it was too late. Only overreaching by the Dutch and a change of government in England prevented Louis XIV from having to agree to a humiliating peace settlement. Callières appears to have played little or no part in the negotiations with eventually led to the Treaty of Utrecht (1713).

ENGLISH AFFAIRS

Callières did, however, stay in in close touch with the former Papal Nuncio, Cardinal Filippo-Antonio Gualtieri, his close ally in the Scottish affair, who had returned to Rome in 1706 and been appointed by the Pope as Cardinal Protector of Scotland.[1] Shortly after his return to Italy, Gualtieri had sent

---

[1] Gualtieri – or Gualterio, but he seems to have used the French version of his name – was from a family of the Papal aristocracy in Orvieto. Born in 1660, Gualtieri had long been a strong supporter of France. Writing from Rome, Claude Bernou had described him to Renaudot as "my intimate friend," and Gualtieri established a connection at that time to Bernou's patron Cardinal d'Estrées, then Ambassador in Rome. Appointed Vice-Legate in Avignon in 1696, in 1700 Gualtieri was chosen from the list of three nominees submitted to Louis XIV by the Pope as Papal Nuncio. His appointment coincided with the election of Clement XI whose attitude to France was far more congenial than that of his predecessor, and he quickly earned the King's gratitude by agreeing to call on his legitimized offspring
(continued)

Callières a *mémoire* in Italian that judging from Callières's reply appears to have been a proposal for direct French intervention in England itself. The Cardinal told Callières that his intention was to send it to send to Queen Mary, but Callières urged that instead it be put in French, copied "in a clear hand," and sent directly and privately to Louis XIV. He assured Gualtieri that ministers would not object, though he would prefer that his own hand in the matter not be revealed:

> Your Eminence is a foreigner who has no claims here that could excite jealousy, and no interest besides that of the King's service. I do not believe that delicacy with regard to our ministers should prevent Your Eminence from giving the King so beneficial a counsel, and I have too good opinion of their zeal and capacity to suspect them of objecting .... As for the translation, I would work on it with M. Lavoisier if I weren't obliged to go to Versailles where I will be until Thursday .... Such great interests should not be outweighed by small scruples of this sort .... I believe that one must always put the public good first.[2]

Gualtieri's scruples aside, Torcy would not have been pleased had he known that Callières was conniving with a foreign envoy behind his back.

In June of 1707, Callières wrote to Gualtieri to say that he would always have the support of France, and "if I can do you any service, I will always be ready to try." In October of that year Callières responded to two letters from Gualtieri, one of which was delivered by the Abbé Passionei, a dashing and ambitious young papal emissary who had brought the news of Gualtieri's election as Cardinal. (Passionei would go on to serve French interests as an undercover agent during the Utrecht peace negotiations.[3])

Callières's letters to the Cardinal contain news of the French court, from the daring kidnapping in 1707 by Flemish partisans of the Marquis de Beringhem, to the death of the Dauphin, but England was their principal focus. In November of 1707, as the Scottish enterprise was getting underway, Callières had sent Gualtieri a letter from Louis XIV (he noted that he had drafted it himself) in which the King thanked Gualtieri for his congratulations on the birth of an heir to Philip V of Spain. In his own letter

---

the Dukes of Maine and Toulouse, which his predecessor had declined to do. This ruined his reputation in Rome, but it earned the lasting gratitude of Louis XIV, and from then on Gualtieri acted more an advisor to Louis than as a representative of the Pope. Gualtieri's extensive correspondence in code with Saint-Simon, much of it sent through Callières, has unfortunately been lost. See the remarkable monograph of A. Baschet, *Le duc de Saint-Simon et le cardinal Gualtieri*.

[2] *Je crois qu'il faut toujours aller au bien public.*

[3] On Passionei see Bély, *Espions et ambassadeurs au temps de Louis XIV*, 189 and *passim*. He became a Cardinal and the Vatican Librarian, and was even regarded as *papabile* at one point.

to Gualtieri, without mentioning the plans for an invasion, Callières expressed the view Marlborough faced a "formidable cabal" in opposition to his plans – accurately enough as it turned out – adding that it was the Duke's own fault for having blocked peace negotiations "for his own reasons," an allusion to Marlborough's reputed venality. By June of 1709, after the failure of the Scottish enterprise, Callières was less optimistic about the European situation, writing that "the disgraces of the last campaign" had emboldened France's enemies to make outrageous demands.

In July of 1710, Callières wrote happily to Gualtieri that Marlborough was under attack over the "great fortune he has gained at the expense of the people," as well as the high-handed ways of his wife Sarah, who had alienated Queen Anne. (The Duchess of Marlborough had been banished by then from the court.) A few days later, he wrote with more hope than good sense that divisions in England had reached the point that "there is no doubt that they will produce a civil and religious war." He thought that Queen Anne was caught between Whigs and anti-war "Anglicans," as Callières called the Tories, and that the latter were likely to gain the upper hand. In this regard, Callières proved to be right.

In September of 1710, Callières wrote to say that he had spoken to the King about the Cardinal in passing on the Cardinal's thanks for the Abbey of Saint-Rémy, a lucrative preferment Louis had granted to Gualtieri:

His Majesty responded with every possible show of his esteem and particular friendship for you. He said he had always loved you, and that he knew you loved him as well. I told him that you had gone to your diocese where your presence was necessary to arrange things so as to be better able to serve him in the future. He responded that he had no doubt of it, with all the grace native to him, as you know. This was in his cabinet, and as I was alone with him I had all the time I needed to tell him what I know of you, and what I think of you.

The image of the two old men talking together about their absent friend is an affecting one. By this time it is clear that Callières had forged a personal relationship of sorts with his royal master.

By the summer of 1711, Callières had persuaded himself that things were finally moving in the right direction in England. Marlborough had been disgraced, as he had predicted, accused of corrupt practices, and Abigail Masham was the Queen's new favorite. In April of the following year, he wrote that he was pleased to hear that Gualtieri was in Rome, "where you can use your talents for our great monarch." (Gualtieri had openly declared his allegiance to France by placing the Bourbon lilies on the door of his residence.)

In January of 1713, there was the prospect of Gualtieri's return to France — "what joy if I see you in May," Callières wrote — and in fact Gualtieri arrived in June. There was even a rumor that the King would appoint Gualtieri his Prime Minister, and Saint-Simon records the nervousness of the King's ministers over the Cardinal's impending arrival, but after some time spent at Marly with Louis XIV, Gualtieri returned to Rome.

By May of 1714, Callières was convinced that the Whigs were resolved to bring over the Elector of Hanover on the death of Queen Anne, and he told Gualtieri that he was persuaded that if the Pretender could only find a way to cross over to Scotland he would find much support: "you know the unhappy state this Prince is reduced to, can't the Pope express himself in some way?" In June, Callières concluded — prematurely and wrongly, as it turned out — that the Whigs had failed in their plan to bring over the Elector of Hanover, and he argued again to Gualtieri that all that was needed was a little external assistance to the Pretender: "If I have dwelled on this, it is because it is the most important thing in Europe."

When despite his confident predictions the Elector of Hanover was crowned George I of England, and in Scotland the Earl of Mar raised the Jacobite standard, once again Callières was hopeful. On August 4, 1715, he wrote to Gualtieri that there were new reasons to predict the success of the Jacobite cause — but he added a disclaimer: "It is true that one can find nothing solid to rely on with regard to the actions of the English, in light of their lack of logic and their bizarre nature."[4] He predicted, accurately, that the Pretender would cross over soon, and "if that happens I think he will begin in Scotland, where he will be safer given its inaccessibility. His greatest problem isn't the crossing, he could do that with a single frigate, but to do so with the money and arms for those that lack them, given that the Highlanders are already armed ...."

The rebellion led by the Earl of Mar had initial success, and the Pretender finally crossed into Scotland in December, with French authorities turning a blind eye and providing covert assistance, but in the absence of a charismatic leader, the rebellion soon lost momentum, the fickle Highlanders gave up the fight, and returned home to their mountains. James Francis Edward Stuart had to be evacuated on a French frigate. Callières wrote sadly to Gualtieri: "I do not doubt that Your Eminence has been deeply touched by the ill success of the enterprise of the King of

---

[4] "*À cause de leur inconséquence et de leur bizarrerie naturelle.*"

England. Though it is true that it was glorious for him, I wish for religion's sake that it had been better."

AT THE ACADEMY

After the failure of the Scottish expedition, Callières gave an increasing amount of time to the *Académie française*, regularly attending its twice weekly sessions, often with only Renaudot and a few others.[5] He was rarely present until 1705, but by 1715 his presence at the Louvre is recorded at most of the Academy's meetings, suggesting that his presence at the King's side was required less and less.

When on September 1, 1715 Louis XIV died, there was a crisis when the Regent, Philippe d'Orléans, informed the immortals that he intended to requisition their space in the Louvre, and he invited them to move upstairs into another room to be shared with the Academy of Science. Callières led the counterattack against this assault on the legacy of the Sun King, the Academy's patron, and on October 4, with the Abbé de Dangeau and the classical scholar André Dacier, he went to see the Duke d'Antin, a prominent member of the Regent's council, to appeal for a reprieve. Dacier's account in the register of the Academy records that "we went, the Abbé De Dangeau, me, and Monsieur de Callières, to the hôtel of the Duke d'Antin, and not finding him home we went to wait for him at the house of Monsieur de Callières."[6] When the Duke returned, he capitulated quickly to the delegation of aging immortals, telling them that in light of infirmities which made it difficult for them to climb stairs, he would rescind the order.[7]

A second problem arose in connection with the Academy's memorial ceremony for Louis XIV, and here again Callières intervened in defense of the memory of his master. The Academy had decided to hold a ceremony in the chapel of the Louvre, and there were to be two eulogies, one in prose and the other in poetry, the first by the Abbé de Caumartin, and the second by Houdart de La Motte, a poet and dramatist. Callières was outraged when both men subsequently tried to back out.[8] With the Regent rapidly sweeping out the old régime with a new broom, it could be

---

[5] A detailed record of his regular attendence is preserved in the Academy's registers, Doucet ed., *Les registres de l'Académie françoise*, 1672-1793. See also Waquet, *François de Callières*, 69.

[6] The Hôtel d'Antin was close to Callières's house on the rue Neuve Saint-Augustin.

[7] Doucet ed., *Les registres de l'Académie françoise*, 1672-1793, 602.

[8] Caumartin was a wit who had infuriated Louis XIV by making fun of the empty-headed Bishop of Noyon on the occasion of his reception by the Academy with a fulsome and over-the-top speech, *S/S*, I, 193-6.

dangerous to dwell too much on the glorious past. Callières had become director *pro tem* of the Academy on October 7 in the regular rotation, and the usually bland record of the Academy's deliberations says that he "insisted strongly" that the ceremony should proceed and the eulogies delivered as planned, referring to the eruption of "great disputes." In the end, Caumartin was let off the hook, but Houdart de La Motte was prevailed on to reconsider, and on December 19, in the chapel of the Louvre, he pronounced both a prose eulogy and a funerary Ode to the Sun King. It was left to a librettist named Antoine Danchet to celebrate the dawn of a new era with a poem in praise not of the Sun King, but of the Regent.

ON NEGOTIATING WITH SOVEREIGNS

Even before the Academy's funeral service for Louis XIV took place, Callières had decided to publish *On Negotiating with Sovereigns*. Callières clearly hoped to publish the book in the King's lifetime, but its implicit criticism of the King's choice of envoys made that impolitic for the King's private secretary. Although he located the examples of incapable negotiators safely in the past, to cast doubt on the French way of negotiation was to reflect on the Sun King's own judgment. As we have seen from the Hooke letter to Callières, the manuscript was circulating within a select circle as early as 1704. There are three manuscripts extant with a dedication to Louis XIV. Jean-Claude Waquet who has made a close study of the various texts concludes that it may have been written while Callières was negotiating in Holland. While this is possible, it is unlikely that Callières could have found either the time or the inclination to compose *On Negotiating with Sovereigns* in Holland, when he had other besetting claims on his time. It is far more likely to have been composed after his return to France in 1698, perhaps during the period before his appointment as principal secretary on the death of Rose in 1701 when his duties required attendance on the King only three months of the year. He would have had considerable leisure then, as well as the motivation to defend his reputation from the attacks on the Ryswick Treaty. The book carries the publication date of 1716, but the *approbatur* from Dacier on behalf of the Chancellor is dated November 13, 1715, the *privilège du roi* was granted on November 16, and it was ceded by Callières to "Michel Brunet, bookseller" on December 10.

The book fell on deaf ears. With the death of Louis XIV the stage was set for a period of reform, as the population recovered from the prolonged bloodletting of the Sun King's wars. Celebration of martial glory gave way to what Lucien Bély has called an ideology of peace.[9] New ideas were in the air, foreshadowing the Enlightenment. During the negotiations at Utrecht, Callières's colleague in the Academy, the Abbé de Saint Pierre, had published a "Proposal for a Universal Peace" in Europe through a grand federation of like-minded states – with a "barrier' for the Dutch in the Spanish Netherlands very much like the one Callières had proposed to Torcy.

The time was also ripe for a further institutionalization of the machinery of foreign policy of the kind that Callières suggests in *On Negotiating with Sovereigns*, with its argument for the careful selection and training of envoys. In the immediate aftermath of the Sun King's death the Marquis de Bonnac, Bonrepaux's nephew and an experienced envoy, sent Torcy a *mémoire* in which he proposed the standardization of the salaries and appointments of ambassadors and other ministers abroad.[10] Torcy's "political academy," a training program for young men of birth at the Louvre preparing to serve in embassies, had already been established. In fact, it was Renaudot, working under Torcy's direction, who drafted its internal regulations.[11] Callières would have been fully conversant with all this and more. His friends Saint-Simon and Chevreuse played central roles in the new régime being set up by the Regent in which a series of councils, the so-called *Polysynodie*, were to supplement if not replace the personal rule of the monarch.

It is possible that despite his age Callières envisioned a role for himself in this new dispensation, perhaps as an ambassador to a major power, and that the book was partly intended to advertise his credentials. There were precedents for men of his age or older having been sent abroad. Honoré Courtin had been 71 when Louis XIV had asked him to go to Holland, about the same age as Callières. It was not to be.

A LAST WORK

At the risk of anticlimax, it must be said that *On Negotiating with Sovereigns* was not the last book published by François de Callières. In 1717, as he lay dying, a book that he may have intended as a companion

---

[9] Bély, *Espions et ambassadeurs au temps de Louis XIV*, 696-749.

[10] Bély, *Espions et ambassadeurs au temps de Louis XIV*, 709-12.

[11] See the article by Maurice Keens-Soper published as an annex to Keens-Soper and Schweizer eds., *François de Callières*, which is based largely on Baschet's *Histoire du dépôt des archives des affaires étrangères*. Renaudot's *règlement* for the Political Academy is in the BnF, *Fonds Renaudot* 7487, 391-6. See also Thuillier, *La premiere école d'administration*.

volume appeared with the title *On the Science of the World, and the Knowledge Useful for the Conduct of Life.*[12] It is a curious mélange, in which advice on correct usage coexists uneasily with thoughts on statecraft, written as a dialogue between a Commander, a Marquise, and other denizens of an aristocratic salon, along the lines of his *ouvrages académiques* a generation earlier rather than the more methodical *On Negotiating with Sovereigns*. *Science du monde* had been Jacques de Callières's term for practical attainments and abilities,[13] as opposed to *science du collège*, or pedantry, and 50 years later his son was still using the term in the same sense. The *approbatur* is dated June 6, 1716, but the manuscript did not go to the publisher Étienne Ganeau until November 6, a delay that was probably the result of Callières's last illness. A review in the *Journal des sçavans* that appeared on March 29 of the following year noted that the book contained many pious sentiments appropriate for a man "not far from his end."

On the Science of the World is not an easy book to summarize, with its 310 rambling pages. There is the familiar condemnation of those "famous thieves admired by the vulgar under the name of conquerors," and a story about the Emperor Trajan, who told his friends at a banquet that they had wasted the day because they had done nothing to serve the public good. The influence of Locke is apparent:

> Sound minds examine things with care to judge them with knowledge, and to classify them in accordance with their degree of certainty: they believe those things that are self-evident, the truth of which can be demonstrated; they reject that which is false; and they suspend judgment on those things that appear to be uncertain, and whose truth they cannot penetrate. One of the great signs of their understanding and intelligence is that they know their limits and always are ready to strengthen them by the help and counsel of others.

This last work was dedicated to the Duke de Chartres, the Regent's son, then fourteen years of age. He is advised to model himself on his father "whose only care is for the public welfare" – suggesting that even at this late stage Callières may still have an interest in public office. As in his earlier books, there was helpful advice on correct usage and pronunciation. An affected court drawl was to be avoided: the imperial city is to be pronounced 'Rome', not '*Roume*', and the name of the country is 'Poland', not '*Pouland.*' Many of its themes are familiar: "It would be less imprudent to entrust the repair of a fine clock or a particularly delicate watch to a

---

[12] *De la science du monde, et des connaissances utiles à la conduite de la vie.*
[13] For example in *Traité de la fortune des gens de qualité.*

blacksmith ... than to employ a man of little wit who is ignorant of public affairs to negotiate some important Treaty with a prince or a foreign state." It was a common error to believe that negotiators had to be deceitful. Ministers of state should take care not to surround themselves with flatterers but with people who are willing to tell them the truth and correct them when they were wrong. Some of this is interesting in light of Callières's own considerable experience with ministers and their advisers, but in the end the moralizing grows tiresome. The book is forgotten today.

Callières's health meanwhile, never robust, was failing. In his letters to Renaudot from 1682-1885, Claude Bernou had worried about his stomach troubles, and in April of 1712, Callières had written to Cardinal Gualtieri that "an illness of two months from which I have scarcely begun to recover has prevented me from writing." Perhaps with the death of Louis XIV and the passing of an age, he found he had little reason to go on. With the exception of a nephew in Normandy from whom he appears to have been estranged and his two surviving sisters there, he had no family of his own. His passion throughout his life had been the "public good," and the Regent was unlikely to make use of his services in the age of the triple alliance with England and Holland. By November of 1716, he stopped attending the meetings of the Academy at the Louvre. He died in his mansion on the rue Neuve Saint-Augustine on March 3, 1717, surrounded by books and his collection of works of art sacred and profane, a refugee from the past.

THE MAN AND THE BOOK

The continued popularity of *On Negotiating with Sovereigns*, some three hundred years after it was written, is a remarkable phenomenon. It would be hard to cite another political text in French from that period still available in print in at least two editions in English translation – much less in a version that can be downloaded in digital form to an ebook reader. Callières has become inextricably identified with what we now call diplomacy and diplomatic practice – terms that would not be invented for another century, and his subject is not diplomacy but negotiation: the practical business of reaching agreements with foreign princes, codes and their uses, how much to put in dispatches, the proper limits of secret activities by envoys, and much else. As he wrote himself in a moment of frankness, politics is the domain of the contingent, and its rules are difficult to codify.

As for an assessment of the man and his life in politics, the reader will make his own, but by now it must be evident that the historical Callières bears little resemblance to the idealized envoy he presents in *On*

Negotiating with Sovereigns. He was clever and hard-working, but far too sure of himself and impatient of authority to make a successful diplomat. In Poland, in his first mission for the Duke of Savoy, he repeatedly offered to serve French interests that were not necessarily those of his master, and this may have created a reputation for duplicity. He was not called on to serve as an envoy abroad again until Louis XIV sent him to Holland some twenty years later. He was an initial success there with his energy and his industry. He liked and admired the Protestant Dutch – too much perhaps for his own good – and he brought the elaborate negotiations at Ryswick to an abrupt standstill with a last-minute gambit over Luxembourg in which his chicanery was exposed, the very thing he warns against in his famous book. Apart from two minor missions to Lorraine, in the second of which he was cast in the invidious part of the conveyor of an ultimatum before an advancing army, the King never sent him abroad again. In *On Negotiating with Sovereigns*, Callières suggests that it is better for an unreliable courtier to be kept close to the person of the sovereign, where he can do less damage, than as his representative to a foreign state. There is considerable irony in the fact that this was precisely what Louis XIV decided to do with Callières himself.

At court, his advice was often at variance with the high-minded counsels of *On Negotiating with Sovereigns*. In the book, he advises against attempts by an envoy to stir up rebellion against the state to which he is accredited on moral grounds – but in his private recommendations to Louis XIV, he suggested that encouraging an internal revolt against the Grand Pensionary, Heinsius, should be one of the tasks of an envoy to Holland, and he had himself in mind for this role. In his advocacy of the Scottish diversion (to give it that name), he was prepared to fight to the last Scot for the sake of French interests, all in the name of peace.

While he was creative, "fertile in expedients" in the phrase of the time, over a long political career he was often unlucky, a grievous sin in a statesman. His patrons tended to die at inconvenient times. But if his enterprises were not always crowned with success, it should also be remembered that in Poland, in Scotland, and in America, he was operating on the periphery of French power, often with inadequate resources or hesitant backing from Versailles.

Through it all he persevered. His career at court brought him to the center of power, and there he was a powerful and prescient voice for peace, presenting in the passionately-worded, cogent, and often prescient recommendations the views of moderates like Chevreuse and Beauvillier, and the case for peace. Saint-Simon testifies to his influence, asserting that Callières could sometimes bring ministers and even the King himself around to his point of view, and that he had the courage to dissent from the prevailing wisdom.[14]

On Negotiating with Sovereigns contains no allusion to the possibility that there might be a tension between the public good, the *bien public* of Callières's letters to the Marquise d'Huxelles, and the requirements of the King's service. But as we have seen, from beginning to end, like many another servant of princes before and since, Callières's political career was an uneasy mix of personal ambition and public duty. Nor will a reader find any reference in *On Negotiating with Sovereigns* to the idea that a negotiator's obedience to his prince may put him in conflict with his conscience, for Callières chose to write as if that conflict did not exist. To acknowledge it even in passing would have been to expose as a fictional character the idealized envoy he presents in *On Negotiating with Sovereigns*, one whose duty to his master is always identical with the public interest, and whose advice is invariably taken,. Sophisticated contemporary readers would have allowed for this, reading *On Negotiating with Sovereigns* as a text in the venerable tradition of works about the perfect courtier. The same cannot always be said for Callières's more credulous modern admirers, too often seduced by the illusion of a high-minded diplomacy conducted by disinterested professionals with which he is so closely linked. They forget that diplomacy is not so much an art as it is the practice of politics on an international scale.

While the man should not be confused with the book, there is much to admire in the long political career of François de Callières, and it would be unfair to be too harsh a judge. Callières overcame setbacks that would have broken a lesser man. He combined a passion to serve the public good with that irrepressible optimism that, as the old saying goes, is as necessary to the diplomat as courage is to the soldier. He served the French state loyally and well, and his constant concern in an age of endless wars was for peace.

Perhaps that is as good an epitaph as any.

---

[14] *S/S* I, 346-7.

MÉMOIRES TO THE KING

This is a selection from what must have been a vast array of state papers produced by Callières during his lifetime. None of them has previously been published, or indeed identified as being from the pen of Callières. The last three come from the Fonds Renaudot of the *Bibliothèque nationale de France*, written when Callières was a senior figure at Versailles, and they are among the papers that Callières preserved and left on his death to Renaudot. The fourth, from the *Fonds Clairambault* of the BnF, was written when he was a young man in late 1673 or early 1674. It would have been an embarrassment to him later, with its insistence to Louis XIV that he be sent undercover to Poland immediately, or else.

Even though they by convention these *mémoires* are addressed to the King as the source of all authority, they were probably not intended to be read by Louis XIV himself. They are too long for that. They were arguments to be deployed by Callières's allies in the *conseil d'en haut*, the policy-making body chaired by Louis XIV, so-called because it met on an upper floor at Versailles. Beauvillier and Chevreuse, as well as Torcy, would have been their intended recipients, and they would have circulated them to like-minded ministers as part of their lobbying in support of a particular policy. They belong to a genre that would be familiar to an official in a modern foreign ministry, starting with an analysis of the situation that appears to be objective and dispassionate but that is really intended to lay the basis for the recommendations that follow, concluding with practical recommendations and next step. Saint-Simon wrote that Callières could often bring the King and his ministers around to his point of view, and these papers provide some insight into how he managed that. The advocacy in them is often strident. Reading them three centuries later in another world, it is easy to forget that once these were matters of life and death, and that every word in them was carefully weighed in an existential context. The detachment of the biographer is cheaply earned.

I have tried without success to find an English translation for *mémoire*. "Memorial" was the contemporary English equivalent but it sounds antiquarian, and memorandum is clearly wrong. The solution has been to leave the term in French.

A. "THE AFFAIRS OF POLAND"[1]

Having informed His Majesty by several *mémoires* given to M. de Pomponne of what I know of Polish affairs, I believe it necessary to inform him again that:[2]

As the House of Austria is working diligently in Poland from all the reports received to form a powerful party against the party of His Majesty, which is powerful but which until now has been deprived of any assistance and even of the consolation of the presence of someone on His Majesty's behalf who could keep it united, it is to be feared that the split in the last election between the senators, the nuncios, and all of the nobility may occur again in the next election, and that with each party insisting on his own candidate, the election will be a double one, split between the son of M. de Neuburg who is the candidate of His Majesty and the Prince of Lorraine the Emperor's candidate. All other factions can be reduced to these two principal ones, next to which the rest have little support among the Poles. In this case, only the fate of arms will decide between the two principal contenders, as was the case between Sigismund of Sweden and Maximilian of Austria, which would cast Poland into a civil war, which would not suit either its present perilous state nor would His Majesty wish to uphold it.[3]

That is what makes me conclude that a third candidate will not only be well-received by the Poles, but that they will find themselves obliged to seek out a third party just as they did in the last election of King Michael in order to avoid this civil war. Since it is in the interest of His Majesty that this third candidate be devoted to him, it seems necessary to me to resolve to have one ready to propose in the event that his Ambassador concludes that it is impossible to bring about a consensus in favor of the son of the Prince of Neuburg, since prudence suggests that in the event of a stalemate we should not fall short lacking this expedient to resolve the matter.

With regard to this third candidate, it seems to me that His Majesty can only choose among three persons who are devoted to his interest, to wit Monsieur le Prince de Conti, Monsieur de Turenne, and Monsieur le Count de Soissons, all of whom are in a position to marry the Polish Queen.[4]

---

[1] *Mémoire pour Sa Majesté sur les affaires de Pologne*, NAQFR 21103, *Fonds Clairambault*, 105-7, ca. late1673/early 1674.

[2] This is added at the top of the paper, apparently as an afterthought.

[3] The syntax is confused, but the sense is that France would not find it easy to intervene against Austria in a civil war in Poland since the Austrians would have the advantage of proximity.

[4] All being bachelors.

The first has his extreme youth against him,[5] but in his favor he is a Prince of the blood of France, and thus a certain pledge of the protection of His Majesty and of a stronger and more durable union between France and Poland than any other candidate, ensuring the secret support for him of the Grand Marshal, who would through this election become in effect the Regent of the Kingdom without having the title, in a position to continue to command the Army and remain in charge of military matters.[6]

Monsieur de Turenne has against him the jealousy of the Grand Marshal, though this could be overcome according to reports, and his age, which is too advanced to enable him to appeal as a husband to the Queen of Poland. In his favor is his great experience of military matters, and Poland's need for such King in order to redress the poor state of its affairs both internal and external. Also in his favor may be counted the services he would be in a position to render to His Majesty in this post against the House of Austria, which are far greater than those a young prince without experience could offer.

The Count of Soissons is a middle ground between the two, less useful it may appear, but much more likely to succeed, since he is the right age to marry the Queen of Poland, and since he is from a foreign House there may be less opposition to him from the Austrian party, which is set against French princes of the blood. He would be much better suited and more useful to His Majesty than the son of M. de Neuburg, who by becoming the brother-in-law of the Emperor might not only attach himself to the Emperor's interests but also induce his father to the Emperor's side on the pretext of saving his lands from the evident ruin that could be caused by the Imperial Army. The good faith of German princes is suspect, as His Majesty has just seen from the violation of the word of a prince of the same House as the Duke of Neuburg who was even more pledged to his word by reason of the blood tie he had contracted.[7] His Majesty can, by contrast, rely on the actions of the other three. The first two are his subjects. With no foreign ties, while the third is from a House devoted to him, and he would leave guarantees of his conduct in the person of Madame his mother and all his family, which would remain in France.

In order to succeed, it seems to me that nothing is more necessary than to send a man to Poland immediately who knows the country with credentials for the Grand Marshal, who could go quickly to his side having

---

[5] Conti was nine years old.
[6] Sobieski.
[7] The reference is probably to Frederick William of Brandenburg, a Hohenzollern who took the Austrian side following the French invasion of Holland in 1672. He had previously agreed with Louis XIV to support Neuburg in Poland.

conferred while passing incognito through Warsaw with the Grand Treasurer[8] from whom he could derive great insights, in order to prepare the way for His Majesty's Ambassador, and to begin to dissipate the cabals of the Prince of Lorraine and strengthen the friends of France on the right side, contriving meetings and councils between them and substituting by his activity for the innate laziness of the Grand Marshal, who though he is well-disposed requires the continued urging of someone in his entourage pretending to be a member of his household[9] to encourage him to carry out the decisions necessary to bring this affair to the desired end. Otherwise the Ambassador who will not be able to arrive until late in the day will find this business in complete confusion[10] and he will find it difficult in the short time remaining to destroy the cabals of His Majesty's enemies unless he is informed by this precursor of what he has uncovered and will continue to uncover by his comings and goings, working under the Ambassador's orders in this vast kingdom where there is work enough for several persons, and where there are already several agents of the Prince of Lorraine on the ground in addition to the Emperor's Resident at Warsaw. They will all be advantaged more than one can imagine by the slightest delay in sending in sending someone to firm up the principal supporters of His Majesty's party, who have been shaken by their offers.

As I have already said, this person should be knowledgeable of the country, but his face should not be well known so that he can continue to come and go in the houses of the principal men of the French party without being unmasked as a French agent, which would ruin all his practices. Moreover, if in accordance with customary practice all foreign envoys are required to withdraw (from Warsaw), he would be able to stay, continuing his practices and gathering intelligence under the Ambassador's orders.

As during my previous stay in this country, I was careful not to be known as what I was to anyone but a few of the principal men of the French part, whose trust I acquired. Having worked with some success on the affair that was entrusted to me, and as I am particularly well-informed with regard to the manner of dealing with these gentlemen in order to advance His Majesty's interests, I flatter myself that I can render good service to His Majesty in this country should His Majesty see fit to send me there immediately. The slightest delay in giving this order would cause notable damage to His Majesty's interests and benefit those of his enemies.

---

[8] Morsztyn.
[9] *Sous prétexte d'être l'un de ses domestiques.*
[10] *Trouvera la matière fort indigestie.*

B. "HOW TO PRESERVE THE PEACE"[11]

Having seen his popularity diminish in England and in all of Europe following the acceptance of the will of the late King of Spain, the King of England will try to restore it by supporting the claims of the Emperor and by working to persuade the English and the Dutch that their security depends on enabling him to offset the combined might of Spain and France, which he represents as being prepared to invade them, or at a minimum to restrict their trade, if they give the King of Spain the time to establish himself in all his dominions, and if France is given a few more years of peace to recover from the great expenses she had to bear during the last war.

The English nation, naturally jealous of the power of France and committed to the maintenance of its maritime trade, is divided between this interest and its desire to preserve its internal privileges and to avoid the extraordinary expenses a new war would bring. Having been exhausted and burdened with debt by the last war, it is reluctant to put arms in the King's hands again, rightly fearing that he may make use of them against the privileges of the whole nation, and to revenge himself against those individuals in England who have opposed his will.

The Dutch Republic sincerely wants to preserve the peace – to question this would be to misunderstand it – but it wants a peace that is secure and lasting. The King of England has acquired a great authority in Holland by playing on the fear of France. He never misses a chance to convince the provinces and cities of this Republic that its only safety lies in the preservation of the barrier established by the last Treaty[12], that this barrier has been broken since the King became the master of the forts that compose it, and that it cannot be restored as long as it is in the power of His Majesty to dispose of it, whether by an exchange with the king of Spain or by governing the Catholic Low Countries in the name of the King his grandson. He convinces them moreover that their trade with Spain and Italy will be lost through the union of the two crowns, and that their only option to ensure their security after his death is to support the Emperor in order to exhaust France in men and money, forcing France to sue for terms.

Torn between their fear of French power and their desire to preserve the peace, the Dutch have chosen to work intensively to prepare their defenses while putting off a declaration of war as long as possible,

---

[11] *BnF*, NAF 7487, *Fonds Renaudot*, 430-441, *Mémoire touchant les moyens de conserver la paix*. The manuscript is a draft, with a few minor edits in another hand. Undated, it must have been written about October of 1701.

[12] Ryswick.

telling the King of England that they are in no position to undertake a war as long as the English nation is not in a state to declare one.

In this situation it is in the interest of the King of England not to be the aggressor, for he would be acting against the intentions of both the English and the Dutch nations, and he is obliged to cultivate them very carefully in order to lead them to his objective. Whatever power he may have it is an error to think that he rules as master. He can only succeed through persuasion, and he will fail if we only take care to destroy his insinuations by providing contrary arguments.

His current plan is to wear us out by forcing us to maintain a large number of troops to keep watch on the troops of the Dutch and their allies while the Emperor makes war against us in Italy, in the hope that our nation, which he knows to be naturally lively and impatient, will soon grow tired of wasting itself in this way, and will choose to declare war on Holland, thereby saving us the expense of maintaining troops by quartering them in the United Provinces or their nearby allies like the Duchies of Juilliers and Cleves, hoping by these conquests to force the Dutch to sue for peace.

When he sees that war has broken out in Holland, he will tell the English that the time for deliberation is over, and that their only option is to grant him all the moneys he asks for to raise an Army by land in order to oppose French conquests as the only way to prevent the ruin of the trade, the liberty, and the religion of the English nation, for which he is prepared to sacrifice himself. These are the arguments he will use to incite them against us. If we make some gains against the Dutch, they (i.e. these arguments) will not miss their mark, and the result will be that instead of forcing the Dutch to sue for peace as we flatter ourselves, they will instead invite all of Europe to come to their assistance, just as in 1672. If we enter under arms into the Duchies of Juilliers and Cleves, the King of England will demand that the King of Sweden implement the defensive Treaty he made after having mediated the peace between Sweden and Poland, and it will be difficult for us to avoid this if we are to support our ally the Elector of Cologne who will fear for his seat. Working with the Emperor, he (i.e. William) will try to induce the entire Empire to declare itself against us for having violated the Treaty of Ryswick by the hostilities we will have begun in these Duchies belonging to Electors of the Empire. By this means he will force the princes who have accepted the principle of neutrality within the Empire to follow the majority at the Diet of Ratisbon where war and peace are decided by majority vote in each of the three colleges.

In order to avoid these pitfalls, which would certainly plunge us into a ruinous and long-lasting war, we must at all costs resist the temptation to gain a few passing conquests over the Dutch and carefully avoid being the first to break the peace, assuring all the princes and states of Europe of the firm commitment of His Majesty to preserve the peace, thereby strengthening the party of armed neutrality within the Empire and adding several additional princes to it by means that His Majesty has at his disposal provided he is prepared for the expense.[13] Nothing could be more useful in the present circumstances, and no matter how considerable such expenses might be, they will not approach the cost of a long war against the greater part of Europe which these alliances are a sure way to avoid.[14]

By taking this course, His Majesty will put the King of England at a great disadvantage, depriving him of the ability to draw from his Parliament the aid he has an indispensable need of in order to make war. The Dutch will soon tire of being the only ones to bear the expenses of subsidies for their allies as well as for the great number of troops they have raised, and they will be satisfied with such reasonable guarantees as the King (of France) is willing to grant them for the preservation of the barrier and for their trade with France and Spain and the other dependencies.

To this end, they must know that the King is still disposed to offer them reasonable guarantees. Before setting out the best means of convincing them of this and entering again into a peace negotiation, whether publicly or in secret, it may be necessary to respond to the objections made to any sort of negotiation:

1 It is said that it is not consistent with the King's dignity to maintain embassies in countries preparing to make war against him and supporting his enemies.

2 That as long as they demand satisfaction for the Emperor it is pointless to negotiate with them, as His Majesty is unwilling to dismember in any way the states of his grandson the King.

3 That once again it would be contrary to His Majesty's dignity to make offers to people who are owed nothing, and that if they seek security it is up to them to ask for it.

4 That they will take any offer of ours as a proof of weakness, and rather than bringing an accommodation closer it will only make one more distant by allowing the King of England to represent to the Dutch that they have only to wait for better terms, and that having made these offers it will be more difficult to make peace with them later.

5 Finally, that this would be to offend the Spanish nation, which does not wish its monarchy dismembered in any way.

---

[13] That is by buying their support through subsidies.

[14] Instead, Louis XIV moved against the Dutch in the Spanish Netherlands, and Callières's dire prophecy was full realized.

To the first objection, if we only maintained embassies to honor those we send them to this would be justified, but as we generally send them to countries we are suspicious of as authorized spies in order to be well informed as to the situation there, in order to establish and maintain networks with the people of the country,[15] to encourage movements against the government[16] and to enable them to oppose plans that they may wish to make against the interests of the Prince who has sent them, it would be an offense against sound policy not to send them, whether or not the occasion presents itself, keeping them in place as long as possible so as not to be the first to break off relations in order to be in a position to blame the other side for the rupture, gaining thereby the support of a large number of other powers who jealous and intimidated will inevitably declare themselves against the aggressor. Applying this general rule to the present situation, nothing would be better suited to the interests of the King of England and more likely to help him persuade the English and the Dutch to join in the league he proposes against France than not to maintain Embassies in their countries, capable of speaking with the principal men in these two nations and of disabusing them of the false ideas that the King of England puts in their head with regard to the plans of His Majesty. (William III) suggests that the Embassies have been withdrawn as a prelude to a declaration of war, and that our aim is to appropriate the Low Countries in exchange for Roussillon, and to acquire as well all the other possessions of the King of Spain in the name of his grandson. This is what the magistrates of Amsterdam are told on his behalf when they argue the need for peace, and we will never overcome these arguments unless we give them proofs to the contrary.

As for the second objection, the response is that as the Dutch need to be united with the Emperor in order to obtain the security assurances they desire they must necessarily give him satisfaction in their public writings and speeches, and we must not expect that they will abandon him before they know the terms the King of Spain is willing to grant them. When we have agreed in person[17] with them it will not be as difficult as it is imagined to gain their agreement without the participation of the Emperor and to separate them from him, just as we did at Nijmegen and at Ryswick

---

[15] *Pour y former et entretenir des intelligences avec les gens du pays.*

[16] In 'On Negotiating with Sovereigns,' Callières writes (Chapter IX): "There are few services that a good subject and faithful minister does not owe to his prince and his country. But obedience has its limits, and it does not extend to acting against the laws of justice and God. They do not allow attacks on the life of a prince, provoking the revolt of his subjects, usurping his territory or inciting civil wars, after having been received under the heading of friendship."

[17] *En tête à tête.*

in addition to Munster, when they negotiated with Spain without the participation of France notwithstanding the great obligations they had, which proves that they can always be separated from their allies if they are given the right terms.

To the third objection, it may be responded that the dignity of His Majesty can scarcely be diminished if takes the initiative to set forth the conditions for peace. On the contrary, it is more lordly[18] to propose the terms, as we did in the last peace treaties, giving a deadline for them to be accepted, than to wait for them to propose more stringent terms like those given to M. d'Avaux.[19]

In response to the fourth objection, if we propose to the Dutch terms they believe are necessary for their security, having rejected their terms as insulting and exorbitant even as the King remains master of the Catholic Low Countries, they will believe as they are told that we intend to appropriate them, and that if they take precautions against this, which they believe would be the ruin of their Republic, far from imputing this to weakness they will seize on reasonable proposals that are made to them with the required dignity with joy, seeing them as the proof of the sincere desire of His Majesty to maintain the peace and not to trouble their security or their trade. Fat from making an accommodation more difficult, as a result of the promises the King of England may make that they will get better terms later, it will be easy to convince them that unless they accept the terms within the deadline proposed they will not obtain more later. The fortunes of war may change the face of things, and the ill health of the King of England who is not expected to live much longer may lead them to fear that they will not always be united with England under a new reign, and that they should not risk the fate of their state, exhausting it by the immense expenses, on the vain hopes, rather accepting our offer of peace and security now.[20]

It is arguable that if we offer them nothing at all this may cause them to sue for peace. Against this, although there are in Holland a number of magistrates who sincerely want peace, especially those of the city of Amsterdam who are the most influential, it would be to misread the nature of their government to believe that they are in a position to make

[18] *Il y a plus d'hauteur.*
[19] The French Ambassador to Holland. Saint-Simon's comment is that "The States (General) in concert with England sought only to distract us while they made their preparations." (S/S I, 811).
[20] Callières does not take up the fifth objection he has listed with regard to the dismemberment of Spanish possessions. There is a note in the margin in another hand, that "the Spanish will have no reason to complain, and this will serve as a response to the fifth objection."

compromise proposals to us. They are only one member of this Republic, and not in a position to propose anything to us. That can only be done by the seven provinces and their *stathoudre* who as the head of the Republic can prevent them from forming such a plan. A majority of the city of Amsterdam and the other well-disposed cities will agree within the assembly of the Dutch states and the estates general may be in a position to agree to proposals that have been made on His Majesty's behalf if their security is guaranteed, notwithstanding the King of England who will not have a majority of the votes unless war is declared.

To those who argue that we may be able to make peace with them later on better terms, the response is that if our offers are rejected within the deadline they will not remain on the table. And even if that were the case, in matters of this importance it is necessary to begin with the best plan possible, and seek to preserve peace on such and such a condition, making the effort to sustain war only if the conditions are too onerous to grant. We can always offer these conditions later without being suspected of weakness, especially as we are the strongest and hold everything in our hands. If our terms are accepted, we obtain peace on conditions preferable to those that have been offered; if they are not accepted we throw all the blame for the rupture on our enemies, and this will help us acquire new friends by establishing our reputation for moderation and justice with the princes and states that are not involved. This wise conduct may give rise to the creation of parties among free peoples like those of England and Holland, which have not yet lost their right to express themselves with regard to that which concerns them, nor the power to change the plans of those who govern them by refusing to give them the means to carry them out.

Finally, it is possible to preserve the peace by giving the Dutch reasonable proposals in which they will see their security requirements, and there is no reason to think that war can be avoided by any other means, as they are not in a position to make proposals to us. They must be told plainly what assurances we can offer them before we undertake a war against them, so as to put them in the wrong before mankind if they persist in the insulting propositions made to M. d'Avaux. Every day we see that the art of negotiation capably carried out can achieve more difficult things than preserving a peace that no one has an interest in breaking, with the exception of the Emperor and the King of England – and there is reason to think that even he is not as far from wanting an accommodation in the languishing state in which he finds himself, if we give him a way to agree to it without losing his credibility and his reputation.

We turn now to an examination of the surest and the quickest means, and those best suited to the grandeur of the King, to enter into a negotiation during the winter in order to reach an accommodation before the next campaign. Since war has not yet been declared against England and Holland, and they still maintain embassies to His Majesty, the King should name two Ambassadors, one to go to London after the King of England returns across the Channel, which will be around the beginning of November, and the other to be sent to Holland at the same time, both to be armed with a draft treaty to be proposed and examined publicly in the seven United Provinces, each of which has a deliberative process, as well as by the English Parliament, which will be in session and to which King William will be obliged to transmit it.[21]

This is the only way to elicit the free opinion of the English and Dutch nations, and to frustrate the tricks of those who under false colors will try to cast them into another war for the ambitions of the House of Austria, for which the Dutch and the English are not foolish enough to sacrifice their lives and goods – provided they can establish the security of their states and their trade through the propositions that will be made to them on behalf of His Majesty and the King of Spain.

It would be good to accompany this nomination with a manifesto to all the states and princes of Christendom, setting forth the reasons that have obliged His Majesty to send these two Ambassadors with the promise of sending them this plan for an accommodation after it has been communicated in England and in Holland, and urging them to be its guarantors. By following this course, His Majesty will persuade all of Europe of his moderation and of the sincere desire he has to preserve its tranquility, and he will encourage all those who love justice to join him in achieving such a good objective.

C. "HOW TO ACHIEVE PEACE"[22]

May 1705

There are two principal ways to achieve peace:

The first is to resolve ourselves to grant the enemies the terns that will oblige them to deal with us without prejudice to the glory and the core interests of His Majesty.

The second is to take the proper measures to gain the acceptance of these conditions without provoking an uprising against the King of Spain.

To expect that our enemies will approach us to seek peace would be to flatter ourselves pointlessly, as it would be to believe that they would wish to make peace without obtaining the conditions that they judge

---

[21] Callières provided draft treaties with Holland between both France and Spain.

[22] *BnF*, NAF 7487, *Fonds Renaudot*, 423-30.

necessary for themselves.

The Dutch – who will always be the easiest to deal with[23] – have been clear with regard to these terms. The first is the relinquishment of the Spanish Netherlands to a prince who is not at all suspect to them, and who could serve as a barrier, reserving for themselves only the forts of Gelderland which they conquered from Spain in order to control navigation on the Meuse as far as Maastricht, which they view as their principal fortress. They also want the forts of Spanish Gelderland because they were a part of the first of the seven provinces that compose their Republic. Even if they were offered the rest of the Netherlands, they could not accept that without exposing themselves to internal divisions between Protestants and Catholics, which would soon cause the downfall of their state.

The second condition they seek is the renewal of all their commercial treaties with Spain, with a ban on the French and any other country on trading directly with the Spanish West Indies so that this trade will only pass through the agency of the Spanish commissioners at Cadiz, as in previous reigns, or a total freedom of trade for all the nations of Europe with the ports of the Spanish Indies.

The third condition is to satisfy the claims of the Emperor, which they believe we recognized in the Partition Treaty, and which they believe they must uphold to a certain point in order to establish an equilibrium in Europe[24] , without which they will not consider themselves to be secure.

These being the real causes of the war the Dutch are waging against us, there is no reason to think that they will agree to peace until they have been given satisfaction on these three points, unless we can reduce them by the force of our arms to abandon their policy.

But as that policy is supported by the greater part of Europe, and as our enemies are much better placed than we are to raise and counter-raise great armies, whether by land or by sea, and as they have more men and ships as well the ability to obtain money at lower interest rates[25], our enemies are better placed than we are to continue the war for several more years, and they appear to be determined to continue to wage war until they get what they want.

This being the situation in which we find ourselves, the longer we put off entering into a serious negotiation with them, the more we will exhaust ourselves in means and men in this painful war without the expectation that will be able to end it under better conditions than we could get agreement to now.

---

[23] *Les plus traitables.*

[24] *Pour faire une balance en Europe.*

[25] In the margin: "The Dutch obtain loans at 4%."

That being the case, it appears that we must not put off deciding what terms might be required and the means of gaining acceptance of these terms.

If we negotiate with the court of Vienna, we can expect that it will not give up its exorbitant claims as long as it is supported by England and Holland. If we deal with England first, it will be no less difficult than the Emperor, and will demand the implementation of the Partition Treaty in order to take control of trade with Spain and exclude us from trade with the Spanish Indies.

The Dutch will be satisfied with much less difficult terms than those their envoys attached to the Emperor will begin by demanding, and we should not be put off by these terms, which it will be easy to reduce through the Good Republicans who have a sincere desire for peace, and who will be satisfied with the terms which are required for their security.

Thus it is with the Dutch that we must negotiate, not only because they are easy to deal with than the others, but because as soon as they are certain of terms that they view as necessary to them they will inevitably bring the Emperor and England along and to satisfy themselves with the terms they think reasonable as they did with the previous treaties.

When the Dutch demand satisfaction for the Emperor, at the same time they leave it to be understood that they will be satisfied as long as they can preserve the Archduke as a King by detaching from the Spanish monarchy a state with the title of kingdom, by which they mean the kingdom of Naples, without making clear all the consequences, which is very different from the implementation of the Partition Treaty which the English will demand, and the claims of the Emperor which extend to the entire monarchy of Spain, which he will only lessen if he forced to do so by the Dutch unless he gets all the Italian states and the Netherlands as well.

The separation (from the Spanish monarchy) of the Netherlands, Naples, and Sicily are therefore the terms on which peace depends if it is negotiated with the Dutch. Thus we need to decide whether it is less damaging to France to agree to this dismemberment of the Spanish monarchy or to continue the war.

There are few persons who will disagree that as the interests of France must be be more dear than those of Spain, peace is preferable to the continuation of a ruinous war to uphold the grandeur of the Spanish monarchy – particularly as by continuing this war it does not appear likely that we can avoid its dismemberment, and that even if we could avoid it with a maximum effort it would be better for France than the maintenance of the Spanish monarchy in its present state. This is easy to show, but it would take us too far from the subject of the present *mémoire*. If we agree that a longer war could destroy France without any certainty that it would

211

preserve the Spanish monarchy in its entirety, that is enough of a basis on which to conclude that we must not put off a negotiation of peace terms any longer, ceding some part of it in order to preserve the greater part while we are still masters of the whole. That being stipulated, it remains only to make the correct choice of the the peace terms and the means of gaining their acceptance by the Dutch without exposing the King of Spain to an uprising from his subjects when they learn that this dismemberment is being negotiated.

This affair can only be negotiated by either general conferences or a private ones, and since general conferences are difficult and infinitely tedious we need to enter into private conferences.

In order for them to be conducted successfully, private conferences must be held between declared and authorized representatives of the King and of the States General. The Dutch are not at all far from agreeing to these conferences, but first they insist on having a basis on which peace is to be negotiated, just as at Ryswick they negotiated on the basis of the restoration of the Treaty of Nijmegen, which His Majesty was pleased to assure them of before the start of the negotiations.

The basis they are seeking now is that they must be assured on behalf of His Majesty that he will be good enough to restore their Barrier, to guarantee their commerce, and to come to an agreement with them as to the satisfaction that will be given to the Emperor.

Until then, both sides will keep their cards hidden[26] with regard to what that satisfaction will comprise. When we have agreed with the Dutch to negotiate on this general basis, only then and not before, will it be the moment to inform the King of Spain that the Dutch having declared to His Majesty what they seek with regard to a conference on how to reach a peace agreement , His Majesty has considered it appropriate to hear their propositions out in order to inform his grandson the King, and that His Majesty will treat his interests as if they were his own.

The Spanish council[27] having been informed of these meetings by His Majesty will have no grounds for complaint, and the King will be in a position to arrange the main peace terms before the Spanish have been informed by taking the following precautions. The person or persons who is entrusted with this delicate negotiation will begin by drawing out the representatives of the Estates General on the terms they seek for their state. They will not fail to say, as was said to the person who first negotiated the Treaty of Ryswick on behalf of His Majesty,[28] that they don't want to

---

[26] *On ne se découvre point.*

[27] The *despacho.*

[28] This was Callières himself, of course.

negotiate for themselves alone, but with the participation of all their allies. He responded that he had the commission and power to negotiate all the interests of their allies, and that he was prepared to reach agreement with the representatives of Holland if they were equally entrusted with the power to negotiate by their allies. They responded that they had only those given to them by their masters. His Majesty's envoy rejoined that it would be necessary to start by reaching agreement on that which concerned them, to which they agreed, even as they protested that any agreement would be contingent on the subsequent satisfaction of their allies. But as soon as the Dutch were assured of obtaining the strengthening of the barrier and commercial advantages, which was what concerned them, they were a great deal less committed to the interests of the Emperor, and they resolved to sign their peace together with Spain and England without the Emperor, who only agreed to sign six weeks later after he saw himself abandoned.

It will be the same with the next Treaty, if we negotiate it with the Dutch. They will bring the rest of their allies along, and they will arrange with His Majesty the terms that have to do with the satisfaction of the Emperor.

But to do this securely and without exposing the King of Spain, the representatives of the States General will have to be told that there will be a discussion of this article only on two conditions.

The first is that before this discussion takes place agreement must be reached on the interests of their masters with regard to trade and the barrier.

The second condition is that after these first two articles are settled, the representatives of the States General must agree that they will join forces with His Majesty to ensure the implementation of these terms both by the Emperor and by the King of Spain all the articles agreed upon, just as they agreed to ensure the implementation of the Treaty of Partition.

Only after the Dutch representatives have made these commitments in the name of their masters will it be time to declare what His Majesty may wish to have his grandson the King cede to the Archduke for the sake of peace, and on no other ground,[29] agreeing to the guarantee of all the princes and states of Europe for the implementation of this concession.

As for the means, the easiest would be to cede the Spanish Netherlands to the Elector of Bavaria, reserving for the King the city and Duchy of Luxembourg, while ceding to the Archduke the Kingdom of Naples without Sicily if possible. As it would be difficult to gain agreement to this without adding Sicily, the ports of this island being necessary to the

---

[29] That is, without reference to the Partition Treaty.

Dutch to serve as entrepots for their trade with the Levant, we will have to be resolved to give it up if absolutely necessary having contested the ground strongly.

There is another way of ceding these territories that might suit all parties, which would be to give Naples and Sicily to the Elector of Bavaria. In exchange the Elector would cede his Duchy of upper and lower Bavaria and the upper Palatinate to the Archduke, for whom a kingdom could be created composed of these territories, just as was done with Ducal Prussia, which is of lesser importance than these lands of the Elector of Bavaria. The Spanish Netherlands would be given to the Elector of the Palatinate, who is the prince the Dutch would most like to see in charge of their barrier because of the Duchies of Julliers and Bergk, which are near these provinces, on condition that he cede to the King the city and Duchy of Luxembourg.

There is also the Duke of Lorraine, to whom the Netherlands could be given while Lorraine goes to His Majesty.

There is little doubt that one or another of these options will be accepted by the Dutch if we begin by satisfying them with regard to their trade, which is the basis of their government. As soon as they are satisfied they will oblige their allies to content themselves with what has been settled on with His Majesty, and there will then be a nearly certain means of obtaining the consent of the English court.

If His Majesty decides that it is for the good of his service to begin to negotiate with the Dutch on this basis, an early success may to be hoped for through the agency of the "good republicans" we know, and a connection can be made through one of their representatives for a meeting on their border, but there is no reason to hope that they might come any further.

D. "THE AFFAIRS OF SCOTLAND"[30]

March 1705

Conflict between the Scots and the English is as old as their two monarchies. They were always separate until 1603, when they were united under King James Stuart, and this union has only served to increase the innate antipathy between them. Currently it derives from the great losses inflicted on the Scots by the English on the occasion of their Darien enterprise; on the losses they cause daily to the Scots by hindering and preventing their trade; on the constant desire of the English to subject the

---

[30] *BnF*, NAF 7487, *Fonds Renaudot*, 360-71.

Scots, as they have subjected Ireland; and from the firm intention of the Scots to preserve their independence. In this resolution they benefit from the advantageous geography of their country, its virtually inaccessible Highlands where the English have never managed to subdue them despite their more numerous armies, which the Scots always find the strength to defeat, subsisting on oatmeal, milk, and turnips, which are found everywhere in their Highlands.

The Scottish lords are the absolute masters of their vassals in the Highlands. They are obligated to follow them to war, and when the lords decide to take up arms they can form up several small armed bodies (*plusieurs petits corps d'armée*), and they have no need of stores or parade grounds to take to the field because what they require for their subsistence is so modest that they can always find it during their passage. A reading of the history of the wars between the English and the Scots is sufficient to demonstrate this. It shows that even the greatest and most fortunate Captain the English have ever had, Cromwell, was never able to conquer the Scots, even with the same victorious armies that conquered England and Ireland, and that he was forced to purchase peace from the Scots with money.

The Scots are the friends of the Irish, as the Highlanders of Scotland are of the same nation and speak the same language. Moreover they have a great ability to provide each other with mutual assistance against their common foe the English, since there are only three leagues of sea between them, which can easily be crossed in small boats between the North of Ireland and the nearest point in Scotland at the peninsula of Kintire.

The Scottish nation has taken the decision to shake off the yoke that the English would impose, and this has been made so public by the recent laws adopted by the Scottish Parliament and their implementation that the English of the court of Saint-Germain, who have always treated as fantasies the reports that have come to us over and over from the principal lordsof Scotland have finally been obliged to admit the truth.

The alarm taken by the English Parliament and the laws it has passed to oppose the laws adopted by the Scottish Parliament and prevent them from taking effect are the irrefutable proof of this, and there can be no question of having to prove that which no one can doubt any longer. The time has come to take advantage of this favorable inclination of a nation as warlike as the Scottish nation to force the King's enemies to purchase peace on terms glorious for His Majesty, by helping the Scots achieve the objectives set out in the law adopted by the last Parliament, which they call the Act of Security.

This Act of Security provides that within twenty days of the death of Queen Anne the last Parliament will reconvene and proceed to the choice of a new King. The King chosen must not be the same as the King of England unless during the lifetime of Queen Anne all the wrongs inflicted on Scotland have been redressed and its independence has been guaranteed, with freedom to trade in all the English colonies and elsewhere, and full protection against the influence of the English and other foreigners. The law provides that the Scottish Parliament will have the right to add other provisions for their government as they see fit, and to trade with France especially by exporting wool, which would be a mortal blow to English trade.

On their side the English have adopted a number of laws in their Parliament that deprive the Scots of the right of residence in England, ban their trade by sea, and order English warships to seize all Scottish vessels until the Scottish Parliament abrogates the Act of Security and recognized Hanoverian succession.

The Scottish Parliament has declared that by meddling in the affairs of Scotland the English Parliament has usurped Scottish sovereignty, and in an address to Queen Anne has begged her to prevent these incursions or it will be obliged to take measures to defend its sovereignty and independence. But since this address the English Parliament has adopted laws against the Scots, and this has so aroused the Scots that they are talking now of demanding from the English the return of the three counties of Northumberland, Cumberland, and Westmoreland, which formerly belonged to Scotland, and which the English hold only by virtue of a lease that has expired.

Since Irish woollen is as good and fine as English, and the Scots are well-placed to obtain it, the English have adopted a law banning the sale by the Irish of woollens to Scotland, knowing well that they would be sold in France, which would ruin the principal trade of England. All these measures taken by the English Parliament against the Scots have had an effect that is the opposite of that intended.

Carrying out their Act of Security, the Scots have bought arms and munitions in Holland and elsewhere. Once a month they review their men capable of bearing arms. Those who fail to appear are subjected to fines, and none are absent. Presbyterians and Episcopalians though divided by religion have joined in opposing the designs of the English. Two well-informed Scottish officers recently arrived from Scotland report that military reviews take place every month, and that they amount to more than 80,000 men. In the Province of Ayre alone they have seen 17,000-armed Scots.

Lacking sufficient sailors the English are obliged to kidnap them forcibly, and last month on the Scottish border eleven Scots were taken to serve in their fleet. The Count of Marchimont, High Sheriff of this border, marched with armed men into England, kidnapped eleven English heads of family and imprisoned them, declaring to the English that they would only be released when the eleven Scots were returned.

Queen Anne, urged by the English Parliament to do everything possible to bring about the revocation of the Act of Security, offered the position of High Commissioner – equivalent to that of Viceroy – to the principal Scottish lords, all of whom refused it, including her two Scottish secretaries of state, because she would have been obliged them to call for the revocation of the Act of Security and the recognition of Hanoverian succession by the next Scottish Parliament. They told her that to advance these proposals would cause a crisis and perhaps a general uprising of the entire Scottish nation.

In light of this state of affairs, several of the principal Scottish lords have sent letters to the Duke of Perth, who is one of the first among them, to determine whether His Majesty will be pleased to grant his protection to the Scottish nation for the preservation of their freedom and independence from the English, renewing the old alliance and the privileges the Scots enjoyed in France before their kingdom was united to England. But they good offices of the Duke of Perth have been contravened until now by a cabal opposed to the Scots at the Court of Saint-Germain, which has done everything in its power to dispose the mind of the Queen against this enterprise and consequently against His Majesty's own court. It seeks to prevent her from listening to those Scots who are well-disposed (*bien intentionnés*), and the insinuations of this cabal have until now achieved all their objectives, which is not only to condemn these proposals as chimerical (*visions*), but also to prevent any effort to determine the truth. But that truth is now beginning to appear more clearly. This can be seen from the anxiety of our enemy as to the current state of Scotland as well as by the measures taken by the English Parliament against the entire Scottish nation.

Another supposed objection to the extraordinary utility that the King could derive from this state of affairs is that His Majesty, burdened as he is with immense expenses for the maintenance of armed forces in all theaters of war, is not in a position to undertake new expenditures to encourage an uprising by the Scots, who are said to require considerable assistance in men and money.

The response to this objection is that if we are persuaded that the Scots are disposed to take up arms, it would be to sin against all the rules of good government to refuse to consider how to bring the Scots to declare themselves, since it is easy to see that their declaration would make it impossible for the English to send troops to Flanders, to Germany, and to Spain, troops that are the most redoubtable we face, and that the Scottish

Diversion would by itself force them to abandon all these far-off enterprises and to recall the better part of their troops, rendering them useless to our other enemies who draw their principal strength from them. This Diversion would end the need for His Majesty to maintain such large armies in so many different countries, and it would be the greatest economy if we could by a modest assistance arm a whole nation, thereby lifting from our shoulders the heaviest of our burdens, since the English are the most dangerous of all our enemies.

In other times, we would have spent millions, and thought them well spent, simply to bring the Scottish nation to the state it is in today. Since Providence has brought it to this state without any effort or expense on our part, how can we refuse to take advantage of this by considering proposals to easily and cheaply bring it to fruition?

Before reviewing these proposals, let us begin by making clear that we are proposing expenditures that are certain to be effective, and that are so modest compared to the great advantages that will derive from them that it is inconceivable that they could be rejected.

First, in order to dissipate the doubts of the court of Saint-Germain and to put the business in good order it seems necessary, if His Majesty pleases, to send immediately to Scotland a man of ability who knows the language and the laws of the country and who is not attached to or in the service of the court of Saint-Germain. His mission would be to with bring the principal Scottish lords to the point of willingness to arm their vassals and renounce their obedience to Queen Anne, exploiting the absence of English forces, in return for the commitment of His Majesty to help them when they have done this. In the event they do not wish to declare themselves immediately, the alternative would be for them to raise the clans of the Highlands (*faire soulever les tribus des montagnards*) who are their clients (*qui sont dans leur dépendance*) and who are safe in their inaccessible country, in order to determine by means of this test whether the rest of the nation in the Lowlands is ready to follow.

He would argue to them that unless they seize on the occasion of the present war to secure their freedom they will not find another occasion after the peace, when the English will no longer be occupied abroad and will make use of all their forces to overwhelm them, and when His Majesty will no longer have the right to come to their aid, having signed a peace treaty with all his enemies. He would tell them on His Majesty's behalf that His Majesty asks only of them that they take the measures they believe best suited to establish their independence from the English who are the enemies of His Majesty as well as theirs. He would carry a letter from the King addressed the estates of the Kingdom of Scotland. Its substance would be that His Majesty having learned with displeasure that the Scottish nation finds itself in peril of being placed under the yoke of the English, who by the laws adopted in their last Parliament have shown themselves determined to overturn the basic laws of the ancient Kingdom of Scotland and to reduce the Scots to the same slavery as the Irish, and knowing of the ancient attachment of the Scots for his forebears, who gave them protection and the right of residence in the Kingdom of France, cannot see them in this peril without offering them his royal protection from the usurpations of the English. Thus His Majesty gives credence and power to the bearer of this letter to reach agreement with the principal men of the Scottish nation, not simply with regard to the assistance that the current state of the war will allow, but also to renew the ancient privileges of the Scottish nation in France.

The letter should be drafted so as to be shown to all those who are well-disposed, but only to be delivered when the estates of the Kingdom have met to determine the form of their government.

It does not appear wise to propose at this early juncture the restoration of their King, as that might be opposed by several of them, whereas they are all in agreement to govern themselves and to shake off the yoke of the English, and this will have a more certain and quick impact for the benefit of His Majesty than to propose in the first instance the return of their legitimate King.

This general letter should be accompanied by a personal letter to the Duke of Hamilton by way of a credential for this emissary in which His Majesty speaks of his esteem for the Duke whom he regards him as the principal chief of his nation, indicating that His Majesty is disposed to enter into a discussion of the means he will suggest for the security and benefit of the Kingdom of Scotland as well as for his own interests. This letter could be accompanied by several others from His Majesty to the principal lords, as designated by the Duke of Perth, those who have written to him to express their readiness to take up arms at the head of their vassals whenever it should please His Majesty to grant them his protection.

Although the King of England is the one principally concerned by this uprising, since it will in all likelihood result in his declaration as King of Scotland, it is essential to negotiate with the Scots only on behalf of the King (i.e. of France) initially, and to conceal the knowledge of all the details of this negotiation from the Court of Saint-Germain. This is because we know from long and unhappy experience that no secret is safe there, and that within this Court are concealed emissaries who would inform the ministers of Queen Anne of every development, all of which is perfectly well known to the Scottish lords. This is one of the main reasons why they dare not open themselves up to this Court, but they will make no difficulty in doing so to the King's ministers as soon as they have been given His

Majesty's word that the Court of Saint-Germain will not be told of the negotiations with them.

We know that the Queen of England[31] has declared that if His Majesty should be good enough to entrust his ministers with the interests of her son the King she will be most content to put her trust in them. It is necessary that this should be done not only for the good of her affairs but also for the service of His Majesty if we are to avoid falling into the difficulties of the past. Nor is it right that because the King and Queen of England are badly served His Majesty should be unable to take advantage of the happy conjuncture of the general discontent in Scotland by attaching that country to French interests to which it was formerly so useful at the time of its major wars with England.

Ireland will in all likelihood join with Scotland against its English oppressors, particularly as the Irish Catholics, deprived of their goods and religious rights by the English, are twenty to one Protestant. They await only the uprising of their brothers the Scottish Highlanders to follow their example. Finally, the English who wage war against us on all sides and who have fomented the rebellion in the Cévennes are more vulnerable to an internal conflict than any other country if we should apply ourselves seriously to undermining their illegitimate government. This is the best and surest way to put them in a position where they are unable to do us harm, and that we have not done so is a great gift to them. Queen Anne's emissaries could render her no greater service than to keep us in our present inaction by treating as fantasies[32] the favorable chance we have of overturning her usurpation, or at the least of dividing her kingdoms. It is certain that the late Prince of Orange had agents at the Court of Saint-Germain who kept him informed of everything that went on there, and it is unlikely that Queen Anne who is served by the most able ministers that England has had for a long time doesn't have the same agents, or that she hasn't acquired new ones. The fact that none of them has revealed being tempted on her behalf is an indication that they have succumbed to temptation.[33]

A foreigner of the first rank who was in the service of our enemies during the last war and who now serves the King of Spain has told well-informed persons (*gens dignes de foi*) that when he was in the enemy camp

---

[31] Mary of Modena.

[32] *Visions*. This was Middleton's term.

[33] While the syntax is tangled the sense is clear. Since none of the ministers of Saint-Germain have come forward to admit having been approached by Queen Anne's agents, and since it is inconceivable that they haven't been approached, some of them must be secretly working for Westminster – an argument from absence.

the best and soundest intelligence he received came from the agents King William maintained at the Court of Saint-Germain. They informed him not only of the plans of Saint-Germain against him, but also of our plans against other enemies and of our order of battle on both land and sea. This foreigner is now totally committed to the King's interests, and he will be willing to give the same testimony directly to His Majesty if He should wish to ask him for it. In that event we offer to reveal his name.[34]

The principal Scottish Lordshave informed the Duke of Perth that if they are to be in a position to shake off the yoke of England they will need five thousand infantry equipped by His Majesty in that country with arms and munitions. The need His Majesty has of his troops elsewhere combined with the difficulty of moving these five thousand to Scotland suggests another option, which we are convinced the Scots will agree to, since it will have the same effect as far as they are concerned.

As they have no lack of able and experienced soldiers, and as those of their former troops quartered in Scotland for the protection of the Kingdom, all of who are Scots paid by the nation, will not fail to follow the actions of their chiefs as soon as they are no longer being paid in the name of Queen Anne and renounced their allegiance to her, we need only send officers to command five thousand troops, which can to be raised in the country in the name of the estates of the Kingdom. We would send the necessary arms with powder and shot along with money for expenses to enable these trained troops to lead the militia who are obligated to follow their lords to war, especially when the cause is to preserve the laws of the entire nation.

Thus we propose to send sixty Irish, Scottish, and French officers, taking them from those that have been discharged from the Irish and other regiments in His Majesty's service. There would be five colonels and five lieutenant colonels for five regiments of a thousand men, and a total of fifty captains of foot to command ten companies of one hundred men for each regiment. As for lieutenants and ensigns, they can be easily found in Scotland if we send blank commissions from His Majesty to be filled in by the colonels if the lords undertake to raise these troops in His Majesty's name. We must also send a few blank commissions for general officers, in case the lords of the country consider it useful to fill them out. In order to transport these sixty officers with arms for five thousand men we will need only one frigate of thirty or forty guns, which can be done in secret provided the Court of Saint-Germain isn't informed.

---

[34] The "foreigner of the first rank" may be the Elector of Bavaria, Maximilian Emmanuel.

As for the funds necessary we ask for no money at all. We propose only that His Majesty draw on the bonds (*contrats*) newly created on the Hôtel de Ville, which bear 20,000 francs in perpetual interest and 20,000 in lifetime interest, for a total of 400,000 francs. We offer to make available (*faire trouver*) these 400,000 francs in four payments of 100,000 francs at the end of every month, provided the interest is paid in advance, which would be 40,000 francs in cash to the holders of the bonds in return for their 400,000 francs. The bonds could be sold by those investors in accordance with their original terms.

Of these 400,000 francs, 100,000 would go to buying the arms and munitions necessary for 5000 men. The remaining 300,000 would be added to by a matching contribution raised from a foreign power[35], which as soon as the Scots have declared themselves against the usurpation will be willing to advance 50,000 francs a month jointly with His Majesty in the form of subsidies, making a total of 100,000 francs a month for a six month campaign, that is the King's 50,000 for a month's pay for the 5000 men, including the officers and general staff, and the other 50,000 a month for the cost of artillery, which can be found in sufficient quantity in the castles of the lords, who are the masters of all the stores of the Kingdom. They have assembly grounds already prepared for the monthly troop reviews they conduct of their vassals, and they can assembly several small armed bodies ready to march on the first day to invade the three counties of the north of England, which have been unjustly retained by the English. They will find good quarters for the subsistence of their troops during the entire campaign, and the English will be in no position to oppose them, with all their troops across the sea. This will cause the ruin of all their enterprises during the campaign, as well as their planned attack on Cadiz and their plan to invade Spain through Andalusia.

Arms would not be bought or subsidies paid until His Majesty's envoy has settled everything with the principal Scottish lords and until His Majesty has obtained sufficient guarantees on their part. Thus there is no risk at all in beginning this enterprise. If it succeeds, as there is every reason to believe it will, it will only cost the King 40,000 francs in cash and 40,000 in income, half from the lifetime bonds issued, and half from the perpetual. This scarcely appears to be a difficulty capable of preventing such a great good as that will redound to His Majesty from this enterprise, which will in all likelihood be followed by a quick and glorious peace, since the Dutch seeing the English occupied at home and unable to come to their assistance will be obliged to negotiate with His Majesty and to accept

---

[35] This is probably a reference to Pope Clement XI, a strong supporter of the Jacobite cause.

the terms he is graciously pleased to offer for the security of their state and their trade.

KEY PERSONS MENTIONED IN THE TEXT

RELATIVES

Jacques de Callières (or Decaillières) (1620?-1662) Father of François. Served the Matignons in lower Normandy as governor of the fort and town of Cherbourg. An Army officer who held a royal commission, he nevertheless fought with the Matignons against loyalist forces during the Fronde. He was also an accomplished humanist who wrote several books, including a popular guide to conduct at court. His legal father was not of noble birth, and Jacques may have been an illegitimate Matignon.

Louis-Hector de Callières (1648-1703) Younger brother of François. A career Army officer from a young age. In 1684, he was appointed Governor General of the fort at Montreal, and from that post he returned to France in 1689 to lobby successfully for an invasion of New York, though it could not be carried out. In 1699, probably in part as a result of the intervention of François with Louis XIV, he became Governor General of New France. On his death Louis-Hector left his heart in a lead box to François.

LONGUEVILLE AND BOURBON-CONDÉ

Louis II de Bourbon, Prince de Condé (1621-1686) Known as Monsieur le Prince, or the Great Condé, he rebelled against Cardinal Mazarin and Anne of Austria and was exiled to Spain. Jacques de Callières celebrated his return to France with a poem dedicated to his sister, the Duchess de Longueville, and from then on Louis XIV kept him to heel.

Anne Geneviève de Bourbon, Duchess de Longueville (1619-1679) A political leader of the Fronde, with her brother Monsieur le Prince. Married to the Duke de Longueville who died in 1663, Governor of Normandy under whom the Matignons held lower Normandy. In 1670, she sold her plate and silver to finance Callières's clandestine mission to Poland.

Charles-Paris d'Orléans, Count de Saint-Paul, in 1671 Duke de Longueville (1649-1672) Son of Madame de Longueville, illegitimate son of the Duke de La Rochefoucauld. Callières dedicated his first book to Saint-Paul, and in 1670 he traveled undercover to Poland to intrigue for

225

his election as King, but as Duke of Longueville died in battle at the crossing of a branch of the Rhine in 1672.

POLAND

Jan Sobieski, King John III of Poland (1629-1696) Callières left a detailed account of his 1674 election as King, which he attended as the envoy of the Duke of Savoy. Sobieski was Initially pro-French, but he tired of the broken promises of Louis XIV and rescued the Hapsburgs at Vienna in 1683. Callières lobbied for appointment as the French envoy to Sobieski, without success.

Jan Andrasz Morsztyn, (1613-1693) Grand Treasurer of the Polish Republic when Callières first met him, he ended his life in France as the Count de Châteauvillain, an estate Callières had acquired for him. A humanist and a literary figure of the Polish baroque period as well as the leader of the French party in Poland, Morsztyn translated Tasso and Corneille into Polish for his private amusement. Callières was intimately associated with Morsztyn from 1670 until his death in 1693, and he negotiated the marriage of his son to a daughter of the Duke de Chevreuse.

Mary Catherine Gordon (1640?-1691) Wife of Morsztyn, a Scot, the daughter of the Marquis of Huntley. Callières met her in 1670 during his first mission to Poland for Longueville. She and Morsztyn are among the the great-grandparents of the last king of Poland.

Jean de Courthonne, Abbé de Paulmiers (died 1674?) A cleric and conspirator of whom little is known except that he headed the mission to engineer the election of Longueville as the Polish King. His code name was "Monsieur du Bourg." He took the view that Callières was not worth the expense, and suspected him of partiality to Morsztyn. Callières wrote a glowing report to Longueville in Paulmiers's name on his own performance in Poland, comparing himself to Corneille's hero Le Cid.

Roger Akakia du Fresne, (died 1683) Clandestine agent for the Longueville candidacy in Poland, imprisoned by Louis XIV as part of a cover-up after he was exposed as a French emissary. Code-named "Monsieur Le Lis." Akakia had previously served as secretary to the French Ambassador to the Ottoman Empire. After his release from the Bastille he would be named the French Resident in Poland, a position Callières had lobbied for unsuccessfully.

Hugues de Lionne, (1611-1671) Louis XIV's able and acerbic Secretary of State for Foreign Affairs, Lionne opposed the candidacy of Longueville as a complication in relations with Austria at a time when he was laying the groundwork for the invasion of Holland, but his own chief clerk, Pierre de Tourmont, managed the affair.

Arnauld de Pomponne (1618-1699) Successor to Lionne at the foreign ministry. Callières wrote repeatedly to him to solicit an appointment in French service, without success. A moderate from a prominent family of Jansenists, close to both Mme d'Huxelles and Mme de Sevigné, he had earlier served as Ambassador to Holland.

Toussaint de Forbin-Janson (1630-1713) Bishop of Marseilles, later Cardinal de Janson. As Ambassador to Poland, he helped engineer the election of Sobieski by the timely disbursement of large bribes. Callières accompanied him to Poland, traveling on a yacht provided by Charles II of England. Despite Callières's attempts to ingratiate himself, Forbin-Janson did not like him, and recommended against his appointment as French Resident in Poland. He served later as Ambassador to Rome. Louis XIV had a high regard for his ability, justifiably so based on his performance in Poland.

Olympia Mancini, Countess de Soissons (1640-1708) Cardinal Mazarin's niece, playmate (if not more) of Louis XIV during his adolescence. Her husband Prince Eugene-Maurice de Savoy-Carignan, Count de Soissons, was related to half the crowned heads of Europe. When he died in 1673, she sought preferment for her elder son, Thomas, and she financed Callières's mission to Poland for the Duke of Savoy in support of his election as King. Exiled from France in 1680.

Louis-Thomas of Savoy, Count de Soissons, Prince of Savoy-Carignan (1657-1702) Olympia's son, and Callières's seventeen year old candidate for election as King of Poland in 1674. Denied a position in French service, he eventually fought against France in the service of the Hapsburgs, and was killed in battle in 1702. His younger brother was the famous general known as Prince Eugene of Savoy.

PATRONS AND FRIENDS

Louis de Rouvroy, Duke de Saint-Simon (1675-1755) The great memoirist admired Callières and wrote that he often spoke truth to power. Callières was thirty years his senior, and acted as his tutor in the mysteries of foreign policy when the young Saint-Simon first came to court. Saint-Simon was close to the Dukes de Beauvillier and Chevreuse, both of whom were Callières's patrons. When Saint-Simon was approached about appointment as Ambassador to Rome in 1705, after his wife Callières was the first person he consulted.

Eusèbe Renaudot (1646-1720) An Abbé in minor orders, proprietor of the *Gazette*, the propaganda organ of Versailles, executor of Callières's will and his will and his lifelong friend, Renaudot is said to have spoken seventeen languages, from Arabic to English. Apart from the *Gazette,* he published little of note during his lifetime apart from theological controversies. He was elected to the *Académie française* on the same day as Callières in 1689 as a reward for his political services.

Marie le Bailleul, Marquise d'Huxelles (1626-1712) An influential Paris hostess, from a prominent family of magistrates, married into the nobility of the sword, twice widowed. The close friend and patron of Callières, she carefully preserved the letters he wrote to her from Holland. Her letters to the Marquis de La Garde in Provence written over a period of some thirty years are a neglected source for the history of the period. Intimate friend all her life of Mme de Sévigne.

Henriette-Adelaïde of Savoy, Electress of Bavaria (1636-1676) The sister of Charles Emmanuel II, Duke of Savoy. Callières stopped to see her in Munich on the way back from Poland with a commission from the Duke. They discussed her passionate desire to marry her daughter Marie-Anne Christine Victoire to the French Dauphin, but that marriage was not concluded until three years later, after her death.

Marie Jeanne Baptiste de Savoie-Nemours, "Madame Royale" (1644-1724) The wife of Charles Emmanuel II, Duke of Savoy. After her husband's death in 1675, she ruled Savoy during the minority of her son, Victor Amadeus. She chafed under French domination, and she gave Callières a commission to travel to England on her behalf, but nothing came of it.

Claude Bernou, Abbé, dates unknown. Renaudot's assistant at the *Gazette de France*. Born about 1634 by his own testimony, he was still working at the Gazette in 1701. Callières figures in virtually all the letters he wrote from Rome to Renaudot from 1683-1686. A geographer, he acted as a publicist for the explorer Robert-René Cavelier de La Salle, ghostwriting his travel accounts.

Robert René Cavelier de La Salle, (1643- 1687) The explorer of the Mississippi. Callières promoted his last expedition in 1684 to found a French colony at the mouth of the great river, and Callières's younger brother Louis-Hector considered joining the expedition but thought better of it. Murdered by his own men.

Charles-Honoré d'Albert, Duke de Chevreuse (1646-1712) An increasingly influential advisor to Louis XIV in the later years of his reign, married to a daughter of the first Colbert. Callières negotiated the marriage of his daughter to Morsztyn's son, and he drew up the plans for the 1708 French invasion of Scotland at the Duke's residence in Paris.

Paul de Beauvillier, Count and later Duke de Saint-Aignan, known as Duke de Beauvillier (1648-1714) Another patron of Callières, governor of the King's sons and minister of state, closely associated with Chevreuse, like Chevreuse married to a daughter of the first Colbert.

Mollo, Francisco, or François The Polish Resident in Amsterdam and a wealthy merchant who operated a back channel for France to the Amsterdam city council off and on from 1692 until the signing of the Treaty of Utrecht in 1713. Mollo may have been a *marrano*, or converted Jew. Callières corresponded with him in cipher from 1702-1707 during the War of the Spanish Succession, and together they promoted the thesis that a separate French negotiation with the Dutch was possible, behind the back of both Bourbon Spain and Holland's ally England.

Sébastien Le Prestre, in 1707 Marshal Vauban (1633-1707) The great military engineer, architect of French defenses. Vauban saw eye-to-eye with Callières about the need for France to confine itself to the "natural borders" of the hexagon, and the two men appear from their correspondence to have been friends, but in a private letter to the playwright Jean Racine, Vauban vilified Callières for offering to return Luxembourg and Strasbourg. It was probably in an effort to meet this criticism that Callières precipitated a crisis in the negotiations and incurred a sharp rebuke from Louis XIV.

Anne de Cominges, in 1698 Dame de La Tresne (died 1708) A close friend of the Marquise d'Huxelles and a daughter of a former French Ambassador to England, she was a bluestocking and an unmarried lady of a certain age with a passionate interest in public affairs when Callières met her. He wrote repeatedly to Huxelles of his fondness for her, but the following year she married a prominent magistrate in Bordeaux with better bloodlines.

COLBERTS

Jean-Baptiste Colbert (1619-1683) Louis XIV's formidable minister, the dominant figure of the early years of the reign, founder of the family's fortunes. Callières was closely connected all his life to the Colberts.

Jean-Baptiste Colbert, Marquis de Seignelay (1651-1690) The son of the first Colbert, he inherited his father's post as Secretary of State for the Navy and Colonies on Colbert's death in 1683. Callières advised Seignelay on American affairs.

Figure 15. Colberts: from left to right, top to bottom: Jean-Baptiste, founder of the family fortunes; his brother Charles, Marquis de Croissy; his son, Marquis de Seignelay, and Croissy's son, the Marquis de Torcy.

Charles François Colbert, Marquis de Croissy (1629-1696) Younger brother of the first Colbert, Secretary of State for Foreign Affairs from 1679 until his death. Acerbic and able, he reprimanded Callières for talking too much.

Jean-Baptiste Colbert, Marquis de Torcy (1665-1746) Croissy' son, Torcy retained the post of foreign secretary from his father's death until the death of Louis XIV. His relationship with Callières was close if occasionally wary.

SCOTLAND

Mary of Modena, Queen Consort to James II of England (1658-1718) After her husband's death in 1701 she presided over the affairs of the exiled Stuart court at Saint-Germain en Laye outside Paris until her son James Francis Edward Stuart came of age. She sent her thanks to Callières for "his interest in her affairs," but he did everything he could to circumvent her and keep the court of Saint-Germain in the dark, convinced that it was penetrated by English agents.

Charles, 2nd Earl of Middleton, (1640-1719) Mary of Modena's Secretary of State. An English convert to Catholicism, Middleton believed that French and Stuart interests were divergent, and that eventually France would sacrifice the Stuarts. He dismissed predictions of an uprising in Scotland as "visions," and Callières suspected him of being in league with elements at Westminster who favored a negotiated Stuart restoration.

Filippo-Antonio Gualterio, or Gualtieri; in 1707 Cardinal (1660-1728) Papal Nuncio to France from 1700-1706, an influential advisor at Versailles and a confidante of Louis XIV and Mme de Maintenon. Gualtieri was strong supporter of the Scottish enterprise, and a political ally of Callières with whom he carried on a correspondence after his return to Italy.

Simon Fraser, in 1716 Lord Lovat (c. 1667-1747) Hereditary chieftain of the Clan Fraser, he believed that he had been cheated of the Lovat title and estates. A wanted man in Scotland, he took service under William III, and eventually fled to France, offering to lead a revolt in Callières continued to trust him despite increasing evidence of his treachery. Fraser was placed under close confinement in France for a decade. Returning to Scotland at the time of the 1715 uprising, he betrayed the Stuart cause, and was rewarded with the restoration of his lands and title. In 1745, he turned his coat again and was executed at the age of 80.

Nathaniel Hooke, Baron Hooke in the Jacobite peerage (1664-1738) Born an Irish Protestant, chaplain to the Duke of Monmouth during his revolt against James II, he took service under Louis XIV, and commanded a regiment in the French Army. Closely connected to Callières, Hooke made two clandestine visits to Scotland as an emissary of Louis XIV to the Scottish lords, and with Callières drew up the plan for the 1708 invasion. He served later as the French envoy to Poland.

BIBLIOGRAPHY

ARCHIVAL SOURCES

Avignon, Bibliothèque municipale:

MS 1419, I-IV (Huxelles letters)

Chantilly, Bibliothèque et archives du musée Condé, "papiers de Condé":

Série R, XIV, "correspondences relatives à la candidature du comte de Saint Pol au trône de Pologne, 1670-1671"

The National Archives, London:

Letters of George Stepney to Sir William Trumbull, SP/1/1/129-142

London, British Library:

additional manuscripts 20368, "correspondence of Cardinal Gualtieri with F. de Callières, Cabt Secretary to the King, 1706-1717"

Manchester, John Rylands Library, Deansgate:

MS French 89-96 (Huxelles letters)

Montreal, Bibliothèque et archives du Canada (online):

MIKAN 3049329

MIKAN 2487003

Paris, Archives des Affaires étrangères, Correspondance Politique:

Angleterre, 217, 218, 219, 222, supplément 1706

Bavière, 19 "négociations de Vitry," 22

Hollande, 159, 162, 163, 164, 207, 208

Pologne, 37, 38, 40

Sardaigne, 64

Paris, Bibliothèque polonaise:

manuscript 13, 311-360, "Relation de mon voyage en Pologne en qualité d'envoyé extraordinaire de S.A.R. en l'année 1674"

Paris, Bibliothèque nationale de France:

Fonds Clairambault, Ms Fr 501, 1016, 1057,1125, 2293,

Ms Fr 21103

Ms Fr 24983

Fonds Renaudot, NAF 7487, 7488, 7492

NAF 3298, "papiers de Callières"

NAF 1663, "négociations de Riswick"

Paris, Archives nationales:

AB XIX 736, Delavaud papers

Fonds Rosanbo, AP 50, carton L, dossiers 3: "lettres de Vauban à M. de Calières, secrétaire de cabinet du Roi, 1694-1697"

Fonds Matignon, Série J 84

Archives de la Marine, B 4, 12

PUBLISHED WORKS MENTIONED OR USED

By François de Callières:

La logique des amans, ou l'amour logicien (Paris,1668).

Épître au Roi, presentée à Sa Majesté le 18 Janvier 1687, avec des vers pour madame la Dauphine, par M. de Callières (Paris, 1687).

Histoire poétique de la guerre nouvellement déclarée entre les anciens et les modernes (Paris, 1688).

Panégyrique historique du Roi: à messieurs de l'académie Française (Paris, 1688).

Des mots à la mode, et des nouvelles façons de parler (Paris, 1692).

Des bons mots et des bons contes. De leur usage, de la raillerie des anciens, de la raillerie et des railleurs de notre tems (Paris, 1692).

Du bon et du mauvais usage dans les manières de s'exprimer (Paris, 1693).

Du bel esprit. Où sont examinés les sentimens qu'on en a d'ordinaire dans le monde (Paris, 1695).

De la manière de négocier avec les souverains. De l'utilité des négociations, du choix des ambassadeurs et des envoyez, et des qualites nécessaires pour réussir dans ces employs (Paris, 1716).[1]

De la science du monde, et des connoissances utiles à la conduite de la vie (Paris, 1717).

By Jacques de Callières:

Traité de la fortune des gens de qualité, et des gentils-hommes particuliers (Paris, 1657).

Histoire du mareschal de Matignon (Paris, 1661).

Le Courtisan prédestiné, ou le duc de joyeuse, capucin (Paris, 1662).

Élégie sur le retour de Monseigneur le Prince, à S.A. Madame la duchesse de Longueville (Saint-Lô, 1660).

Other works cited or consulted:

Amiel, Olivier ed., *Lettres de Madame, duchesse d'orléans, née princesse Palatine* (Paris, 1982).

Archives de l'assistance publique, documents pour servir à l'histoire de l'Hôtel-Dieu de Paris (Paris, 1881).

D'Aubigné Françoise, eds. Théophile Lavallée, et Laurent Angliviel de la Beaumelle, *Correspondance générale de madame de Maintenon* (Paris, 1865).

---

[1] A comprehensive list of the editions in various languages can be found in Waquet, *François de Callières*, 270-2.

Barbour, Violet, *Capitalism in Amsterdam in the 17th Century* (Baltimore, 1950).

Barnett, Correlli, *The First Churchill: Marlborough, Soldier and Statesman*. 1st American ed (New York, 1974).

Barthélémy, Edouard de, 'La Chronique de Traité de Ryswick', *Revue Britannique* V (1879): 177-208.

Barthélémy, Edouard de, *La marquise d'Huxelles et ses amis, Mme de Sévigné, etc* (Paris, 1881).

Baschet, Antoine, *Le duc de Saint-Simon et le Cardinal Gualtieri, mémoire sur la recherche de leur conversation*, Cabinet historique (Paris, 1878).

————, *Histoire du dépôt des archives des affaires étrangères au Louvre en 1710, à Versailles en 1767, à Paris en 1799* (Paris, 1875).

Beaulieu, Alain, *The Great Peace* (Montréal, 2001).

Bergin, Joseph, *Crown, Church and Episcopate under Louis XIV* (New Haven, Conn., 2004).

Berridge, G. R., H. M. A. Keens-Soper, and Thomas G. Otte, *Diplomatic Theory from Machiavelli to Kissinger, Studies in Diplomacy* (Basingstoke, Hampshire and New York, 2001).

Berridge, G. R., *Diplomacy: Theory and Practice*, 3rd ed (Basingstoke, Hampshire and New York, 2005).

Bély, Lucien, *Espions Et Ambassadeurs Au Temps De Louis XIV* (Paris, 1990).

————, *Le Roi mon maître. Le service du roi à l'étranger vu à travers l'oeuvre de François de Callières, hommage à Arlette Jouanna* (Montpellier, 1996).

————, 'Les larmes de Monsieur de Torcy. Un essai sur les perspectives de l'histoire diplomatique à propos des conférences de Gertruydenberg (mars-juillet 1710)', *Histoire, économie et société*, 1983, Volume 2, numéro 3, 429-56.

Bouquet, H. L., *l'Ancien college d'Harcourt et le lycée Saint-Louis* (Paris, 1891).

Brooks, William S., *Philippe Quinault, Dramatist* (Bern, 2009).

Bulloch, John Malcolm, *The Gay Gordons* (London, 1908).

Burger, Pierre-François, '*Renaudot*', in *Dictionnaire de journalistes, 1600-1789, sous la direction de Jean Sgard* (Oxford, 1999).

Byrne, Thomas, 'From Irish Rebel to Bourbon Diplomat: The Life and Career of Nathaniel Hooke (1664-1738), unpubl. thesis, National University of Ireland, Maynooth, 2006.

Call, Michael, 'The Battle for Molière's Corpse/Corpus', in William Brooks and Rainer Zaiser eds., *Theater, Fiction and Poetry in the French long Century* (Oxford, 2007).

Cambridge History of Poland (Cambridge, 1950).

Chesterfield, Earl of, *Letters*, Vol I (New York. 1901)

Churchill, Winston S., *Marlborough, His Life and Times* (Chicago, 2002).

Chevrier, F. A., *Mémoires pour servir à l'histoire des hommes illustres de Lorraine*, Tome II (Brussels, 1754).

Clark, Sir George, 'From Nine Years War to Spanish Succession', in *New Cambridge Modern History* (Cambridge, NY, 1990).

Colbert, Jean-Baptiste, Marquis de Torcy, 'Mémoires', in Petitot et Monmerque, eds, *Collection Des Mémoires relatifs à l'histoire de France*, V. 67 (Paris, 1828).

Connor, Bernard, *The History of Poland*, printed for J.D. by Dan Brown (London, 1698).

Corp, Edward T., *A Court in Exile: The Stuarts in France, 1689-1718* (Cambridge, UK; New York, 2004).

Correspondance générale de Mme de Maintenon, Tome IV (Paris, 1865).

Les Correspondants du duc de Noailles, lettres inédites de Le Verrier, Renaudot, et Valincour (Paris, 1905).

Courtilz, Gatien de Sandras de, *Annales de la cour et de Paris sur les années 1697 et 1698* (Cologne, 1701).

Cousin, Victor, *Madame de Longueville*. 2 vols (Paris, 1853).

Cruickshanks, Eveline, ed., *Ideology and Conspiracy: Aspects of Jacobitism, 1689-1759* (Edinburgh, 1982).

Daire, Eugène Louis François, *Économistes-financiers du XVIIIe Siècle. Vauban, projet d'une dime royale* (Paris, 1843).

Dangeau, marquis de, *Journal du marquis de Dangeau*, (Paris, Firmin-Didot, 1854-1860) 19v., available in digital form (.pdf) from Gallica, the website of the Bibiothèque nationale de France.

Dechêne, Louise, *La correspondance de Vauban relative au Canada* (Montréal, 1968).

Delanglez, Jean, *Some La Salle Journeys* (Chicago, 1938).

Delavaud, Louis, 'Un arrangement international sur les bombardements', *Revue générale de droit international public* 16 (1909): 698-705.

Dingli, Laurent, Colbert, *Marquis de Seignelay, le fils flamboyant* (Paris, 1997).

Doucet, Charles Camille, *Les régistres de l'académie Française*, 1672-1793 (Paris, 1895).

Duchêne, Roger, ed., *Correspondance De Mme De Sévigné*. 3 v. vols ([Paris], 1972).

Duchêne, Roger, *Madame De Sévigné ou la chance d'être femme* (Paris, 1982).

Duffo, Fr., *Lettres inédites de l'abbé Renaudot au ministre J.-B. Colbert. (Années 1692 à 1706)* (Paris, 1931).

Erlanger, Philippe, *Louis XIV* (Paris, 1965).

———, *Le Régent* (Paris, 1938).

Fawtier, Robert , 'La Correspondance de la Marquise d'Huxelles et du Marquis de La Garde', *Bulletin of the John Rylands Library* 9, no. 2 (1925).

The Federalist Papers 19, Project Gutenberg Etext [www]

Forbin, Claude, comte de, *Mémoires, Collection des mémoires relatifs à l'histoire de France*, eds. Petitot et Monmerqué, T. LXXV (Paris, 1829).

Fosseyeux, Marcel, 'Deux Académiciens Collectionneurs', *Mercure de France* I, no. VII (1912): 568-81.

Fraser, Simon, *Memoirs of the Life of Simon Lord Lovat* (London, 1797).

Fuchs, James Lawrence, 'Vincenzo Coronelli and the organization of knowledge: the twilight of seventeenth century encyclopedism', unpubl. thesis, 1983 (Microfilm 84/2051, Library of Congress)

Fumaroli, Marc, *The Poet and the King: Jean de La Fontaine and His Century* (Notre Dame, Ind., 2002).

————, *La Querelle Des Anciens Et Des Modernes* (Paris, 2001).

Gibson, John C., *Playing the Scottish Card* (Edinburgh, 1988).

Godefroy, Maxime, 'Testament De Louis-Hector De Callières', *Revue Catholique de Normandie* (1899).

Grimblot, Paul, ed., *Letters of William III and Louis XIV, and of Their Ministers; Illustrative of the Domestic and Foreign Politics of England, from the Peace of Ryswick to the Accession of Philip V of Spain, 1697 to 1700*, 2 v. (London, 1848).

Hauteville, Gaspard de Tende de, *An Account of Poland* (London, 1698).

Hazard, Paul, *La crise de la conscience européenne, 1680-1715* (Paris, 1935).

Hein, H. J. van der (ed), *Het Archief van der Raadpensionaris Anthonie Hensius* (The Hague, 1867-80).

Herbert, Harvey Rowen and Nicolas Arnauld Simon, *The Ambassador Prepares for War. The Dutch Embassy of Arnauld de Pomponne* (The Hague, 1957).

Hoff, B. van 't, ed., *The Correspondence, 1701-1711, of John Churchill, First Duke of Marlborough and Anthonie Heinsius, Grand Pensionary of Holland* (Utrecht, 1951).

Israel, Jonathan, *The Dutch Republic: Its Rise, Greatness and Fall, 1477-1806* (Oxford, 1995).

Jusserand, Jean-Jules, *A French Ambassador at the Court of Charles II, Gaston Jean-Baptiste, Le Comte De Cominges* (New York, 1892).

Keens-Soper, H. M. A. and K. W. Schweizer (eds), *François de Callières: The Art of Diplomacy* (Leicester, 1983).

Klaits, Joseph, *Printed Propaganda under Louis XIV: Absolute Monarchy and Public Opinion* (Princeton, N.J., 1976).

Leach, Catherine S., *Memoirs of the Polish Baroque: The Writings of Jan Chryzostom Pasek, a Squire of the Commonwealth of Poland and Lithuania* (Berkeley, 1976).

Legrelle, Arsène, *Notes et documents sur la paix de Ryswick*, (Lille, 1894).

————, *La diplomatie française et la succession d'espagne* (Gand, 1888).

————, *Louis XIV et Strasbourg; essai sur la politique de la France en Alsace, d'après des documents officiels et inédits* (Paris, 1884).

Leibel, Jean, 'La famille du chevalier de Callières, gouverneur en la Nouvelle France', vol. 2, no. 4, *Cahiers De La Sociètè Historique* (Montréal, 1983).

Lempereur, Alain Pekar, *De la manière de négocier avec les souverains, édition critique* (Geneva, 2002).

Letters (1694-1700) of François De Callières to the Marquise d'Huxelles, ed. Laurence Pope (in collaboration with William S. Brooks) (Lewiston, N.Y., 2004).

Logié, Paul, *La fronde en Normandie* (Amiens, 1951, 1952).

Lynn, John A., *The Wars of Louis XIV, 1667-1714* (London and New York, 1999).

Mackenzie, W. C., *Simon Fraser, Lord Lovat, His Life and Times* (London, 1908).

Macray, William Dunn, *Correspondence of Colonel N. Hooke, Agent from the Court of France to the Scottish Jacobites, in the Years 1703-1707*, 2 v. (London, 1870-71).

Margry, Pierre, *Découvertes et établissements des français dans l'ouest et dans le sud de l'Amérique septentrionale (1614-1754) Mémoires et documents Originaux*, 6 v. (Paris, 1876).

Mesnard, Paul, *Oeuvres de J. Racine.* vol. VII (Paris, 1870).

Milosz, Czeslaw, *History of Polish Literature* (Berkeley, 1983).

Montpensier, Anne Marie Louise d'Orléeans, duchesse de, 'Mémoires', in *Collection Des Mémoires Relatifs À L'histoire De France*, tome XLIII (Paris, 1828).

Morgan, William Thomas, 'Economic Aspects of the Negotiations at Ryswick', *Transactions of the Royal Historical Society* XIV, (1931): 225-49.

————, 'The Expedition of Baron De Pointis against Cartagena', *American Historical Review* 37, no. 2 (1932).

Moulin, M. H., *Les deux de Callières, Jacques et François* (Caen, 1883).

Nicolson, Harold, *Diplomacy* (London, 1939).

————, *The Evolution of Diplomatic Method* (New York, 1953).

Nute, Grace Lee, *Caesars of the Wilderness* (New York, 1943).

Ochmann-Staniszewska, Stefania, *Listy Jana Andrzeja Morstina* (Wroclaw, 2002).

Omont, H., *Inventaire sommaire des manuscrits de la collection Renaudot conservés à la Bibliothèque nationale* (Paris, 1890).

Oreskó, Robert, Marie Hatton Ragnhild, G. C. Gibbs, and H. M. Scott, *Royal and Republican Sovereignty in Early Modern Europe* (Cambridge, 1997).

_____ 'Maria Giovanna Battista of Savoy- Nemours, Daughter, Consort, and Regent of Savoy' in Orr, Clarissa Campbell, ed., *Queenship in Europe* (Cambridge, 2004).

Pagès, G., 'Les frères Formont', in *Revue historique*, tome 46, mai-août 1891.

Parkman, Francis and David Levin, *France and England in North America*, 2 vols. (New York, 1983).

Parkman, Francis, *La Salle and the Discovery of the Great West*, vol. I (New York, 1983).

Pepys, Samuel, *The Diary of Samuel Pepys*, eds Robert Latham and William Matthews, 12 vols (Berkeley, 1970).

Pequet, Antoine, *De l'art de négocier avec les souverains* (The Hague, 1738).

Petitfils, Jean Christian, *Fouquet* (Paris, 1998).

Picavet, Georges, *La diplomatie française au temps de Louis XIV, 1661-1715* (Paris, 1930).

Piganiol De La Force Jean Aimar, *Description de Paris, de Versailles, de Marly, de Meudon, de S. Cloud* (Paris, 1742).

Pradel, Abraham du (Nicolas de Blégny), *Livre Commode des addresses de Paris pour 1692*, 2 tomes (Paris, 1878).

Price, J. L., *Culture and Society in the Dutch Republic during the 17ᵗʰ Century* (London, 1974).

Puttfarken, Thomas, *Roger De Piles' Theory of Art* (New Haven, Conn. and London, 1985).

Ranum, Orest, *National Consciousness, History, and Political Culture in Early-Modern Europe* (Baltimore and London, 1975).

Ravaisson-Mollien, François, *Archives de la Bastille, règne de Louis XIV (1675-1686)*. vol. 8 (Paris, 1866).

Recueil de ce qui s'est passé au sujet de la guerre, tant des Anglais que des Iroquois, depuis l'annéé 1682, manuscrits de Paris publiés sous la direction de la Société Littéraire et Historique de Québec (Montréal, 1871).

Recueil des harangues proncées par messieurs de l'académie française, (Amsterdam, 1709).

Recueil des instructions des ambassadeurs, IV, Pologne (Paris, 1888).

Rigault, H., *Histoire de la querelle des anciens et des modernes* (Paris, 1859).

Richetti, John T., *Life of Daniel Defoe: A Critical Biography*, (Oxford, 2005).

Roman, J., *Le Livre de Raison du Peintre. Hyacinthe Rigaud* (Paris, 1919).

Rousset, Camille, *Histoire de Louvois et de son administration politique et militaire,* tome I (Paris, 1886).

Rouxel, Albert, *Chroniques de l'élection de l'Académie française, 1634-1841* (Paris, 1886).

Rowlands, Guy, 'Louis XIV, Vittorio Amedeo II and French Military Failure in Italy, 1689-96', *The English Historical Review*, vol. 115, no. 462 (Jun., 2000), 534-69.

Roy, Pierre George, *Le projet de conquête de la Nouvelle-York de M. de Callières en 1689* (Québec, 1919).

Rule, John C., ed. *Louis XIV and the Craft of Kingship* (Columbus, Ohio, 1969).

Rule, John C., 'Louis XIV, Roi-Bureaucrat', in John C. Rule, ed., *Louis XIV and the Craft of Kingship* (Columbus, Ohio, 1969).

Rule, John C., 'The King in his Council: Louis XIV and the *Conseil D'en Haut*', in R. Oresko, G. C. Gibbs, and H. M. Scott, eds., *Royal and Republican Sovereignty in Early Modern Europe: Essays in Memory of Ragnhild Hatton* (Cambridge, 1997).

Saint-Simon, Duke de, *Mémoires de Saint-Simon.*, ed. A. De Boislisle avec la collaboration de L. Lecestre (Paris, 1929).

Saint-Simon, Duke de, *Mémoires; Additions au Journal de Dangeau* ed. Ybes Coirault (Paris, 1983).

Sainte-Marie, Père Anselme de, *Histoire généalogique et chronologique de la Maison Royale de France, des Pairs, des Grands Officiers de la Couronne et de la Maison du Roy* (Paris, 1725).

Satow, Ernest Mason, *A Guide to Diplomatic Practice*, 2 vol. (London, 1917).

Schweizer, Karl W., *François De Callières, Diplomat and Man of Letters, 1645-1717* (Lewiston, N.Y., 1995).

Sedgwick, Alexander, *The Travails of Conscience: The Arnauld Family and the Ancien Régime* (Cambridge, Mass. and London, 1998).

————, *Jansenism in Seventeenth-Century France: Voices from the Wilderness* (Charlottesville, 1977).

Sgard, Jean, *Dictionnaire des Journalistes 1600-1789* (Oxford, 1999), 'Eusèbe Renaudot' by Pierre Burger.

Somerset, Anne, *The Affair of the Poisons* (London, 2003).

Sonnino, Paul, *Louis XIV and the Origins of the Dutch War* (Cambridge, 1988).

Sourches, Louis-François de Bouschet, Marquis de, *Mémoires du marquis de Sourches sur le règne de Louis XIV,* 13 vols. (Paris, 1882).

Sternberg, Giora, 'Epistolary ceremonial: corresponding status at the time of Louis XIV', *Past and Present*, vol. 204, no. 1, August 2009.

Thomas, Henry Thynne, Joel Cartwright James, Crawford Lomas Sophie, Maxwell Lyte Arthur, Macmullen Rigg James, Marjorie Blatcher, Matthew Prior, and Edward Seymour, "Calendar of the Manuscripts of the Marquis of Bath Preserved At Longleat, Wiltshire," *Historical Manuscripts Commission*, 1908.

Thuillier, Guy, *La premiere école d'administration: l'academie politique de Louis XIV* (Geneva, 1996).

Veenendaal, A. J., 'The War of the Spanish Succession in Europe', *New Cambridge Modern History* (Cambridge, NY, 1990).

Villefore, Joseph-François Bourgoin de,, *La vie d'Anne Geneviève De Bourbon, duchesse de Longueville* (Amsterdam, 1739).

Virol, Michèle, *Vauban: de la gloire du roi au service de l'État* (Seyssell: 2003).

——————, *Les oisivetés de monsieur de Vauban* (Paris, 2007).

Voltaire, *Histoire de Charles XII* (Paris, 1821).

Waliszewski, K., *Marysienka* (Paris, 1898).

Warkentin, Germaine, 'Radisson, Pierre-Esprit (1639/40?–1710)', *Oxford Dictionary of National Biography*, Oxford University Press, Sept 2004; online edn, Jan 2008 [http://www.oxforddnb.com/view/article/59805, accessed 19 Jan 2010].

Waquet, Jean-Claude, *François De Callières, L'art de négocier en France sous Louis XIV* (Paris, 2005).

Weddle, Robert S., *The Wreck of La Belle and the Ruin of La Salle* (College Station, 2001).

Wilson, Lester Newton, 'François De Callières (1645-1717) Diplomat and Man of Letters', unpubl. thesis, University of Illinois, 1963.

Wood, Peter H., 'La Salle: Discovery of a Lost Explorer', *American Historical Review* 89, no. 2 (1984): 294-332.

Zoltvany, Yves F., 'Louis-Hector de Callières' in *Dictionary of Canadian Biography* (Toronto, 2005).

INDEX

R

Racine, Jean, 92
Radisson, Pierre, 54–55, 57
Reichberg, Baron, 39
Renaudot, Eusèbe
  Académie française and, xix, 61,
    64, 191
  Bernou and, 195
  death of Callières and, xxi
  on Lorraine, 134
  as patron, 49–51
  portrait of, 50 *fig*
  Ryswick and, 102, 112
  Stuart court at Saint-Germain and,
    155
  Torcy and, 193
Renaudot, Théophraste, 49
Retz, Cardinal de, 107
Richelieu, Cardinal, 61
Rigaud, Hyacinthe, 128
Rizzini, Abbé, 48
Rochefoucauld, François VI, Duke
  de La, 12
Rose, Baron, 105–106, 123, 181
Rose, Toussaint, *le président Rose*,
  48, 127
Rouillé de Marbeuf, Pierre, 144, 148
Rouville, Louis, Marquis de, 48
Royale, Madame, Marie Jeanne
  Baptiste de Savoie-Nemours,
  Regent of Savoy, 41 *fig*, 42–44, 73
Ryswick Conference and Treaty,
  46n2, 55, 72–73, 100 *fig*, 109–110,
  112–113, 115–116, 160, 192

S

Sainctot, Nicolas II de, 106–107
Saint-Pierre, Charles Irénée de
  Castel, Abbé de, 193
Saint-Simon, Louis de Rouvroy,
  Duke de
  on *Académie française*, 61
  on Callières, 44, 128, 196–197
  on Cély, 106
  Cominges and, 96, 98
  on Gracé, 182

  Gualtieri and, 188n1, 190
  on Huxelles, 47
  on Maintenon and Trémoille, 134
  on negotiations, 101
  in new régime, 193
  position of secretary and, 127
  Ryswick and, 73–74, 112
  on Stuart Pretender, 184
  War of the Spanish Succession
    and, 140
Saint-Thomas, Charles Victor
  Joseph Carron, Marquis de, 42, 43,
  46–47
Savoy, Charles Emmanuel II, Duke
  of, 28–29, 30, 34, 88, 111
Savoy, Marie Jeanne Baptiste de
  Savoie-Nemours, "Madame
  Royale", 41 *fig*, 42–44, 73
Savoy, Marie-Adelaïde de, Duchess
  de Bourgogne, 62, 88
Savoy, Prince Eugen Jean François
  of, Count de Soissons, 26, 40, 137–
  138
Savoy, Victor Amadeus II, Duke of,
  73, 137, 160–161
Saxe, Maurice de, 106n15
Scotland
  English relations and, 169–171,
    175
  loss of independence of, 167, 177
  rebellion and, 159–162, 165–166,
    178–181
Sedgemoor, Battle of, 168
Seignelay, Jean-Baptiste Colbert,
  Marquis de, 51, 54, 56, 62, 71, 155
Servien, Ennemond de, 42
Sévigné, Marie de Rabutin Chamtal,
  Marquise de, 20–21, 26n3, 48, 98
slave trade, 137, 150
Sobieski, Jan, King John III of
  Poland
  Callières on, 39
  death of, 104
  election of, 9n7, 34, 40
  Mollo and, 77
  Morsztyn and, 46

History of International Relations Diplomacy and Intelligence

Editor: Katherine A.S. Sibley

15 Laurence Pope, *François de Callières: A Political Life*. 2010. (monograph)
                    hardback, ISBN 978-90-8979-039-2
                    paperback, ISBN 978-90-8979-040-8

14 Kimberly Jensen and Erika Kuhlman (ed.s), *Women and Transnational Activism in Historical Perspective*. 2009. (edited volume)
                    hardback, ISBN 978-90-8979-037-8
                    paperback, ISBN 978-90-8979-038-5
13 Priscilla Roberts (ed.), *Lord Lothian and Anglo-American Relations, 1900-1940*. 2009. (edited volume)
                    hardback, ISBN 978-90-8979-034-7
                    paperback, ISBN 978-90-8979-033-0
12 John W. Young and Raj Roy (ed.s), *Ambassador to Sixties London: The Diaries of David Bruce, 1961-1969*. 2009. (source publication)
                    hardback, ISBN 978-90-8979-013-2
                    paperback, ISBN 978-90-8979-030-9
11 Nigel J. Brailey, *Imperial Amnesia: Britain, France and "the Question of Siam"*. 2009. (monograph)
                    hardback, ISBN 978-90-8979-014-9
                    paperback, ISBN 978-90-8979-026-2
10 Bruce Russell, *Prize Courts and U-boats: International Law at Sea and Economic Warfare during the First World War*. 2009. (monograph)
                    hardback, ISBN 978-90-8979-011-8
                    paperback, ISBN 978-90-8979-025-5
9 Tor Egil Førland, *Cold Economic Warfare: CoCom and the Forging of Strategic Export Controls, 1948-1954*. 2009. (monograph)
                    hardback, ISBN 978-90-8979-012-5
                    paperback, ISBN 978-90-8979-024-8
8 Gregory Russell, *The Statecraft of Theodore Roosevelt: The Duties of Nations and World Order*. 2009. (monograph)
                    hardback, ISBN 978 90 04 17445 0
                    paperback, ISBN 978-90-8979-023-1
7 Michael Salter, *US Intelligence, the Holocaust and the Nuremberg Trials*. 2009. (monograph)
                    2 volumes, hardback, ISBN 978 90 04 17277 7
6 Simon Davis, *Contested Space: Anglo-American Relations in the Persian Gulf, 1939-1947*. 2009. (monograph)
                    hardback, ISBN 978 90 04 17130 5

History of International Relations Diplomacy and Intelligence

Editor: Katherine A.S. Sibley

ADST-DACOR

DIPLOMATS AND DIPLOMACY SERIES

Series Editor: MARGERY BOICHEL THOMPSON

Since 1776, extraordinary men and women have represented the United States abroad under all sorts of circumstances. What they did and how and why they did it remain little known to their compatriots. In 1995 the Association for Diplomatic Studies and Training (ADST) and Diplomatic and Consular Officers, Retired, Inc. (DACOR) created the Diplomats and Diplomacy book series to increase public knowledge and appreciation of the role of diplomats in world history. The series seeks to demystify diplomacy through the stories of those who have conducted U.S. foreign relations. Laurence Pope's biography of François de Callières, the 40th volume in the series, fulfills these aims with scholarly élan.

OTHER TITLES IN THE SERIES

Herman J. Cohen, *Intervening in Africa: Superpower Peacemaking in a Troubled Continent*

Charles T. Cross, *Born a Foreigner: A Memoir of the American Presence in Asia*

James E.Goodby, Dmitri Trenin, and Petrus Buwalda, with Yves Pagniez, *A Strategy for Stable Peace: Towards a Euroatlantic Security Community*

Brandon Grove, *Behind Embassy Walls: The Life and Times of an American Diplomat*

Parker T. Hart, *Saudi Arabia and the United States: Birth of a Security Partnership*

John H. Holdridge, *Crossing the Divide: An Insider's Account of Normalization of U.S.- China Relations*

Cameron R. Hume, *Mission to Algiers: Diplomacy by Engagement*

Bo Lidegaard, *Defiant Diplomacy: Henrik Kauffmann, Denmark, and the United States in World War II and the Cold War 1939–1958*

Dennis Kux, *The United States and Pakistan, 1947–2000: Disenchanted Allies*

Jane C. Loeffler, *The Architecture of Diplomacy: Building America's Embassies*

ASSOCIATION FOR DIPLOMATIC STUDIES AND TRAINING
ARLINGTON, VA

 ## ADST-DACOR

DIPLOMATS AND DIPLOMACY SERIES

Series Editor: MARGERY BOICHEL THOMPSON

William B. Milam, *Bangladesh and Pakistan: Flirting with Failure in Muslim South Asia*

Robert H. Miller, *Vietnam and Beyond: A Diplomat's Cold War Education*

David D. Newsom, *Witness to a Changing World*

Ronald E. Neumann, *The Other War: Winning and Losing in Afghanistan*

Howard B. Schaffer, *The Limits of Influence: America's Role in Kashmir*

Ulrich Straus, *The Anguish of Surrender: Japanese POWs of World War II*

James Stephenson, *Losing the Golden Hour: An Insider's View of Iraq's Reconstruction*

Nancy Bernkopf Tucker, *China Confidential: American Diplomats and Sino-American Relations, 1945–1996*

ASSOCIATION FOR DIPLOMATIC STUDIES AND TRAINING
ARLINGTON, VA

CPSIA information can be obtained at www.ICGtesting.com

264481BV00002B/20/P

9 789089 790408